10⁹⁵

The Problem
of
Political Obligation

The Problem
of
Political Obligation

A Critique of Liberal Theory

Carole Pateman

University of California Press
BERKELEY   LOS ANGELES

First published 1979 by John Wiley & Sons Ltd. This
paperback edition published in 1985 by the University of
California Press.

Library of Congress Cataloging-in-Publication Data

Pateman, Carole.
  The problem of political obligation.

  Reprint. Originally published: Chichester;
New York: Wiley, c1979.
  Bibliography: p.
  Includes index.
  1. Allegiance 2. Liberalism 3. Democracy
I. Title.
JC328.P27 1986   323.6'5'01   85 8719
ISBN 0 520 05650 7 (pbk.: alk. paper)

Printed in Great Britain

For Roy

Acknowledgements

I first began work on this study during my periods as Visiting Fellow in the Political Science Department, Research School of Social Sciences, Australian National University, and I am grateful to have had such congenial surroundings in which to gather my thoughts together. I am also grateful to participants in seminars in North America, Australia and England to which I have presented papers on this topic, and to the many people with whom I have discussed my ideas.

I owe special thanks to Brian Barry for commenting on the manuscript in its various stages, and also to my namesake, Trevor Pateman, and to Michael Masterson. I should also like to thank Harry Beran, Michael Jackson, Zbigniew Pelczynski, Hanna Pitkin, Raymond Plant, Peter Singer and Michael Walzer for their comments on particular arguments or chapters. The final argument is, of course, my own. My biggest debt is expressed in the dedication: to my husband, who has demonstrated that there is nothing immutable or 'natural' about the prevailing sexual division of labour, and who typed successive drafts, made invaluable comments, and who has provided the support over the years which has made my academic work possible.

Contents

Promises are the uniquely human way of ordering the future, making it predictable and reliable to the extent that this is humanly possible.

H. Arendt, *Civil Disobedience*

Only *political superstition* believes at the present time that civil life must be held together by the State, when in reality the State is upheld by civil life.

K. Marx and F. Engels, *The Holy Family*

Introduction

Political obligation, even in Oxford,
is now an old-fashioned topic.

J. Plamenatz, *Consent, Freedom and Political Obligation.*

Most recent discussions of the political authority of the liberal democratic state and the political obligation of its citizens are based on one of two assumptions: that general problems about political obligation have now been resolved or are easily resolvable; or that no such problems exist. One aim of this book is to show that the latter assumption is unfounded and that political obligation is inherently problematic. My larger aim, which is both more substantive and more controversial, is to show that political obligation in the liberal democratic state constitutes an insoluble problem; insoluble because political obligation cannot be given expression within the context of liberal democratic institutions. The problem of political obligation can be solved only through the development of the theory and practice of participatory or self-managing democracy.

There are few contemporary theorists who would dispute that citizens of states ruled by modern tyrants, by repressive and cruel military regimes, or by ruthless authoritarian parties, may legitimately doubt that their governments have a rightful claim to their obedience. But the liberal democratic state is different; the nature and the basis of its authority are such that, although specific laws or policies of government may sometimes be open to question, the general political obligation of citizens is beyond doubt. Some writers have claimed that this is so far beyond doubt that to suggest that a general problem may exist shows only that one is philosophically confused.[1] The majority of theorists do not try to eliminate the problem in this way. They regard political obligation as a genuine problem since they agree that it requires justification, and there is no point in looking for a justification of something unless there is some difficulty about it. However, most political theorists also agree that a justification can quite easily be provided; the problem of political obligation is not an intractable one and can be solved with relative ease. That is to say, it is widely assumed that citizens in the liberal democratic state do have a justified political obligation.

Political theorists are also widely agreed upon the form of justification that is required. For three hundred years, political theory 'has been characterized, ... above all by *voluntarism*, by an emphasis on the assent of individuals as the standard of political legitimacy'.[2] Contemporary writers on political obligation typically appeal to voluntarist arguments. Like their predecessors the social contract theorists, they offer justifications for political obligation that rest upon the voluntary consent, assent, choice, agreement, and promises of individuals. Theorists differ about precisely which individual actions best indicate that such agreement or consent has been given; whether it is given through voting, for example, or through the acceptance of benefits, or through participation in liberal democratic institutions, and I shall be discussing various formulations of voluntarism and the relation between them in detail in later chapters. The point to be emphasized here is that a specific conception of 'obligation' is implied by voluntarist arguments. 'Obligation' means self-assumed obligation; or a moral commitment that is freely entered into by individuals, and freely taken upon themselves through their own actions. This view of obligation is linked to a wider conception of social life, or an ideal of the good society, which Rawls has nicely summed up as coming:

> as close as a society can to being a voluntary scheme, ... its members are autonomous and the obligations they recognize self-imposed.[3]

Voluntarist social contract and consent theories began to emerge as general theories of social and political life round about the seventeenth century; they developed with, and helped constitute, modern liberal societies. Until the modern era political 'obligation' was not a central category of political thought. In earlier times political life was conceived of in terms such as virtue rather than obligation; the ancient Greeks, for example, lacked the conception of individual moral responsibility which is essential for the idea of self-assumed obligation.[4] Some reasons for the emergence of voluntarist theories, and their connection to the development of liberal individualism, are discussed in Chapter 1, but it is necessary to make these brief comments here in order to establish that 'political obligation' has a history. Today, the subject tends to be discussed in an ahistorical fashion, which encourages the assumption that there are few general difficulties about political obligation in the liberal democratic state.

An ahistorical approach has been fostered by trends within post-war political theory. Under the combined impact of behavioural political science and linguistic or analytical philosophy, political theorists tended to lose confidence in the validity of their own enterprise and in the importance of 'traditional' or 'normative' problems. More recently, political theory has made an excellent recovery from these doldrums, and there is now some exciting work being done. Interest in political obligation has also revived over the last decade or so, and a number of books and articles have been devoted to the topic, but most discussions have failed to reflect the new approaches and advances so visible in other areas. The influence of linguistic philosophy, in particular, is still very strongly felt and there is a widespread belief that the important questions about political obligation are of the order: how do we use the term 'political obligation'? This approach neatly begs the question whether 'obligation' should be used at all in the political context. Behaviourists and empirical theorists have shown little interest in political obligation. However, one recent example illustrates very well that such an approach to this subject is likely to result in the uncritical conclusions typical of mainstream empirical political science. The problem of political obligation is taken to be to 'discover the pattern of attitudes ... toward the obligation to obey'—thus taking it for granted that there is indeed such an obligation in liberal democracies. The finding that 'the American citizen is a thoughtful and rule-oriented person', and that political authorities can generate a *feeling* of obligation, will come as no surprise to followers of empirical studies of electoral behaviour.[5]

Without an appreciation of the historical tradition within which most theorists of political obligation are presently working, it can more easily be doubted whether political obligation really does pose a genuine problem. This is because the absence of an historical perspective renders it virtually impossible to show *why* political obligation in the liberal democratic state is a problem, what the character of the problem is, or why voluntarist arguments continue to be so prominent. Before contemporary or classic social contract arguments can be examined, it is therefore necessary to undertake some preliminary groundwork to establish that there actually *is* a problem of political obligation to be discussed, and why this is so. This groundwork is tackled in Chapters 1 and 2. There is also much more to be said, and many questions to be asked, about the concept of 'obligation' itself, before any systematic analysis can be undertaken of arguments about political obligation in the liberal democratic state.

Theorists of political obligation rarely consider, for example, why the practice of obligation is a valuable one, or what it implies about the capacities and potentialities of individuals; they rarely consider why they are concerned with political *obligation* rather than political *obedience*. Again, promising is usually taken to exemplify 'obligation', and moral philosophers have devoted a good deal of attention to promising in recent years, yet the relationship between obligation in everyday life and political obligation is rarely examined in any detail. It appears that the term is used in the same sense in both cases. Political obligation is often said to be based on a promise, an agreement, a contract or consent; it thus seems to be a particular form of obligation as we know it in our everyday lives. However, as we shall see, political theorists actually have a very ambiguous attitude to voluntarism in political life. It is frequently argued that even if citizens cannot, with any plausibility, be said to have promised or consented, they are, nevertheless, politically obligated in the liberal democratic state. (Clearly, a problem about political obligation would otherwise have to be acknowledged.) But this suggests that political obligation and the obligation consequent upon a promise in everyday life are not the same after all.

Furthermore, the concept of self-assumed obligation is rarely examined to see what it implies about the character of social relationships, or what is required if the practice of self-assumed obligation is to exist throughout the whole of social life. It is taken for granted that obligation is central to everyday and political life in liberal democracies; but is it? Liberal theorists are reluctant to present theoretical and empirical evidence to show that this is really the case. They rarely treat their own ideals and values as seriously as they deserve and take a hard look at the practical requirements, especially the *political* requirements, for social life to be a voluntary scheme. That is to say, they fail to consider the possibility that liberal democratic institutions do not—and cannot—give expression to liberal ideals. This also means that one crucial aspect of the problem of political obligation is usually completely neglected. It is conventionally treated as a theoretical or philosophical problem, but it also has an integral *empirical* dimension. The problem of political obligation is, in large part, a problem of the feasibility of democratic social and political change.

Another necessary piece of groundwork arises because the origins of the conception of self-assumed obligation are tangled up with the emergence of the theoretical perspective of abstract individualism, and there is still a long way to go before this entanglement is broken. If some theorists now claim that general problems about political obligation are mere figments of disordered philosophical imaginations, abstract individualism suggests, on the contrary, that there are inherently insoluble problems surrounding the ideal of self-assumed obligation (the most famous of which concerns the obligatory nature of promises). If, in fact, there were such insoluble problems, then the idea of 'obligation' would be an incoherent one, and there would be no point in continuing to discuss political obligation. It is therefore necessary to show that these apparent problems are actually artifacts of a specific theoretical perspective, and that the concept of self-assumed obligation is not, despite its origins, irretrievably linked to abstract individualism. It is useful to note, at this point, that there are a group of writers who form an exception to my general characterization of theorists of political obligation. These are the philosophical anarchists (Wolff's *In Defense of Anarchism* is probably the best known recent expression of this theoretical position). They argue precisely that political obligation constitutes an insoluble problem. However, as I shall show in Chapter 7, this argument is as unsatisfactory in its own way as the attempt to sweep the problem away.

It may appear, at first sight, that recent discussions of political obligation have little in common. A series of discrete appraisals and criticisms of individual arguments may thus appear to be the most that can be achieved. However, once the initial groundwork has been completed, it becomes possible to see that a distinct pattern of argument, and an argument with a long history, runs through recent writings. Although theorists may canvass, often in an eclectic fashion, plausible justifications for political obligation, or analyse the concept of 'obligation', or discuss a particular author's arguments, recent discussions rest on a set of shared assumptions and arguments. It is therefore possible to criticize them in a systematic fashion. My purpose is precisely to present a *critical argument* about political obligation in the liberal democratic state. Although my discussion will cover some familiar ground, for example making use of conceptual analysis, and examining the arguments of the classic contract theorists, these investigations form part of an overall critique of the liberal theory of political obligation. Such a critical argument is possible only in the light of an appreciation of the existence of a *problem* about political obligation. A critical starting point allows a specific and systematic interpretation to be made of the classical writers that, in turn, enables contemporary discussions to be put into a wider perspective. It is only from a critical perspective that some crucially important and complex questions can be raised about the relationship between liberal democratic theory and liberal democratic practice, or between the realities of the liberal democratic state and the way that it is presented in theoretical discussions of political obligation.

I have been referring to 'liberal' theory and to 'liberal democratic' theory, and I now want briefly to say something about this terminology. Most anglo-american political theory is liberal democratic theory, or the theory of the institutions of the liberal democratic state. My argument is concerned with political obligation in the context of the liberal democratic state, and so it is also necessarily an argument about liberal democratic theory. The term 'liberal democracy' is sometimes used as if it were a combination or synthesis of liberalism and democracy; it has also, and most importantly, become popularly and academically identified with 'democracy' itself. It is widely assumed that 'democracy' can be nothing other than our existing liberal democracies. Part of my argument is that this identification is mistaken, and that, from the time of the classic contract theorists, a democratic as well as a liberal account of political obligation has been available to us. Indeed, the democratic account is also a critique of the liberal tradition of argument, and of liberal claims about the form of institutions which actually gives expression to the practice of self-assumed obligation.

'Liberal democracy' is not, therefore, a synthesis of 'liberal' and 'democratic' ideas and practices. Liberal democratic societies are in origin, and remain today in institutional form and ideology, essentially *liberal* societies. Their one democratic element was introduced when universal suffrage was granted. We are inclined to forget how recent an innovation this is—in Britain, for example, one person, one vote was finally established in 1948, and women were enfranchized in Switzerland only in 1971—or how relatively tenuously it is grounded. In one of the most influential discussions of liberal democratic theory, Schumpeter argues that there is no necessary connection between 'democracy' and universal suffrage, and that women, or certain religious or racial groupings, can be denied the vote in a 'democratic' system.[6] In this study I shall distinguish 'democratic' from 'liberal' or 'liberal democratic', using the latter two terms interchangeably as the historical context requires.

My argument about political obligation can also be seen as a specific 'case study' of the more general deficiences of contemporary liberal democratic theory. Criticisms of liberal democratic theory for its complacent ideological character are, by now, a virtual commonplace. Arguments about political obligation illustrate very well why this criticism is made so frequently. In fact, as I shall show in Chapter 5, arguments about consent and voting are little more than restatements of the familiar, and comforting, conclusions that empirical democratic theorists have drawn from voting studies. Discussions of political obligation also show, however, that the criticism that most liberal democratic theory is merely an ideological defence of the *status quo* is more fundamental and damaging than is often supposed. The obvious objection is that it is not at all clear exactly what this criticism implies. I shall by-pass the many disputes over the term 'ideological' itself; what I am concerned with in this study, out of the many possibilities, is the sometimes unstated, but nevertheless pervasive, claim that liberal democratic institutions do in fact operate as liberal democratic theory tells us that they do; that they actually embody and realize central liberal values and ideals. In the liberal democratic state, it is claimed, theory and social reality are not out of step, or at least, not unreasonably so. To paraphrase John

Rawls, one might say that the institutions 'nearly' give expression to liberal aspirations. A central part of this claim is that the appropriate way to characterize the relationship between citizens and the state is in terms of 'political obligation'. The practice of political obligation, it is usually accepted, is institutionalized in the liberal democratic state. This is the specific claim that I shall be questioning.

That this claim is rarely challenged is not a matter than can easily be rectified. If it could, there would be little bite in the criticism that most discussions of political obligation have an ideological character. The failure is bound up with the attitude of political theorists to the liberal democratic state, an attitude most clearly revealed in the extreme claim that there is no problem whatsoever about political obligation. If the relationship between citizen and state is completely unproblematic then it, and the state, must be accepted as they are. However, if theorists and citizens can only passively accept what exists, the result is that the liberal democratic state is 'naturalized'. It is regarded as if it were a natural feature of the world that individuals can do no other than accept as they find it. A critical and questioning stance towards the state is entirely misplaced and there can be no prospect of further democratic development or change. This reification of the state is not confined to writers taking the extreme position on political obligation. A tendency to treat the state as if it were a natural fact about the world is characteristic of liberal democratic theory in general. The liberal democratic state is taken for granted and is an unexamined premise of most anglo-american political theory.

Such a totally uncritical attitude to the liberal democratic state has two consequences that are of particular relevance for my argument. First, it is not accidental that unasked questions abound in discussions of political obligation. When the state is treated as it were nothing but a natural feature of the world, then certain questions cannot be asked. It becomes meaningless, or ridiculous, to ask critical questions when social reality appears to be not only as liberal democratic theory tells us that it should, but as if there were no possibility that it could be otherwise. Even where political obligation is admitted to be a problem, it is extremely difficult for most theorists to ask questions that might reveal its magnitude, since that would also begin to undermine their most basic assumptions about the liberal democratic state.

The second consequence of the reification of the state is that political theorists who are heirs to a long tradition of liberal argument about the proper relationship between citizens and the state (and who place themselves within its compass through their voluntarist arguments) are now denying, or tending to deny, a central postulate of that tradition. Liberal theory, and its conception of self-assumed obligation, was born in conflict with divine right and patriarchalist theorists who insisted that relationships of subordination and authority were God-given or natural. It is absolutely basic to liberal theory that political authority is conventional. The conception of political 'obligation' as a relationship that individuals voluntarily take upon themselves—and so can refuse, reject or change—makes no sense outside of a conventionalist view of at least a large number of human relationships and, most especially, of political relationships. (How can one freely assume or refuse a relationship that exists because it is God's will that it be so, or because it is part of the natural order of things?) To reify the state, and suggest that it must merely be accepted like a natural feature of the world, is to cut the ground from under the feet of any idea of political 'obligation'. A logical result of this, albeit a radical revision of liberalism, is the demand that the term be expunged from the vocabulary of the political theorist.[7]

Discussions of political obligation tend to be characterized by a marked lack of theoretical self-consciousness.[8] This extends to a singular lack of curiosity about the precise character of the arguments of the classic social contract theorists, and their continuing relevance and significance, especially ideological significance.[9] Consideration of the contract theorists' arguments sometimes amounts to little more than a ritual reference to Locke's theory of consent, and citation of a few well-thumbed passages from the *Second Treatise*. It is true, of course, that contract theory has received new attention since the publication of Rawls' *A Theory of Justice*. However, what is not usually appreciated is that, although Rawls' argument differs substantially from his contract predecessors, it still falls into the tradition of *liberal* contract theory, rather than 'the' social contract tradition. One of the consequences of the assimilation of 'democratic' theory into 'liberal democratic' theory is that the existence of *two* contract theories is usually ignored. The classic theorists tend to be discussed as if they were all talking about the same social contract, namely the liberal contract. But Rousseau rejects the liberal contract. His theory sets out an alternative, democratic social contract, that has a different structure from the liberal contract and very different implications. Contemporary theorists of political obligation pay little attention to Rousseau, and thus can conveniently ignore that his theory provides a brilliant critique of liberal arguments about political obligation. Rousseau rejects the liberal claim, that now seems so 'obvious' and in accord with common sense, that the practice of political obligation is actually institutionalized in the liberal state. One might have expected that political theorists would be anxious to meet such a long-standing challenge to the liberal theory of political obligation.

An examination of social contract theories also throws some interesting light onto the other side, so to speak, of political obligation: namely, onto arguments about political disobedience. The political life of citizens is not completely subsumed under the practice of political obligation or in actions of obedience—however much some political theorists, and many rulers, have wished, and continue to wish, it to be. Discussions of political obligation and political disobedience, or, more broadly, the question of citizen political action, tend to be compartmentalized off from each other, but there are some striking historical continuities in the arguments used in both areas. Almost all of the recent literature on political disobedience has been concerned with civil disobedience. This is, of course, partly a reflection of the political events of the 1960s. But the preoccupation with civil disobedience is also due to the concern of many writers to circumscribe as tightly as possible the political activities that are held legitimately to be open to citizens of liberal democracies. A very uneasy relationship exists between the desire of liberal theorists to leave no room for doubts about political obligation in the liberal democratic state, and their simultaneous wish, as good liberals, to uphold the rights of citizens. The idea of 'civil disobedience', which follows fairly directly from the contract theorists' discussions of the right of individuals to resist governments, appears to allow them to do both. However, like earlier arguments about the political rights of subjects, the idea of civil disobedience raises some very awkward, and largely unrecognized, questions about the extent to which citizens can be granted meaningful rights of political action if political obligation is to be treated as generally unproblematic.

One of the nice ironies of contemporary discussions of political obligation is that, despite the efforts made to deny that a difficult problem exists, the existence of a problem is continually revealed by theorists' own arguments. This is shown particularly well by one argument that is becoming increasingly popular. Writers on political obligation have recently begun to argue that political obligation is primarily owed, not to the state, but to fellow citizens.[10] Now, throughout this 'Introduction' I have referred to the political obligation of citizens to the state, and I am following liberal theorists in this formulation. For three hundred years, they have presented political obligation as a 'vertical' relationship between each citizen and the state. The writers who are claiming that political obligation is owed primarily to fellow citizens do not, it should be emphasized, give any indication that they see any difficulties in reconciling their argument with the assumption that citizens have a justified political obligation in the liberal democratic state. Nevertheless, they are presenting a completely different picture of political obligation from the traditional liberal one. Political obligation now appears as a 'horizontal' relationship between citizens.[11]

If that is an accurate representation of the relationship between citizens in the liberal democracies, then it invites the response that the claims of the state are left hanging in thin air. If political obligation is owed to fellow citizens, on what grounds is it also owed to the state? How are the vertical and horizontal relationships linked to each other? This argument, therefore, immediately gives rise to an obvious *problem* about political obligation in the liberal democratic state. The claim that political obligation is primarily owed to fellow citizens is a particularly striking example of the way in which liberal democratic theorists' own arguments bring to the surface problems that have apparently been satisfactorily disposed of. More generally, one of the major points that I intend to establish during the course of my argument is that reliance on voluntarist justifications of political obligation is a tacit acknowledgement that problems exist. Indeed, in the political context, use of the concept of 'obligation' itself constitutes a problem.

Another major theme of my argument concerns differential political obligation. Even if it were the case that political obligation was generally unproblematic, the question whether political obligation is differentially distributed would still remain, and it has important implications for liberal democratic theory and the liberal ideal of social life as a voluntary scheme. It is taken for granted by almost all writers on political obligation that all citizens, no matter what their social status, enjoy (or are burdened with) an equal political obligation. Yet, from the outset, liberal theorists have had a great deal of difficulty in incorporating all the inhabitants of the liberal state under the umbrella of their arguments justifying political obligation. This difficulty is usually glossed over, but it has recently, and most graphically, been highlighted in Rawls' *A Theory of Justice*. Rawls argues, and his argument is discussed in detail in Chapter 6, that only the most socially advantaged members of liberal democracies can be truly said to have a political obligation. Most of the population have merely an involuntary natural duty to obey—an argument which sits very oddly with the characterization of liberal democracy as a voluntary scheme.

The argument that all citizens are equally obligated looks reasonable enough once universal suffrage is admitted to the liberal state. All individuals then occupy a formally equal status as citizens. The equality of citizenship seems to transcend the substantive social differences and inequalities that divide individuals, and so it appears to provide a sound basis for an equal political obligation. The question always remains, however, whether social inequalities really are irrelevant to political obligation. It obviously arises in an acute form if a minority exist who, in practice, are denied all the rights of citizenship that are theirs in principle. In such a case it might be argued that the minority have no obligation at all. The possibility of a differential political obligation also arises in another fashion. It is widely believed that there are 'natural' differences between the sexes that prescribe completely different social and political roles for men and women (differences socially and legally recognized in a multitude of ways). Women, it is held, are 'naturally' unfitted for political life; their 'natural' place is outside the political sphere. But contemporary theorists of political obligation do not stop to consider whether, given these beliefs and current social practices, their arguments have any relevance to women, even though a few theorists have doubts whether claims about political 'obligation' can be extended to the working class. Beliefs about the proper social place of the sexes pose a very awkward problem for arguments about political obligation in the liberal democratic state. If they are not challenged, a sexually differentiated account of the individual's relationship to the liberal democratic state is appropriate. Yet, if such an account is provided, the contradiction is exposed between the formal equality of liberal democratic citizenship and the allegedly 'natural' social place of women.

This is an appropriate point at which to note that I have consciously attempted to write this book in a non-sexist fashion. This is difficult because, as I shall show, most of the writers I am dealing with, whether contemporary or classical, almost invariably assume that the 'individual' and the 'citizen' are male. It is therefore quite accurate to write 'he' in many places. Non-sexist writing is made all the harder because language is a form of life, embodying the discriminations, inequalities and prejudices of our own lives, and it is hard to avoid the masculine voice without falling into clumsy constructions.

Chapter 1

Problems and Questions

To seek a general justification of political obligation ... is to pursue a
meaningless question.

T. McPherson, *Political Obligation*.

An examination of books and articles on political obligation, and the chapters
devoted to the topic in political theory textbooks, is revealing more for what is
omitted than what is discussed. A good deal of attention is paid to the justification of
political obligation in the liberal democratic state, but there is little consideration
given to the question of *why* such justification is required, or whether political
obligation is indeed a problem. This is a curious omission, and now that the
argument is being advanced that it makes no sense to ask for a general justification of
political obligation, the silence on this basic point is all the more remarkable.
Theorists have not always been so reticent. The social contract theorists were well
aware that a large problem existed about the political authority of the liberal state
and the political obligation of its citizens, and they were quite clear about its origins.
But political theorists have now become so impressed by the development and
consolidation of the liberal democratic state that they have apparently forgotten this
fact, and seem unable to come to grips with the significance and implications of the
social contract theorists' answer to this problem.

In order to understand why the social contract theorists were faced with a
problem of political obligation, and why this problem remains acute for theorists of
the contemporary liberal democratic state, it is necessary to establish why the
conception of 'obligation' is central to the liberal ideal of social life, and why social
life is seen as a voluntary scheme. The most useful way to approach this question is
to look more closely at 'obligation' itself. Contemporary writers see obligation as self-
assumed obligation; they follow Hobbes, who wrote that there is 'no Obligation on
any man, which ariseth not from some Act of his own'.[1] Thus the first, and
fundamental, question that needs to be tackled is why 'obligation' is conceived of in
this way; why is it that individuals only have an obligation if they have voluntarily
taken it upon themselves through their own actions? The answer to this question is
central to the problem of political obligation in the liberal democratic state.

Obligation and Liberal Individualism

In the 'Introduction' I noted that it was from about the seventeenth century that
'obligation' first became a central category of political thought. The idea of self-
assumed obligation emerged and developed as part of the wider development of

liberal or market society, and of a specific conception of the individuals who inhabited that society. 'Obligation' is central to the theory and, to an extent—an extent that will be examined during the course of my argument as a whole—the practice of liberal democracy. However, political theorists and moral philosophers often present their analyses of 'obligation', and other social and political concepts, as if they were discussing a general, abstract idea that has the same significance in any historical period or social context. Concepts are treated as if they existed in an independent, timeless world of their own, instead of forming part of and helping to constitute specific social relationships and specific forms of social life.[2] Despite the enormous differences between present-day conceptions and the way in which people saw themselves and their socio-political relationships in ancient times, Socrates, for example, is often presented as if his trial exemplified some contemporary problems about 'political obligation', and as if he were little different from a civil disobedient of the 1960s. Analysis of concepts as if they were independent of specific social relationships is part of the ahistorical approach of theorists of political obligation to which I drew attention in the 'Introduction'. This approach allows theorists to take contemporary liberal democratic institutions for granted, so that they form an essential and uncritically accepted, but disregarded, background to their analyses. Theorists can, therefore, appear to be discussing an abstract idea of 'obligation', instead of a conception that forms part of their own lives.

From an ahistorical perspective there appears little that is new or especially noteworthy about the idea of self-assumed obligation; there seem to be no interesting questions to be asked about why we should see 'obligation' in this way. All that can be said about 'obligation', treated in the abstract, is that we use the term in a particular way. But once it is seen as part and parcel of the development of a specific form of social life, as helping to constitute a liberal form of society—which also requires a specific conception of individuals and their relationships—then it becomes clear that there is good reason why 'obligation' is self-assumed obligation.

Arguments about consent and social contracts can be found in political writings from ancient times, but this is not to say that the classic social contract theorists were doing no more than seizing upon and elaborating some traditional ideas. In earlier times such ideas appeared intermittently and formed only part, and a minor part, of wider political theories. It is only in the modern period that consent and contract become central conceptions, and social and political life in their entirety become seen in terms of voluntarism and convention. The voluntarist ideal itself depended upon, and helped shape, the development of liberal individualism.[3] The notion that individuals were born free and born equal to each other, that they were 'by nature' free and equal, formed an integral part of the complex development of liberal society and its market economy. How could individuals freely enter contracts, make equal exchanges, and pursue their interests in the market, if they were not so conceived? This conception of individuals was the starting point of the social contract argument, and individual freedom and equality is central to the liberal political ideal today. The idea of 'natural' freedom and equality marked a dramatic shift from a view which had prevailed for many centuries. Before about the seventeenth century, humans had been seen as part of a cosmic, divinely-ordered and 'natural' hierarchy of inequality and subordination. Within this context there was scant room for general questions to be posed about political authority and political obligation. The scope of a given ruler's right of command might be challenged but, in general, rulers were seen as part of God's way with the world. The crumbling of this world view had major and revolutionary consequences.

Once the belief gained currency that individuals were not 'naturally' arranged unequally and in subordination one to another, but, on the contrary, were 'naturally' free and equal, some enormous questions emerged about their mutual relationships. In particular, questions began to be asked about the basis of their political relationships, about political authority and political obligation. The social contract theorists had to address themselves to these questions; most importantly, they had to find an answer to the fundamental political problem of *how and why any free and equal individual could legitimately be governed by anyone else at all.*

The full implications of this subversive query have, even today, not yet fully worked themselves out; consider, for example, the argument of the feminists that there is no good reason for the widely held belief that a free and equal individual woman should be under the authority of the man whom she marries. The ideal of individual freedom and equality has led the philosophical anarchists to conclude that no claim to authority and no claim that political obligation exists can ever be justified. This is not the liberal response. Liberal theorists argue that an acceptable answer to this crucial problem of government can be found. My own argument agrees with the liberal theorists. Their reply provides the only rational and acceptable answer—but it is an answer which has implications for arguments about political obligation in the liberal democratic state which liberal theorists cannot pursue.

If individuals are 'naturally' free and equal to each other, then there is a potential problem about all their social relationships, because any of these might be seen as compromising that freedom and equality. For instance, a relationship of obligation places a restriction upon the individual's freedom because it binds him or her to perform (or refrain from) a certain action at some later date. How could such a restriction be justified? Clearly, it is compatible with the initial postulate of freedom and equality only if the individual *voluntarily* places herself in that relationship. The relationship of obligation is justified because the individual has created it for herself in full knowledge of what it involves; 'obligation', properly, is self-assumed. This explains why philosophers so frequently present promising as paradigmatic of obligation. In making a promise the individual deliberately undertakes 'an act of her own' that voluntarily creates a relationship of obligation, and commits her for the future. A promise is the clearest and most explicit example of self-assumed obligation. Free and equal individuals can justifiably have obligations if and only if they have taken them upon themselves. The concept of self-assumed obligation is a necessary corollary of the liberal ideal of individual freedom and equality.

'Obligation' is self-assumed obligation because this is the only conception that is compatible with (and, in turn, has helped shape) the liberal view of individuals and their social life. It can now also be seen why the relationship between the citizen and the liberal state is characterized in terms of 'obligation'. The same answer can be

14

given in political life, as in everyday life, to the subversive question that emerged together with liberal individualism: free and equal individuals have voluntarily to consent, agree, contract or promise to enter into a relationship of political obligation. Voluntarism does not undermine 'natural' freedom and equality, but exemplifies a striking, and radical, contrast with force, coercion, and beliefs about divinely-ordained or 'natural' hierarchies of subordination, as a basis for political life. With the establishment of liberal individualism the relationship between subject and government has to be transformed into one of *obligation*, into which individuals freely enter and in which they are morally bound by virtue of their own free action and commitment. Government can no longer rest on mere political *obedience*, however engendered, for obedience is required irrespective of the individual's own actions or judgement.

It is now possible to answer the question of why political obligation poses a general problem. It does so because it always and continually requires a justification of a very specific kind, a voluntarist justification. A free and equal individual can always question political authority and political obligation in general terms; political obligation can never be taken for granted. To establish this, however, is only to argue against those political theorists who eliminate the need for the justification of political obligation by denying that it constitutes a genuine problem.[4] Of more importance, and political interest, is the claim that political obligation in the liberal democratic state is unproblematic in the sense that it can always be justified in the manner required. There are features of liberal democracies, it is claimed, that will always make it reasonable to argue that citizens do assume their political obligation for themselves. In an unselfconscious and uncritical fashion most political theorists are committed to some form of voluntarist justification of political obligation, which is necessary if their commitment to the liberal ideal of individual freedom and equality is not to be jeopardized. But voluntarist justifications lie at the heart of the problem of political obligation in the liberal democratic state; *far from providing a solution, they define the problem*. To show that this is the case, it is necessary to consider exactly how, and to what extent, political obligation can exist in the liberal democratic state. This is the task I am undertaking in this study as a whole, but it can be elucidated initially by looking more closely at the relationship between promising and political obligation.

Promising and Political Obligation

In everyday life, promising exemplifies the activity of assuming obligations. In the next chapter I shall be discussing in detail some of the real and pseudo-problems surrounding the social practice of promising, and their importance for the question of political obligation; at present I am concerned only with the frequently drawn comparison between, or assimilation of, promising and political obligation. Political obligation, as discussions of the social contract illustrate, is often presented as if it is a certain kind of, or as if it is like, or rests upon, a promise. If political obligation is a form of promising, or if it can be validly compared to a promise, then there is no doubt that it is indeed 'obligation', like the obligations that individuals assume in their everyday lives. On the other hand, political theorists have also argued that political obligation is significantly different from promising. Pitkin has argued, for example, that political obligation differs from promising because it need not be 'explicitly taken on oneself' and, unlike a promise, 'its *content* seems to be a subordination to the judgement of others'.[5] In addition, doubt is thrown on the very notion of political 'obligation' since it is often argued that, whether or not individuals have performed some act of their own, they are, nevertheless, justifiably politically obligated in the liberal democratic state.

For example, in a book devoted to showing that obligations, properly, arise from individual commitments, it is asserted in a footnote that the 'act of making a commitment is not, in general, a necessary condition for legal [political] obligation'.[6] More strikingly, Tussman, in *Obligation and the Body Politic*, argues that liberal democracies are like voluntary associations, membership being based on consent. However, he also argues that some citizens have not consented. Tussman calls the latter 'child-bride citizens', and claims that, like minors, they are justifiably obligated without their own consent.[7] Tussman does not enlighten us about the basis of the 'child-brides' ' political obligation. His argument clearly illustrates the dilemma facing those theorists who try both to retain a voluntarist justification of political obligation, and to cling to the assumption that a justified obligation exists in the liberal democratic state. Consent theory has long been embarrassed by the fact that it always runs into difficulties when confronted by the demand to show who has, and when, and how, actually and explicitly consented in the liberal democratic state. Attempts to comply with that demand frequently end in an admission that some citizens (perhaps many) have not done so, and this conclusion immediately threatens the assumption that political obligation is unproblematic. Theorists of political obligation then tend to follow one of two alternatives. They can fall back on the claim that self-assumed obligation or consent is, at best, only partially relevant; the obligation of some citizens—the 'child-brides'—rests on some other basis. This alternative, however, begins to move completely away from voluntarism for at least part of the population.

The second alternative is to resort to what I shall call *hypothetical voluntarism*.[8] This interpretation of voluntarism has a long history and it plays an extremely important role in the liberal democratic state. The contrast between voluntarism and hypothetical voluntarism can be illustrated quite simply. The idea of self-assumed obligation, on the face of it, leads to some fairly straightforward conclusions about individuals, their capacities and their social relationships. It implies that an obligation can exist only if individuals have knowingly and deliberately, after reasoned reflection about the consequences of taking such a step, decided to enter such a relationship. In turn, this implies that individuals have the capacity to act responsibly, to evaluate their actions, and to make rational choices about what they ought to do. Or, to put this in a different idiom, obligation is a relationship willed by individuals themselves. The acts of one's own that constitute an obligation are thus explicit undertakings and commitments. Promising clearly illustrates all these features; a person making a promise has to decide when to do so, understand what the action entails, and decide upon the content of the obligation. A major focus of attention in discussions of obligation, therefore, might be expected to be individuals' own knowledge of, and interpretation of, what they are doing.

In most arguments about political obligation, however, 'obligation' is interpreted in terms of hypothetical voluntarism. The acts of one's own with which political theorists are usually concerned are not explicit undertakings, but the implicit or tacit consequences of actions. These consequences are interpreted not by the individual, but by the theorist; an hypothesis or inference is offered about the meaning of the actions. The performance of certain actions is said to give rise to, or the hypothesis is offered that they give rise to, political obligation. Consent and obligation is inferred from the fact that individuals voluntarily engage in certain activities—irrespective of the way in which the individuals themselves may understand what they are doing. One advantage of hypothetical voluntarism for the political theorist is that a very broad view can be taken of the requisite 'acts of one's own'; acceptance of benefits, and participation within liberal democratic institutions, for instance, can form the basis for the hypothesis about obligation. This broad view is illustrated in the following two definitions:

> the word 'obligation' has, I suggest, paradigm use both in the context of talk about promises or agreements, and in the context of talk about acceptance of benefactions.[9]

Similarly, it is argued that obligations

> arise as a result of our voluntary acts; these acts may be the giving of express or tacit undertakings, such as promises and agreements, but they need not be, as in the case of accepting benefits.[10]

It should be noted that both these examples initially refer to promising. We all understand that in making a promise an individual is assuming an obligation to do, or refrain from, certain things. Just because we know what promising 'means' it can also make sense to hypothesize that other actions, which are not usually so understood, can be interpreted in this way.

I shall be considering in detail, in later chapters, some recent examples of hypothetical voluntarism. At present, Locke's famous argument about tacit consent will provide a good illustration of this approach. In the *Second Treatise of Government*, Locke argues that people tacitly consent, or tacitly assume their political obligation, when they walk along the highway. That is to say, Locke is arguing that it is a reasonable hypothesis, or inference, that a given voluntary action (walking along the highway) is one of the 'acts of one's own' through which a political obligation is assumed. One of the objections that is often made to Locke's argument is that people do not see their action in this light, and do not connect walking down the road with consent. But, as we shall see later, Locke's hypothesis is no more far-fetched than many other examples of hypothetical voluntarism to be found in contemporary discussions of political obligation. Locke's claim about tacit consent also illustrates why hypothetical voluntarism provides an alternative for theorists embarrassed by the problems surrounding claims about consent in the liberal democratic state. An obvious attraction of hypothetical voluntarism is that it can easily be made all-inclusive, so that no one is left outside its scope (we all walk along the road—therefore we all consent). This avoids the dilemma of the political theorist who is left with 'child-bride' citizens to account for. It also appears to solve the problem of how to retain a voluntarist justification while leaving undisturbed the assumption that political obligation in the liberal democratic state is unproblematic. This, however, is achieved at the cost of the comparison of political obligation and promising. The obligation arising from a promise is actual, not hypothetical. Promising stands at the opposite pole from hypothetical voluntarism, and so the question remains whether or not political 'obligation' is self-assumed obligation.

Despite all the references to promising in discussions of political obligation, the relationship between this social practice and political obligation is rarely explored in detail. Nor are the political implications of the comparison between promising and political obligation pursued. The ambiguous attitude of many theorists to this comparison is inevitable because their own assumptions allow them to follow only two courses: either partially to abandon voluntarism, or to fall back on hypothetical voluntarism. They are unable to consider any other alternatives because these require a critical approach to political obligation and the liberal democratic state. In short, they can give no serious attention to a simple, but crucial and fundamental, question: *what is the political counterpart of the social practice of promising?*

The answer to this question is also simple, or, more accurately, it is simple up to a point. It is all too easy to suppose that the answer supports the prevailing consensus about political obligation in the liberal democratic state. *The political counterpart of promising is voting.* The points already made about self-assumed obligation and promising are relevant to voting and political obligation. The result of voting, like that of promising, is an obligation; an obligation to carry out the undertaking that has been entered into by virtue of engaging in the social practice of promising or the political practice of voting. Voting enables citizens to decide on the basis of their own deliberations and judgement to create a relationship of obligation in their political lives. It must be emphasized that the general and abstract connection between voting and obligation does *not*, by itself, say anything about the specific form of voting that enables citizens to assume their political obligations for themselves. It can be agreed that 'there is a conceptual connection between voting and consenting',[11] but it does not follow directly from this, as is so often assumed, that, therefore, liberal democratic voting gives actual expression to this conceptual relationship.

Earlier, I cited Pitkin's statement that political obligation differs from promising because it involves the individual's judgement being subordinated to that of others. Now, this will always appear to be the case if the 'act of one's own' giving rise to political obligation is taken to be a liberal democratic vote. The point of liberal democratic voting is that citizens vote for representatives whose task it then is to make political decisions for them. In other words, citizens alienate their right of political decision-making, and, therefore, a few representatives decide upon the content of citizens' political obligation. If the leap is made from the general relationship between promising, voting and obligation, to the conclusion that the 'voting' in question is liberal democratic voting, political obligation and promising, despite their initial similarity, will necessarily appear to differ. And to differ precisely because the *content* of political obligation, unlike that of a promise, involves a 'subordination to the judgement of others', to the judgement and decision of representatives.

There is, however, another form of voting which does provide a political counterpart to promising; namely, direct or participatory democratic voting. If the political practice of voting is to complement and supplement the social practice of promising, and enable citizens to order their political as well as their social lives for themselves, then citizens must be able to decide when to assume an obligation and their own judgement must decide its content. Participatory democratic voting allows them to do these things. An important difference between participatory voting and promising needs to be noted at this point; the decision about political obligation is made by individuals in their collective or political capacity as citizens, not as individuals in their private or everyday lives, but this does not invalidate the comparison with promising. In a participatory or self-managing democracy, citizens, collectively, exercise political authority over themselves in their capacity as private individuals; or, to make this point in a different way, in voting they are subordinating themselves to their own collective judgement, not to the judgement of others. Furthermore, just as a promise creates a relationship between the person making the promise and the person(s) to whom it is owed, so participatory democratic voting creates a relationship of political obligation that is owed by each citizen to his or her fellow citizens; there is no one else to whom it could be owed.

To establish that there is a political counterpart to the social practice of promising has some extremely far-reaching consequences for arguments about political obligation. It is to argue that it is not merely fanciful or metaphorical, or only of limited relevance, to compare political obligation and promising; it is to claim that a political relationship could be created that involves 'obligation' in the same sense as relationships of obligation in the sphere of everyday life. But the argument that there is a political practice through which citizens can assume their political obligation for themselves does not support the claim that such a practice already exists in the liberal democratic state. On the contrary, the argument leads to a quite different conclusion: that political obligation, arising from the explicit acts of citizens, will exist only in a participatory form of democracy.

There is, of course, a great deal more discussion required to support this conclusion. However, the interpretation of social contract theory, and the critique of contemporary voluntarist arguments which follow, are possible only when the existence and character of the problem of political obligation has been outlined. The problem remains obscured unless certain questions are posed, questions which can find no place in most discussions of political obligation. In particular, the relevance of the comparison between promising and political obligation has to be confronted; either political 'obligation' is indeed 'obligation' in the same sense as promising, or it is not—and, if it is not, the relationship between the citizen and the liberal democratic state must be characterized in other terms. The multitude of references to promises, consent, voluntary agreements, and acceptance of benefits, in recent discussions, do not, in themselves, establish anything about political obligation. It has to be shown that citizens do actually consent or agree, or, at least, that it is possible for the relationship between citizen and liberal democratic state to rest on this basis, if the term 'political obligation' is to be more than a useful ideological device.

For three hundred years liberal theorists have argued, for very good reason, that political obligation, like other obligations, must be freely assumed by citizens themselves. By focusing on voting as the 'act of one's own' which gives rise to political obligation, it appears that the difficulties and ambiguities of voluntarism can be avoided. Present-day liberal democracies are based on universal suffrage, and universal voting appears to be the obvious mechanism through which all citizens can assume their political obligation. However, the nature of liberal democratic voting is such that any comparison with the obligation arising from a promise looks very odd indeed. But, it might be said, it is surely possible to promise to obey someone else; liberal democratic voting is like a promise to obey.

If this is so, then the relevant analogy for liberal theory is not between political obligation and promising as a generalized social practice, but between political obligation and one specific form of promising: namely, promising to obey. The essence of liberal social contract theory is that individuals ought to promise to, or enter an agreement to, obey representatives, to whom they have alienated their right to make political decisions. The essence of Rousseau's critique of this argument is that such a contract is necessarily illegitimate. Now, a promise to obey is not merely one particular form that the social practice of promising can take; it is a very special and singular kind of promise. Promising, as I have shown, is important to liberal theory because it brings into being a relationship that, at one and the same time, is an expression of individual freedom and equality, yet commits individuals for the future. Promising also implies that individuals are capable of independent judgement and rational deliberation, and of evaluating and changing their own actions and relationships; promises may sometimes justifiably be broken. However, to promise to obey is to deny or to limit, to a greater or lesser degree, individuals' freedom and equality and their ability to exercise these capacities. To promise to obey is to state that, in certain areas, the person making the promise is no longer free to exercise her capacities and decide upon her own actions, and is no longer equal, but subordinate.

These consequences of promising to obey are most starkly revealed in the extreme case of a promise or agreement to become a slave. Slavery involves the total alienation and denial of freedom, and the master becomes the slave's absolute superior. Most people in liberal democracies today, theorists or otherwise, would regard such a promise as one that ought not to be made. Yet, if we are willing to argue that this specific promise to obey is illegitimate, then more careful consideration should be given by political theorists, and citizens, to the significance of other promises to obey for the realization of liberal ideals. To see liberal democratic voting as a promise to obey is, of course, to claim only that obedience is due in a certain area of life, and about certain matters. Moreover, it will be pointed out, citizens can vote their representatives out of office, and have other ways of making their influence felt. This view of liberal democratic voting draws attention to its similarities with another example of promising to obey. In an employment contract, the employee agrees to obey the orders of the employer in return for wages, but (in principle, if not always in practice) employees have some choice about whom they contract with, and can bargain about the conditions of the contract (and can break it). However, liberal democratic voting is also similar to another familiar example of promising to obey. In the traditional, Christian marriage service, the wife promises to obey her husband in all conjugal matters—for life. Voters may be able to reject representatives, but in so doing they are also choosing new decision-makers; liberal democratic voting is a series of renewals of the promise to obey.

These comments have assumed that liberal democratic voting can validly be compared to, or seen as, a promise of some kind. But there are general difficulties with this comparison. In a recent empirical study of political participation, issue is taken with the many empirical investigators who have cast doubts on the rationality of voters. It is pointed out that the liberal democratic electoral mechanism is such that voters can choose neither whom they vote for, what they vote about, nor when they vote.[12] And, it might be added, their only means of modifying what they have done is to perform the same action again when they are next invited to do so. The comparison with promising can be turned round the other way; if promising were like liberal democratic voting, to promise would be to perform an action that could be engaged in only periodically, at times and about matters chosen by others; to make a promise would be (until the opportunity were offered to do the same thing again) to give others the right to decide upon the content of one's obligations. If promising were like this, the conception of self-assumed obligation would be meaningless.

These problems about the comparison between promising and liberal democratic voting could be avoided if voluntarism were abandoned. If this step were taken, it would also be to abandon the claim that the liberal democratic state actually embodies liberal ideals; citizens are not merely required to obey, but are morally bound through a voluntary commitment of 'obligation'. There is a problem about political obligation in the liberal democratic state precisely because voluntarism cannot be avoided. It is always open to citizens to question the liberal claim about political obligation; to ask why, if obligation is so important, their voluntary commitment is so frequently merely inferred, or limited to only part of the population. Citizens can always ask why political obligation cannot be like promising, and why they cannot assume their political obligation through participatory democratic voting. The problem of political obligation has an integral empirical dimension. The relevant questions are not only theoretical or philosophical—what do we mean by 'political obligation'?—but are also concerned with the possibilities of social and political change and the development of alternative forms of democratic political organization.

Consent and Self-Assumed Obligation

I have, so far, used the terms 'promise', 'self-assumed obligation', 'consent' and 'agreement' as if they were interchangeable. Historically, 'consent' is the most familiar term, and it is widely used today, but the supposition that consent *is* self-assumed obligation places severe limits on the scope of discussions of political obligation and arguments about the democratic organization of political life. To see why this is so, it is necessary to make explicit the distinction between self-assumed obligation as the free creation of a relationship, and self-assumed obligation as consent. This distinction is basic to my argument as a whole. A promise is an example of self-assumed obligation as the free creation of a relationship of obligation. The social practice of promising enables individuals to create a new relationship where none existed before, and the content of the promise is a matter for their own judgement. Consent, however, must be *to* something. In the case of obligation it is consent to an already existing relationship of obligation. The individual is asked by another, or a group, to take an obligation upon herself. The content of that obligation has already been defined by others, and the individual has to decide whether or not consent should be given, whether or not that particular obligation ought to be assumed.

'Consent' is the basic concept in most discussions of political obligation precisely because theorists are usually concerned with the justification of political obligation in the liberal democratic state. They are concerned with a situation where, they claim, citizens can be said to consent to the decisions of representatives about their political obligation. 'Consent' is central because to consent is the only way in which it is open to citizens to assume their political obligation in a liberal democratic state. Thus, again, political obligation appears to involve the subordination of the citizen's judgement and will to that of others. Nor is the consent in question always the explicit and actual consent to which I have just referred. A person can decide not to make a promise and, similarly, can refuse to consent. However, as noted earlier, to leave open the possibility that citizens may not consent poses problems for the assumption that political obligation is unproblematic. The 'consent' in current discussions of political obligation is usually the implied or tacit consent of hypothetical voluntarism. Chapter 5 is devoted to contemporary consent theory so I shall not discuss this here.

What should be said, however, is that 'consent' has become so firmly associated with political obligation in the context of the liberal democratic state that it is rarely considered what its meaning and role might be in a different democratic context; a context where the fundamental form of self-assumed obligation is not consent, but the free creation of obligations. The role of consent in this situation can be briefly indicated by reconsidering participatory democratic voting. Citizens can freely create their political obligations through participatory voting as they create obligations in everyday life through promising. But a participatory vote is unlikely always to be unanimous; what then is the position of the minority? In my previous comments on participatory voting I passed over this question, but it can now be seen that the minority have to decide whether or not they ought to *consent* to the decision of the majority. The political obligation of the minority will arise through self-assumed obligation as consent, not directly through the creation of an obligation. The question of minority consent is explored later, especially in Chapter 7. At this stage, there is another distinction to be drawn in order to put contemporary discussions of consent and, more generally, voluntarist arguments about political obligation in historical perspective.

'Consent theory' and 'social contract theory' are often treated as if they are merely different labels for the same thing, and this hinders an understanding of the relationship of the problem of political obligation to classic liberal social contract theory.[13] The idea of the social contract gives a voluntarist explanation of how 'in the beginning' free and equal individuals can rationally and justifiably join together in a political community and put themselves under political authority. However, this is only part of the *liberal* contract story. It is a preliminary to the second stage of a two-stage agreement. The second stage of the contract is of fundamental importance for liberal democratic theory; it is at this point that it is assumed that political authority, initially in the hands of the community, must be given up to a few representatives. Once the second stage is concluded, representatives are authorized to decide upon the political obligations of the members of the community.

The idea of the social contract offers a voluntarist justification for the political obligation of those who take part in it, but it does not, as the patriarchalists were well aware, solve the problem for those who come after. If they, too, are free and equal individuals, then they cannot be bound by the agreements of their ancestors. It is at this point that liberal contract theory becomes *consent* theory. It is also at this point that a pattern is set for contemporary voluntarist arguments. The next generation can justifiably be bound by the political arrangements of their forefathers if they voluntarily consent to them. It is important to keep in mind, however, that these arrangements have already been legitimized through the social contract, and it is for this reason that the liberal contract theorists then have recourse to hypothetical voluntarism. The question they ask is not whether the next generation consent, and how their consent is given. Rather, they assume that consent ought to be, and is, given; the question with which they are concerned is how the next generation can plausibly be said to consent, or, on the basis of what hypothesis can it be argued that they consent? There is a direct parallel here with contemporary voluntarist arguments. Contemporary theorists take the authority of the liberal democratic state for granted. They assume that there is no problem about consent to political obligation. They therefore ask the same hypothetical voluntarist question, about how consent can plausibly be said to be given, as their predecessors.

Nevertheless, a crucially important difference remains between the liberal contract theorists and more recent writers. The contract theorists used the social contract story to provide an answer to the enormous *problem* about political obligation that liberal individualism had brought with it. It was impossible for them to gloss over the fact that the problem existed. Contemporary hypothetical voluntarism, in contrast, derives from theorists' inability or unwillingness to admit that any really difficult problems exist. This difference highlights the tremendous shift, of the utmost theoretical and practical importance, that has taken place over three centuries in liberal political thought.

This shift also means that attitudes to the liberal ideal of social life as a voluntary scheme are not as straightforward as they may appear. A sharp separation is made in liberal theory and practice between the private and political spheres of social life, and voluntarism is interpreted in the light of this separation. 'Voluntarism' has a different significance in the two spheres. The private or everyday sphere is presented unambiguously as a voluntary scheme in which individuals freely decide for themselves, assume obligations, and pursue their interests. There are some important questions to be asked about this characterization of the private sphere but, at present, the crucial point is that voluntarism in private life, in contrast to the state, is not seen as partial or hypothetical—promising is different from political obligation. Indeed, this distinction is inevitable when the liberal democratic state is treated as if it were a natural feature of the world. Nevertheless, it is claimed that political life is still part of the voluntary scheme, and that liberal ideals are given expression in the liberal democratic state. It is this claim that I am challenging.

Chapter 2

Self-Assumed Obligation and Abstract Individualism

> What would be useful ... is a new, critical account of political obligation that visualizes the independence and responsibility of active citizenship against a background of sociological insight into the nature of political culture.
>
> H. Pitkin, *Wittgenstein and Justice.*

In Chapter 1, I noted that the liberal ideal of individual freedom and equality can lead to general problems about social relationships; any relationship might be seen as compromising that ideal. If individuals are seen abstractly, in separation from each other and their social relationships, these problems can assume enormous proportions and prevent a coherent understanding of moral and social life. This is shown nowhere more clearly than in Hobbes' theory, which I shall explore in the next chapter. At present, I am concerned with the specific case of relationships of obligation. The idea of self-assumed obligation and the theoretical perspective of abstract individualism share a common historical origin. This means that they tend to be seen as if they are integrally associated with each other and, in turn, this ensures that discussions of obligation are dogged by a series of unnecessary difficulties. Any examination of the political implications of the idea and practice of self-assumed obligation must therefore deal with its entanglement with abstract individualism. I want to show that there is no permanent connection between self-assumed obligation and abstract individualism but also, and more importantly, that the latter stands in the way of the development of a coherent conception of the practice of obligation. It does so by generating some problems, and a pseudo-problem about the binding nature of promises, that appear insoluble from an abstractly individualist perspective. These problems then appear as obstacles in the way of any attempt to treat self-assumed obligation seriously as a political practice. Indeed, if the pseudo-problem about the obligatory nature of promising were genuine, the idea of self-assumed obligation itself would be rendered incoherent.

An important first step in any discussion of political obligation is thus an appreciation of the need for a theoretical alternative to abstract individualism. This is especially necessary because of the tendency of political theorists uncritically to accept the liberal democratic state as a 'given' in their analyses. In so doing, they are implicitly discussing individuals as if they could be separated from their institutions—and so abstract individualism is very hard to avoid. In showing that the so-called problem of promising is an artifact of abstract individualism some indication can be given of the theoretical alternative that is required. It is then possible to make a crucial distinction between 'ought' and 'obligation', and to differentiate between the various kinds of rules that govern liberal democratic social life.

Because so many political theorists argue from an abstractly individualist perspective, 'the great scandal of modern political science' lies at the heart of liberal democratic theory, including discussions of political obligation.[1] The scandal is that of possessive individualism, and Macpherson's phrase brilliantly encapsulates the character of the attributes that are presented as belonging 'naturally' to individuals. When the attempt is made to see individuals in complete abstraction and isolation from each other, to see them as 'ineluctably *separate*' units, they necessarily appear as 'naturally' free and equal to each other.[2] They also appear to be possessors of property, including the property they own in their personal attributes and capacities. However, if such an individual is to be a recognizably human person 'he' must be given some specific characteristics (the 'individual' in liberal theory usually has been, and continues to be, seen as male; a male who possesses even the property that a female has in her person). The characteristics must be those that individuals would have 'naturally', and the problem is, of course, how can it be known what these are.

The answer is that it cannot be known; individuals may be 'born free and born equal', but they are neither born as fully-fledged persons nor are they born outside a network of social relationships. The 'natural' characteristics attributed to the individual by liberal theorists are social, and they are, moreover, the characteristics of individuals who are to assume their obligations for themselves, freely enter contracts and pursue their own interests. This is not accidental; abstract individualism is precisely what it says, an abstraction from social reality. The reality in question is that of the capitalist, market economy and the liberal democratic state, and the postulated characteristics are those of the inhabitants of such a society. In the previous chapter I stressed that concepts are constitutive of social life, but this does not mean that it is impossible to treat them completely otherwise. This seems all the more plausible a procedure when the belief that individuals are, and should be, primarily concerned with their self-interest and profit is central to the institutions of contemporary liberal democracy. This suggests that individuals 'naturally' act as abstract individualism claims that they do. It is because abstract individualism is, at the same time, both a reflection of, and an abstraction from, aspects of liberal democratic social life that it remains so important in liberal democratic theory.

The view of individuals' 'natural morality' presented by abstract, possessive individualism, especially in its most radical versions, gives rise to the problems with which I am concerned here. If the individual is seen in the abstract, in complete isolation from other beings, then all 'his' judgements and actions are based solely on his own subjective viewpoint—what other viewpoint is there for such a creature? That is to say, the individual's reasoning will be entirely self-interested; he will act if, and only if, he judges it to be for the benefit of himself and his property. The 'natural morality' of the abstractly conceived individual is completely possessive, so that when a decision has to be made, for example whether or not to assume or fulfill an obligation, the outcome will depend entirely upon the individual's subjective judgement of personal advantage and profit. This view of individual motivation has bedevilled discussions of self-assumed obligation from the outset.

The 'Problem' of Promising

In my discussion of promising and political obligation in Chapter 1 it was taken for granted that there was no problem about the obligatory nature of promises, or, more generally, about the fact that one is committed to fulfill an obligation once it has been assumed. Yet many moral and political philosophers have seen a problem here; it has been claimed that a genuine doubt exists whether there is an obligation to carry out one's promises. In his famous objection to social contract theory, Hume writes that 'we are bound to obey our sovereign, it is said, because we have given a tacit promise to that purpose. But why are we bound to observe our promise? ... you find yourself embarrassed when it is asked, *Why are we bound to keep our word?*'.[3] Doubts about the binding nature of promises and contracts are based on the apparent fact that if, properly, obligations are self-assumed, then the obligation to perform them must be self-assumed too. An infinite and insoluble problem of why individuals should ever thus commit themselves then appears to open up, and it seems to undermine the very foundations of the idea of self-assumed obligation.

This 'problem' of the binding nature of promises is, as some theorists have recently begun to argue, a purely philosophical puzzle.[4] It has its origins in the conceptual confusion arising from a theoretical perspective that attempts to treat individuals as abstractly situated beings. It is not a genuine and real problem like that posed by conflicting obligations, or the problem that can arise if an individual begins to wonder whether a promise should be broken. The spurious nature of the 'problem' can be seen by approaching it through the question of why anyone should doubt whether they are ever bound by any of their promises. The only individual who would inevitably and always have such doubts is the abstractly conceived individual. Or, more accurately, the completely possessive individual could never admit that promises usually bind; self-interest must dictate just the opposite. In fact, such an individual could never agree that there are good reasons for any general constraint upon individual action or upon the individual's will. From a purely subjective, self-interested viewpoint such constraints make no sense. But, it might be disputed, the possessive individual would have a good reason to keep promises (or, at least, not to break them if the breach of faith would become public knowledge) because it always pays to have a reputation for keeping promises. However, a desire for such a reputation does not, in itself, mean that the possessive individual must change his outlook. No recognition that promises bind is required; merely the ability to deceive others into believing that self-interest has been tempered while breaking promises at every opportunity. More importantly, such a limitation upon absolute self-interest, or its replacement by a long-term view of self-interest as 'constrained maximization', makes sense only if abstract, possessive individualism itself is modified.[5] This limitation presupposes a different perspective from that of the individual in isolation. It requires that the individual is already interacting with others and taking their reactions—'his' reputation—as well as pure self-interest, into account.

The 'problem' of promising dissolves if promising is seen not as a discrete activity of separate individuals but as a *social practice*, a practice in which individuals engage during the course of their communal life together. The social practice of promising *is* the practice of assuming and keeping obligations. The words 'I promise' would be meaningless if it were not generally understood that to promise is to assume an obligation, to commit oneself to perform or refrain from a given action. There could be no such practice as promising if any single promise did not *presuppose* that promises oblige. The meaning of 'I promise' is not purely subjective and individual but is social and inter-subjective. It is 'constitutive of the social matrix in which individuals find themselves and act', and it forms part of the relationship of obligation that is created through the making of a promise.[6] If this were not so, it would be impossible for children to learn how to promise.

The fact that promising is learnt is something that, astonishingly, abstract individualism has to disregard. The abstractly conceived individual is assumed to come into being fully equipped with moral and social capacities so that 'he' can, at one and the same time, meaningfully utter the words 'I promise' and yet deny that promises are binding.[7] This reduces the social practice of obligation to a series of discrete and inconsequential utterances. Other individuals can have no consistent expectations about the consequences of the statement. The most that can be said is that the individual may or may not *feel* obliged as a result of saying the words. Actually, however, people learn during their moral and social education in childhood, and beyond, that the meaning of a promise is that they have assumed an obligation. Within the context of inter-subjective meanings an individual can, so to speak, step forward and establish an objective relationship of obligation. When a promise has been made others know that the individual has assumed an obligation 'in much the same way as [they know that] someone who puts on a coat, has a coat on'.[8]

To see promising as a social practice means that the 'problem' of promising should not arise. But not all theorists who make use of the idea give up the attempt to separate individuals from their social relationships, and the 'problem' can then arise in a different guise. For example, in *A Theory of Justice*, Rawls relies heavily on the notion of a social practice. However, Rawls also argues that when a person says 'I promise' she or he has invoked the 'rule of promising', which is a non-moral rule, constitutive of the social practice of promising. A further rule, the moral 'principal of fidelity', or the rule that promises ought to be kept, is required to account for the binding nature of the words.[9] I discuss Rawls' account of the social practice of promising in detail in Chapter 6. The relevant point here is that the 'problem' of promising emerges in Rawls' argument because it can be asked why the individual should accept or consent to the 'principle of fidelity'. The latter rule is explicitly treated as independent of, not constitutive of, the social practice of promising, and so self-assumed obligation appears to be a matter of individuals recognizing or consenting to the rule (recall the discussion of 'consent' in Chapter 1). Such a conclusion can also follow from another argument that is aimed at showing that the 'problem' of promising arises from conceptual confusion. This occurs because the argument, which I shall call the conceptual argument, is usually not framed carefully enough, and the concepts of 'ought' and 'obligation' are not distinguished.

The conceptual argument runs as follows: a coherent conception of 'social life' necessarily involves ideas such as 'obligation'; unless it is generally understood that people have an 'obligation' to keep their promises then there can be no understanding of what it means to 'be a member' of a society, and no understanding of what 'social life' demands. (It might be added here that this understanding derives from the process of education. To learn to say 'I promise' implies that the individual understands the meaning of 'I', and this is because he or she has also learnt what 'we' and 'being a member' means.) It is because an abstractly individualist theoretical perspective cannot encompass these necessary conceptual connections that it generates the 'problem' of promising.[10] The conceptual argument, and the philosophical and sociological traditions from which it derives, is a valuable antidote to abstract individualism, but it does not, in itself, tell us as much about obligation as its proponents usually suppose. In particular, as I shall show in Chapter 6, no substantive conclusions can be drawn about political obligation from these conceptual points.

One aspect of the conceptual argument that requires further consideration is the use of 'obligation'. Strictly speaking, the conceptual point about 'social life' should be made in terms of 'ought'. There are certain basic concepts that are internally related to the idea of 'social life'; and there are also certain basic practices of mutual aid and forbearance without which it would be difficult to see, empirically, how social life could exist—and no one has shown this better than Hobbes. These are practices involving trust in all its aspects, and actions such as helping the injured, the sick and the aged, and not wilfully injuring others. That is to say, they are practices and actions that it is generally right or morally worthy to perform; they are actions that we *ought* to perform. It is 'obvious' that we ought to perform these actions because of their direct connection to fundamental human needs, wants, interests and values. If this were not a self-evident connection a large problem of social order would arise. It is because these practices and actions are so basic to social life that it is easy to suppose that not only ought we to perform them when the occasion arises, but that we have an obligation to do so. The concept of 'obligation' is often used, as it is in the conceptual argument, as if it were indistinguishable from 'ought', or as if it were coextensive with the whole of morality. But surely, it will be objected at this point, there is no good reason to make this distinction; surely we have, for example, an obligation to help an injured person?

It is true that in everyday speech we frequently use 'obligation' in this fashion. There is, however, a very good reason for maintaining a clear distinction between 'ought' and 'obligation'.[11] The distinction is essential if due account is to be given to the mutuality and communality of our social life, and to individual freedom, equality and individuality. To conflate 'ought' and 'obligation' is implicitly to deny that obligations, properly, are self-assumed, at least in the sense of the free creation of obligations. To claim, for example, that we always have an obligation to help an injured person is implicitly to claim that we have obligations irrespective of any acts of our own. It is to assume that obligations exist independently of individuals' words and actions. It follows from this view of obligation that the most that individuals can do is to accept, recognize, or consent to, already existing obligations (compare Rawls' treatment of 'the principle of fidelity'). Self-assumed obligation as the free creation of obligations then disappears; all that is left is consent to pre-existing obligations, and, if the individual is to act as a morally responsible person, it appears that consent ought to be given. The distinction between 'ought' and 'obligation' is thus closely bound up with the distinction between the two forms of self-assumed obligation discussed in Chapter 1. It is also closely related to hypothetical voluntarism, for if 'obligations' that ought to be recognized, or consented to, exist independently of individuals' actions, it is an easy step to the inference that such recognition is given.

Moreover, if 'ought' and 'obligation' are not distinguished, no account can be taken of a crucially important aspect of relationships of obligation. Pitkin has directed attention to the fact that individuals are, at one and the same time, both superior to and subject to their obligations. We are bound by our obligations, but we also create them, and can, if necessary, break them.[12] She presents this as a paradoxical fact about obligations, but rather than paradoxical it is central to our conception of obligation and all that it implies about individuals' capacities for rational judgement and action. The real paradox is that, if 'ought' and 'obligation' are not distinguished, we are left with only two alternatives, both of which, in different ways, attempt to separate individuals from their social practices. On the one hand, the use of 'obligation' in the conceptual argument reduces individual choice to the acceptance or recognition of independently existing 'oughts' and 'rules' ('obligations'); individuals are bound but they do not create their obligations. On the other hand, abstract individualism focuses on individuals' capacity to create obligations, but it can say nothing about the rules and oughts. Individuals are superior to their obligations but their binding nature is incomprehensible. If the two dimensions of self-assumed obligation are to be given their due weight, then neither the mutuality of social life nor individuals' creative social capacities must be emphasized at the expense of the other.

When a person makes a decision 'this is what I ought to do'—and this will usually be a considerably more complex matter than in the 'self-evident' examples referred to earlier—such a decision can form the basis for a further step to be taken. The person may now have a good reason for assuming an obligation to perform the action. The point of taking this further step, and part of the value of the practice of self-assumed obligation, is that it takes the individual beyond an individual moral judgement to a 'public' declaration of a commitment to a certain course of action. It is only when an obligation has been created that one is publicly committed. It may be this aspect of obligation that encourages the assimilation of 'ought' and 'obligation'; by making a public commitment the individual stands open to the moral judgement, and perhaps censure, of others in a direct fashion. A very wide usage of 'obligation' is a way of emphasizing the moral seriousness and importance of certain kinds of actions. Be that as it may, it is important to stress that the commitment arises because a new relationship has been created. Relationships of obligation depend upon, and arise from, the complex web of inter-subjective meanings and constitutive rules of social life, but they also transcend them. Individuals are not completely submerged in their rules, meanings and oughts, but are also superior to them, and use them as a necessary basis from which they judge, choose and act, and create and change their social relationships. People are committed by, and responsible for, the relationships they have created. But they can also evaluate their past actions and try to make good unintended or unforeseen consequences; this is why it makes perfectly good sense to say 'I have an obligation but I (now) see that I ought not to keep it'.

The persistence of abstract individualism in liberal and liberal democratic theory can partly be explained by the existence of this moral and social consciousness and capacity for critical reflection. The consciousness and capacities that enable us voluntarily to assume obligations are also those that enable us to single out an aspect of this process and *imagine* that an individual could be completely abstracted from, and separate from, social relationships. It is because we are both superior to, and bound by, our obligations that we can formulate the general 'problem' of promising. At the time of decision whether a promise ought to be made an individual is, in relation to that particular decision, in a position like that attributed to the abstract individual: the individual is unbound and not yet subject to any constraint. But it is only *as if* the individual were in the position of the abstract individual. It is only when a particular decision is abstracted from the 'background' provided by the social practice of promising, and generalized as a 'natural' condition, that the 'problem' of promising emerges. Then the superiority of individuals to their obligations appears paramount and the fact that they are bound by them appears as an inexplicable puzzle.

Because of the central place of individual freedom and equality in liberal theory there is an enormous temptation to make such a generalization; and there is also a temptation to solve the resulting problems through the conceptual argument. But this is to go straight from the frying-pan into the fire. If there is also a failure to distinguish 'ought' from 'obligation', the 'problem' of promising is dissolved at the expense of the complex dialectic of individuals and their social relationships and the free creative social and political capacities of individuals. A difficult and precarious path has to be trodden between these two alternatives if we are to arrive at an appreciation of the value of the practice of self-assumed obligation, and to understand the contribution it can make to the realization, and transformation, of the liberal idea of social life as a voluntary scheme.

The Problem of Arbitrariness

In Chapter 1, I argued that the voluntarist ideal is not so wholeheartedly accepted by liberal democratic theorists of political obligation as one may assume at first sight. One reason for this is a belief that liberal voluntarism provides a very precarious basis for social life, especially in the political sphere. The following question illustrates this: why can individuals be expected to enter into obligations when it is appropriate for them to do so? There appears to be nothing to prevent individuals from arbitrarily picking and choosing when to assume obligations, or refusing to do so, from mere whims and fancies; thus the prospect of an orderly social life appears to be placed in jeopardy. This difficulty, unlike the 'problem' of promising, is a genuine problem in that it reflects the uncertainties that surround all human action. However, that having been said, it also remains the case that from an abstractly individualist viewpoint this problem appears to be insoluble, and to place a major obstacle in the way of any socio-political changes aimed at bringing a self-managing or participatory form of democracy into being.

From an abstractly individualist perspective, furthermore, not only does self-assumed political obligation appear empirically unrealistic, but the entire practice of obligation is placed in question. The difficulties seem to be further compounded if a distinction is drawn between 'ought' and 'obligation', or if emphasis is placed on individuals' consent to their obligations, because consent appears so fragile and capricious. Social life appears to be placed on a much firmer footing if individuals believe that they have obligations whether or not they have voluntarily assumed them. For instance, this seems to be in Flathman's mind in *Political Obligation*, when, discussing the example of an injured person, A, requesting another, B, to call an ambulance, he comments that 'neither the legitimacy of A's request nor B's obligation to comply with it depends on B's consent'.[13] This formulation illustrates the remarks I made earlier about the typical use of 'consent' in discussions of political obligation and its relationships to the conflation of 'ought' and 'obligation'. I shall leave aside the oddity of talking about the 'legitimacy' of the injured person's request; the important point is that to refer to the irrelevance of B's consent in this context immediately makes it appear that B has an 'obligation' irrespective of anything that B does. However, we can all agree that in this situation B ought to call an ambulance, and it can be agreed that it would be shocking if B failed to do so and, if so, she or he would justifiably be open to censure. It can also be agreed that B's conduct is worse if, having agreed to A's request, B then failed to call the ambulance (if B had not agreed someone else would have called it ...). Since these perfectly acceptable ways of talking about the request are available, the only reason to refer to 'consent' and 'obligations' seems to be to gain assurance that B will act as he or she ought. If B's consent is irrelevant, and B can be said to have an obligation, then we can apparently be more sure of B's conduct.

This certainty is illusory. Even if obligations did exist independently of individuals' actions, and even if consent were never mentioned in the context of obligations, this does not rule out the possibility that B may still fail to fulfill the obligation because of normal human moral failings such as weakness of will, or because B is a person who enjoys seeing people suffer, or enjoys inflicting suffering. Whether or not 'ought' and 'obligation' are distinguished, or consent emphasized, there can be no guarantee that B will act as she or he ought. Nevertheless, we can be reassured that it is as reasonable to expect B, where necessary, to assume and fulfill obligations as it is to have other expectations of B, providing only that B is not conceived as acting from the 'natural morality' of the possessive, abstract individual. If B always and only acts from subjective judgements of self-interest, then there is no reason for B to believe that injured people ought always to be helped, or that there are certain circumstances where obligations ought to be assumed. One way of stating this point is that B, as an abstract individual, will *always* be a free-rider. It is only if self-assumed obligation is seen from a non-abstractly individualist conceptual perspective that it can be understood why individuals do not actually always act in arbitrary and self-seeking ways, why 'consent' does not necessarily imply capriciousness, and why self-assumed obligation does not pose problems that are inherently insoluble.

To understand self-assumed obligation as a social practice is to begin to move away from abstract individualism and it is also, as I have already stressed, to focus attention on the importance of moral and social education. An essential part of this education, for adults as well as children, is to learn about the circumstances in which obligations ought to be assumed, or refrained from, and to learn about the proper content of obligations; there are some things to which one ought not to commit oneself. B will have learnt what generally ought to be done if a person is injured, and although this does not eliminate all uncertainty from B's conduct, it does show why it is reasonable to expect B to act as a minimally decent, if not always as a splendid, Samaritan.[14] Nevertheless, it should be added that the extent to which people in fact act as minimally decent Samaritans, and the extent to which they actually assume obligations where this is appropriate, depends upon the form and character of the institutions within which individuals interact; it depends upon the extent to which people are encouraged to act in given ways. I noted above that widespread adherence to abstract individualism derives partly from the fact that within liberal democratic institutions, especially capitalist economic production, individuals are expected to act self-interestedly. Thus, in fundamentally important areas of their lives, individuals are educated to act in a fashion that is often not compatible with mutual aid and forbearance and voluntary cooperation.[15]

Before turning to the problem of political obligation one further comment is in order. The problem of arbitrariness looms largest when the individuals in question are male. It is widely believed that men and women 'naturally' have different characters. The 'individual' in liberal and liberal democratic theory has usually, if often implicitly, been regarded as male, because the 'natural morality' attributed to females is not a possessive morality like that of the males who interact in the market. Female motivation has been, and still is, held to be based on love, altruism and self-sacrifice, characteristics necessary to persons whose 'natural' social role is held to be one of nurturing and caring within the family. In the 'Introduction' I drew attention to the question of differential political obligation that is raised by the allegedly 'naturally' apolitical character of women but, ironically, most aspects of the 'natural morality' attributed to them make them better suited to engage in the social practice of self-assumed obligation than the possessive male of liberal abstract individualism.

Participation in the social practice of promising presupposes that individuals—of both sexes—have some capacity for self-reflection and an ability to evaluate their own actions. The development of a critical self-consciousness is a further aspect of the process of moral and social education. Individuals learn to look critically at their own actions, and also at the rules and principles that order their social practices and the institutions of liberal democracy. It is this latter capacity that allows questions to be asked about the binding nature of the rule of fidelity, and it is a capacity that must be developed if a democratic political practice is to be established, where citizens decide upon, and can criticize and change, the rules that govern their social and political lives. Although political theorists pay homage to individuals' ability to ask radical and critical questions about the rule of fidelity, they have a very different attitude to other rules—as they must, given their fundamental assumption that political obligation in the liberal democratic state is unproblematic. They also assume that, even if it were possible for people to develop the requisite political capacities, it would not be feasible for them to be exercised; it would be to place political life at the mercy of whim and caprice, of arbitrary choice and refusal, and would thus be to court disaster. For example, Flathman, who in his analysis of 'obligation' places great emphasis on the need for individuals critically to deliberate about their actions and to have good reasons for taking on obligations, also states that

> it would be exceedingly difficult to achieve or sustain a stable society if obedience to rules could rest only on the sort of rational grounds we have been emphasizing. Habit, impulse, mindless acceptance of the status quo ... all serve to bring about obedience without a sense of being imposed upon; ...[16]

There is little doubt that all these factors help explain why people obey rules of all kinds in liberal democracies. They may or may not *feel* imposed upon. But that is not the relevant question if political *obligation* in the liberal democratic state is being discussed. Owing to their uncritical attitude to the liberal democratic state, contemporary writers tend to be more concerned with individuals' subjective feelings than with the question of whether they are actually being imposed upon. However, if individuals are free and equal, it is the latter question that is fundamental. There can be no justification for the imposition of 'obligations' upon free and equal individuals, and for someone else to decide upon the rules that will order their social and political practices. Relationships of political obligation, and the rules that constitute and follow from these relationships, must be freely created and maintained by the voluntary commitments of those involved. To be sure, when political obligation is self-assumed, individuals are unlikely to have a sense of being imposed upon, but this subjective aspect is secondary to, and far less important than, the fact that they are not actually imposed upon. The reduction of liberal voluntarism to a matter of subjective feelings, irrespective of the basis of those feelings, encourages hypothetical voluntarism. If the relevant fact appears to be that citizens in the liberal democratic state have no sense of being imposed on, or if there is no obvious manifestation of such a feeling, then it is easy to go further and make inferences about political obligation from various aspects of social and political interaction.

If it is assumed that rational evaluation of, and voluntary commitment to, rules is not a feasible basis for political life, and that habit or mindless acceptance of the *status quo* has to be relied upon, there is little or no room for self-assumed obligation in the political sphere. Habit is often presented as if it were tantamount to voluntary acquiescence, or tacit consent, to authority. Hume, for example, commenting on the origins of government 'in the woods and deserts', says that the exertion of authority by chieftains 'produced a habitual and, if you please to call it so, a voluntary ... acquiescence in the people'.[17] Locke, as I shall show, argues in a very similar way. But to claim that individuals can be said tacitly to consent, and to assume their political obligation because they habitually carry out their daily lives in a certain way, is to stretch hypothetical voluntarism to its furthest limits. The point of talking about 'habit' is usually to contrast it with actions that are undertaken selfconsciously, after reflection and consideration. One might deliberately choose habitually to act in a certain fashion, but the action would hardly be called a habit until one had stopped thinking about it and it was no longer a matter of choice. Moreover, to extend hypothetical voluntarism to include habit is to raise, in a particularly acute form, questions about individuals' own interpretation of their actions.

At this point it will be useful to make some comments about the concept of duty. Like 'ought', 'duty' is frequently used as if it meant the same thing as 'obligation', and with much the same consequences. Arguments and pronouncements about duty are also very useful in 'bringing about obedience without a sense of being imposed on' and, like arguments about habit and mindless acceptance of the *status quo*, they encourage citizens to see the rules and institutions of liberal democracy as if they were natural features of the world, independent of their judgements and actions. Duties are not dependent upon individuals' actions; the notion of 'my station and its duties' perfectly sums up the idea of a 'duty'. One occupies a station and, therefore, must accept the duties that accompany it and help define it. The performance of duties is 'not ... contingent on the mere opinion or choice of this or that subject'.[18]

It might be argued, against this, that today in liberal democracies we can choose our stations, and hence can be said to assume our duties (even if it is odd to say that we assume our habits). The genuineness of this choice is far from self-evident, especially when some persons, notably women, are regarded as 'naturally' fitted for certain stations. But even if this point is granted, it begs some very important questions about duties. The implication is that, if we can choose our stations, then there is no more to be said about the rules that constitute the station and define its duties. Once the choice has been made the rules (duties), and the way in which they are arrived at, must be accepted. This is to treat the rules governing economic and other institutions as if they were like the rule constituting the social practice of promising. This brings me to another very important reason why, despite much recent discussion by moral and political philosophers of the concept of 'rules' and 'social practices' (largely under the impetus of Wittgenstein's work), there have been few advances in arguments about political obligation in the liberal democratic state.

These arguments are usually conducted from the assumption that the rules governing social life are all of the same status, and that individuals' relationships to these rules can all be treated in the same way. This is explicitly stated by Rawls, for example, who argues that the 'rule of promising', which is constitutive of the social practice of promising, is 'on a par with legal rules and statutes, and rules of games'.[19] The consequence of this view is that questions and doubts about any rule are all regarded as equally valid and meaningful, or as equally invalid and meaningless. This is so, whether the questions and doubts are about the 'rule of promising', or about the rules constituting the institutions of the liberal democratic state. By failing to differentiate between various kinds of rules and between various dimensions of social life, political theorists leave themselves no alternative but to apply arguments about promising directly to questions of political obligation. If it is argued that it is a symptom of conceptual confusion to ask whether promises really oblige, it is also argued that to ask whether a justified obligation exists in the liberal democratic state arises from the same confusion, and that the problem of political obligation can be dissolved in exactly the same way as the 'problem' of promising. Alternatively, if doubts about promising are held to be genuine, then it also appears as if voluntarism in political life is an unrealizable ideal. The philosophical anarchist conclusion may then be drawn that individual freedom and equality are necessarily incompatible with political authority and political obligation.

In order for the nature and extent of the problem of political obligation in the liberal democractic state to be appreciated, it is necessary to differentiate between rules, like the rule of fidelity, that are constitutive of social life itself, and rules that are necessary to the existence of specific forms of social and political institutions, that are open to modification and change in a way that promising is not. It is virtually impossible to imagine the existence of human social life without the rules constituting promising, but it is not so difficult to imagine it without the rules that govern the institutions of the liberal democratic state. It is because of the socially fundamental character of the practice of promising, and its implications for mutual trust and keeping faith, that the conceptual argument about 'obligation' and 'social life' can be put forward. But to agree that it is a sign of conceptual disorder, a misunderstanding of the use of language, and of the meaning of 'social life', to doubt that promises oblige, is *not* also to agree that the same argument can be used to dismiss questions about obligation in the context of other forms of rules. If it is true that 'there is no reason to suppose that promising is more "natural" or basic than obeying authority', this is only in the sense that much the same 'natural' capacities are required for individuals to engage in the practice of promising and to obey authority—at least, if the authority in question is of a specific form.[20] If all societies need both the practice of promising and a form of political authority to make decisions about the collective life of their members, the importance of the words 'a form of' cannot be ignored. Individuals will need to develop and exercise their critical capacities in political life only if the authority in question is based on a freely created and maintained relationship. The liberal democratic form of political authority is only one possible form. While it is meaningless to ask if promises oblige, it makes very good sense to have doubts about political obligation in the liberal democratic state and to ask questions about the form of authority in other liberal democratic institutions. For example, it is far from nonsensical to ask questions about the prerogative of private owners and their managers to impose rules in the workplace, or to question the validity of the belief that it is husbands and fathers alone who should exercise authority in the household.

A view of social life and its constitutive rules as being all of a piece, and the other approaches to obligation discussed in this chapter, all contribute to the tendency for recent discussions of political obligation to oscillate between two theoretical extremes. At one extreme, attention is focused on the abstractly conceived individual, equipped with a purely possessive 'natural morality', and apparently insoluble problems of arbitrariness loom large. The second extreme appears to dissolve the problems of obligation through the conceptual argument. But it is possible to be too impressed by conceptual considerations. The arguments of some theorists suggest that social life is nothing more than a multiplicity of language games, and that all social rules are like those governing linguistic usage. Both these extremes encourage the reification of 'rules' and 'oughts' which it appears that individuals must accept, as they must accept the rules of linguistic usage, and both encourage the reduction of the problem of political obligation to a question of subjective feelings. Nor is this surprising, as each extreme is the inversion of the other, and neither acknowledges the complex, dialectical relationship between individuals and their practices, institutions and rules. To do so is a difficult undertaking, but unless the need for such an undertaking is recognized, and unless some attempt is made to carry it through, political obligation in the liberal democratic state will continue to be treated as unproblematic, and self-assumed obligation will continue to be seen as giving rise to insoluble problems.

One of these problems, of course, concerns the feasibility of a democratic political practice within which citizens rationally evaluate, decide upon, and freely commit themselves to, the rules that order that practice. There will appear to be insoluble problems surrounding participatory democracy all the time individuals' relationship to rules is deemed to be governed by a possessive 'natural morality'. To look at the problems from a different theoretical perspective, a perspective that gives a central place to the process of moral, social and political education, does not, it hardly needs to be said, solve any of the problems by itself. But it does begin to show that a solution may be possible, which is a major step forward in thinking about political obligation. Moreover, it also directs attention to the empirical aspects of problems about self-assumed obligation that are ignored in the two extremes of the conventional approach: for example, to the question of how individuals might best educate themselves in the practice of self-assumed obligation, develop their actual and potential capacities for rational deliberation and decision-making and a critical self-consciousness about their own, and collective, social creations. Despite contemporary theorists' tendency to treat the liberal democratic state as if it were a natural feature of the world, political institutions are, as the social contract theorists emphasized, human creations. People have had to learn how to take part in liberal democratic institutions, and to learn what it means to be a liberal democratic citizen (an historical process in which the learning has been aided by no little coercion and violence). If people are capable, on the most mundane level, of learning how to take part in the social practice of promising, and, on a wider plane, have been able to transform themselves and their conceptual and socio-political worlds into contemporary liberal democracy, it does not seem entirely fanciful to suggest that they might also be capable of building a democratic political order based on self-assumed political obligation.[21] It would not be built out of nothing, but would be rooted in, yet transform and transcend, some central liberal ideals and practices.

Political theorists who show such great ingenuity in formulating voluntarist justifications for political obligation might have been expected to be keenly interested in exploring the possibilities of such a development—were it not for their totally uncritical attitude to the liberal democratic state. Here lies the real paradox: that political theorists are so eager and willing to ask general and radical questions about promising, and yet are so unwilling to question the rules that govern the institutions of liberal democracy, and to question the existence of political obligation in the liberal democratic state.

Chapter 3

Political Obligation and the Sword of Leviathan

A society as conceived by individualism has never existed anywhere.

L. Dumont, *Homo Hierarchicus*.

The problems of political authority and political obligation to which the emergence of liberal individualism gives rise are nowhere better laid bare than in Hobbes' *Leviathan*. It might be thought that Hobbes' theory is hardly the place to begin an examination of the historical roots of liberal voluntarism; Leviathan is not a liberal ruler. Nevertheless, Hobbes 'had in him more of the philosophy of liberalism than most of its professed defenders'.[1] His theory is based on central liberal assumptions and values, and his radically abstract individualism presents a particularly clear statement of the problems surrounding self-assumed obligation. Hobbes' uncompromising individualism leads him to the extreme solution of absolute rule and unconditional political obedience, but, because he takes his arguments to their logical conclusion, they are all the more instructive for contemporary discussions of political obligation in the liberal democratic state. In particular, his arguments throw some interesting light onto the costs of assuming that political obligation is unproblematic.

The interpretation of Hobbes' theory, and especially his theory of obligation, is a matter of some controversy. However, much argument, especially over the status of the laws of nature, is due to a failure by many of his commentators to distinguish 'ought' from 'obligation'. Nor is the radically voluntarist character of Hobbes' theory always appreciated. It is true that his conception of 'consent' stands at the limits of hypothetical voluntarism, and that he ends by claiming that all rulers who preserve order, no matter what the ostensible basis of their power, rule by virtue of their subjects' 'consent'. But the peculiarities of Hobbes' conception of 'consent' do not mean, as some writers have argued, that he is not a consent theorist at all. Voluntarism—self-assumed obligation, consent, and the social contract—is at the heart of *Leviathan*. In this chapter I shall comment further on the general significance of liberal social contract theory. Hobbes' version of the contract story, notwithstanding its singular features, establishes a pattern of argument followed by subsequent liberal theorists.

Hobbes aimed to place his argument about political obligation on such a certain footing that his conclusions could no more be doubted than the conclusion of a geometric theorem. It is possible to arrive at demonstrable conclusions about commonwealths because, as in geometry, we are arguing about something which is the artificial creation of humans themselves. In *Leviathan* Hobbes does not work through the whole process of his method of 'resolution' and 'composition', but begins from the result of an imaginative 'resolution' of a commonwealth into a collection of individuals, which are themselves 'resolved' into machines in perpetual motion; he then takes his readers through the process of 'composition'.[2] It should be emphasized that Hobbes' methodology leads him to base his argument on a radically abstract and atomistic individualism. Machines in perpetual motion, or mere physiological entities, have no natural connections with each other. Hobbes not only removes the bonds of civil law from his individuals but all bonds and relationships whatsoever. His conception of the 'condition of meer nature', as he calls the state of nature, is thus a logical abstraction in the most complete sense. But any logical abstraction is an abstraction from an actual form of social life. The entities have to be reconstituted as individuals before they can be seen in their 'natural' state or as subjects in a commonwealth, but the allegedly 'natural' characteristics with which Hobbes equips the entities during the process of 'composition' are socially familiar ones. How else could he claim that his readers had only to look into themselves and examine their own passions and fears to find his argument irresistible? Hobbes' individuals' 'natural' qualities are admirably suited to people living at a time when the traditional social order, bolstered by claims about the divine right of kings and patriarchal arguments, was beginning to pass away and the first stages of the market economy and a liberal society and state were making their appearance.

The State of Nature

The 'problem' of promising discussed in Chapter 2 is a particular case of the general problem of moving from the perspective of a single, isolated individual to a coherent conception of social life and its multiplicity of social practices. The general problem is a consequence of radical, abstract individualism, and it is exemplified in Hobbes' account of the state of nature. His account makes sense only because he (and his readers) implicitly presupposes the social attributes, relationships, and practices that he attempts to strip away. Hobbes' state of nature shows us a world as it would be if inhabited by individuals who are each confined within a purely subjective viewpoint. Since each one is considered singularly, individuals can have no other outlook than an entirely private and self-interested one. They are possessive individuals who judge the world, and others, solely in terms of subjective evaluations of self-interest, in terms of the protection and enlargement of what they own, including, most importantly for Hobbes, the protection of the property they have in their own bodies and lives. The well-known features of Hobbes' state of nature are a direct consequence of this radically individualist perspective.

Hobbes' natural individuals are able to reason and they can speak to each other. Without speech, Hobbes says, 'there had been amongst men, neither Commonwealth, nor Society, nor Contract, nor Peace, no more than amongst Lyons, Bears, and Wolves' (IV; 100).[3] For the nominalist Hobbes words, 'names', depend on the will and the judgement of the individuals who are speaking. Meaning is a matter for private judgement. In the natural condition *everything* is a matter of individual private judgement. Hobbes argues that 'True and False are attributes of Speech, not of Things' (IV; 105). The same things affect individuals differently, and affect the same individual differently at different times, so their names will be of 'inconstant signification' and it will therefore be an arbitrary matter how individuals evaluate others and their environment. What one person calls cruelty another will call justice, and similarly with 'good' and 'bad'; everyone calls 'good' whatever it is they happen to desire, and things that they are trying to avoid are called 'bad'. There is nothing that 'naturally' leads to any consistency in naming, and in 'the condition of meer Nature, ... private Appetite is the measure of Good, and Evill' (XV; 216).

Hobbes' examples of the subjective attribution of meaning are of moral words. However, there is no good reason why 'private appetite' is not the measure of *all* words. Unconnected, atomistic individuals have to decide for themselves what their words mean, and this makes it extremely difficult to see how language would ever arise at all. If, as Hobbes argues, society requires speech, the development of speech also requires a set of social relationships. Speech is learnt, it is not generated anew each day by isolated individuals.[4] This is just one example of Hobbes implicitly presupposing what he has ostensibly abstracted from his argument. He is implicitly falling back on a conception of social individuals and social relationships in order to get his imaginative reconstruction off the ground at all. In reading these passages of *Leviathan* we, and Hobbes, implicitly assume a social background of agreed meanings, or a language, in which only the meanings of moral words remain to be arbitrarily assigned. Without this assumption the state of nature would not be inhabited by speaking individuals, but his machines or, rather, as Rousseau saw, dumb animals who are potentially human.

Hobbes also assumes that although there is no agreement about the meaning of moral words in the state of nature, his individuals, nevertheless, do possess a capacity for understanding what these words would mean in a condition of social peace.[5] Indeed, he must make this assumption; if his individuals did not have this capacity they could not enter into civil society. It is not individuals or their 'natures' that change during the transition from the state of nature to civil society, but their socio-political situation. Therefore, if individuals did not *already* understand what kinds of relationships were indicated by words such as 'justice', 'obligation', 'peace', 'promise' and 'contract', there could be no social contract and no political obligation in civil society.

Hobbes argues that individuals will try to obtain as much as possible of whatever they desire and call 'good'. He calls the means to fulfil these desires 'power', and this can be all kinds of things, from riches, or strength, to a reputation of power (X; 150–1). Insofar as individuals are able to satisfy their desires through use of their power they obtain 'felicity' or a 'continual prospering'. Hobbes sees the striving for felicity as a continual struggle, the fulfilment of one desire being merely a step on the way to another. To keep felicity and power at a constant level demands more power, and so Hobbes arrives at his famous statement of the 'generall inclination of all mankind, a perpetuall and restlesse desire of Power after power, that ceaseth onely in Death' (XI; 161).

These characteristics of individuals have been established before Hobbes deals with the 'natural condition' of mankind in Chapter 13 of *Leviathan*.[6] He then considers what will happen when they come together with no social rules or civil laws to regulate their interaction. It is at this point that Hobbes introduces the postulate of a fundamental equality between individuals. In fact, this postulate necessarily follows from the assumptions of abstract individualism. Seen singularly, each with the same 'natural' attributes, individuals must be regarded as equals; there is no reason why 'naturally' they should be otherwise. It should be noted that Hobbes regards the sex of the individual as irrelevant; individuals are equal whether they are male or female (XX; 253). Hobbes is extremely unusual in the consistency of his individualism on this point and in his willingness to challenge the patriarchal claim that women are 'naturally' weaker than, and thus subordinate to, men (although Hobbes' challenge does not extend to his argument about civil society). Each individual, whether male or female, is strong enough to kill another, and with experience, all are equally capable of the reasoning and cunning required to use their strength to kill. If two individuals both desire the same thing, and only one of them can enjoy it, 'they become enemies; and ... endeavour to destroy, or subdue one an other' (XIII; 184).

Each individual in the state of nature has a natural right to everything that is required for self-preservation. Since individuals judge their needs entirely subjectively, it follows that there can be no general limitation upon their natural right. Hobbes' individuals have a natural right to all things—even to each others' bodies; 'there is nothing he can make use of, that may not be a help unto him, in preserving his life against his enemyes' (XIV; 189–90). No one, except the individual concerned, can judge whether the natural right has been properly exercised in a given case.

The paradox of a situation where individual private judgement is paramount is that the absolute freedom of the right to everything involves no real liberty or rights at all. Instead it leads to complete insecurity and a condition of pure arbitrariness. Individuals will attack each other at random at any time in their competition to attain felicity. It will always be advantageous for an individual to act first, to make what would today be called a pre-emptive strike, in anticipation of another's actions: as Hobbes states, 'there is no way for any man to secure himselfe, so reasonable, as Anticipation; that is, by force, or wiles, to master the persons of all men he can' (XIII; 184). In the state of nature there can be no ideas of 'justice', no notions of 'mine' and 'thine', and no matrimonial laws; all will take what they can get and keep it for as long as they can. The natural condition is therefore a state of mutual war between individuals; war will break out every time any individual judges it advantageous to attack another. It is, as Hobbes describes it in one of the most famous passages in the whole literature of political theory, a nasty, brutish condition. Life is short where there is 'no place for Industry; ... no Culture of the Earth; ... no Navigation; ... no commodious Building; ... no account of Time; no Arts; no Letters; no Society' (XIII; 186).

'No Society'—but it is usually assumed that the absence of a 'common power' in Hobbes' state of nature implies only that a political sovereign, a government, or state, and a set of civil laws, is lacking. But Hobbes' individualist state of nature lacks much more than this. It has no social or moral rules or relationships; that is to say, it is not a social state. The task of Leviathan is correspondingly enormous; his sword has to bring into being not only a civil government but social life itself. This tends to be overlooked because it is usually erroneously assumed that a 'common power' would not exist in a society where people voluntarily and willingly complied with rules and laws, and no specialized, external rule-enforcement agency was required. Yet, if offences did occur, these people would be prepared to take action against the offenders, although it need not be violently coercive action: 'In order that a society should be describable as having no "common power" it would have to be positively committed to abstaining from *any* sort of action which could bring any substantial evil on the heads of offenders'.[7] In other words, all 'societies' will have a common power. Indeed, outside of a society the conception of an 'offender' makes no sense, for an 'offender' presupposes that there is something, namely a framework of ordered social relationships, to be 'offended' against. Without such relationships, all that remains is a collection of atomized individuals in Hobbes' asocial natural condition. They have no social constraints on their wills, judgements, and actions, and therefore no conception of an 'offence'.

The sociological and anthropological oddity of Hobbes' picture of the state of nature, and the radical task that Leviathan is called upon to perform, is usually underestimated precisely because the social and moral relationships that Hobbes has attempted to strip away are implicitly read back in. One of the questions that has greatly exercised Hobbes' commentators is whether moral obligations exist in his state of nature. As we have seen, Hobbes' individuals have the capacity to understand what an 'obligation' is, but, nevertheless, his state of nature is extremely unlikely to contain obligations.

Obligation in the State of Nature

Hobbes' individuals are unrelated to each other in their natural condition and they therefore have to create *all* their social relationships for themselves, including relations of obligation. Hobbes states there is 'no Obligation on any man, which ariseth not from some Act of his own; for all men equally, are by Nature Free' (XXI; 268). Paradigm cases of such acts are a contract, a promise, a covenant, consent. An individual takes on an obligation by giving up the right to all things, either by general renunciation, or by transferring it to some specific person or persons. Once this is done, 'he is said to be OBLIGED, or BOUND, not to hinder those, to whom such Right is granted, or abandoned, from the benefit of it' (XIV; 191).

Hobbes goes on to argue that, once the individual is bound, it is self-contradictory not to perform the obligation. It would be 'absurd' if it were not carried out. This is just one example of how Hobbes hopes to make his argument as watertight as a geometric theorem. It is 'absurd' to question the conclusion of a theorem and, similarly, because all voluntary acts, according to Hobbes, are performed only because individuals expect that they will result in some good to themselves, it is 'absurd' to try to hinder their consequences. One aspect of the right to everything cannot be renounced or transferred to form part of an obligation. No individual can give up the right of self-preservation or self-protection. Hobbes goes so far as to say that anyone who appears not to want to preserve their life, 'is not to be understood as if he meant it, or that it was his will; but that he was ignorant of how such words and actions were to be interpreted' (XIV; 192).

Hobbes distinguishes two basic forms of self-assumed obligation: a contract, where there is a mutual transfer of rights; and a covenant, where one party is trusted by the other to perform their part of the agreement at some later date.[8] The 'bonds' of an obligation are constituted by the appropriate words and actions that indicate that a contract or covenant has been made. However, these bonds have no strength 'from their own Nature'; words alone are not sufficient to hold individuals to their obligations. Bonds constituted by words 'are too weak to bridle mens ambition, avarice,anger and other Passions', all of which lead men to break faith (XIV; 192). If obligations are to be fulfilled, individuals must be sufficiently fearful of the consequences of breaking them, and the only completely effective fear is that brought about by the sword of an absolute sovereign. It should be emphasized, however, that Hobbes is *not* saying that words cannot create an obligation—to say 'I contract ...' or 'I promise ...' *is* to put oneself under an obligation. Rather, words alone are not enough to bring about the *keeping* of obligations.

In the state of nature words are so ineffective that it is very unlikely that any agreements will be kept. In discussing the example of a covenant, Hobbes says that 'upon any reasonable suspicion, it is Voyd'. Individuals have only their own subjective judgements of the possible actions of others to guide them. It is always advantageous to anticipate the actions of others, so that the slightest hint that one individual will not keep an agreement, or that it would be disadvantageous for an individual to perform his or her side of the covenant, will mean that the words have become void.[9] Fear of what the other person will do (or fail to do) means that covenants are unlikely ever to be fulfilled: 'He which performeth first, does but betray himselfe to his enemy' (XIV; 196).

Hobbes says that the reason for the fear must be something that arises after the making of the covenant, but there seems no good reason, given Hobbes' characterization of the state of nature, why any covenants should be entered into. It is difficult to see why the words 'I covenant ...' should ever be spoken and why obligations arising from covenants should ever exist in the state of nature. If the words are to be spoken meaningfully, individuals must understand that covenants involve trust on the part of one party at least, and their experience would have shown them that it is never beneficial to oneself to trust anybody. That is the first lesson of prudence that comes with experience; to trust someone, to perform your part of the covenant first, is to betray yourself to an enemy. The prudential thing to do would be *to enter no covenants at all*. If an individual could always be sure that he or she would never perform first, then it would be beneficial to enter a covenant— because he or she would always break the trust. However, other individuals would also learn that this is advantageous, and so would demand to perform second or be trusted. ... Thus it is extremely unlikely that there would be obligations arising from covenants in Hobbes' state of nature because there is little reason for covenants to take place.

This conclusion might be contested in the light of Hobbes' own affirmative answer to the problem: 'where one of the parties has performed already; ... there is the question whether it be against reason, that is, against the benefit of the other to performe, or not' (XV; 204).[10] The important point here is the exact force of Hobbes' reference to 'against reason'. If the 'benefit' is to be assessed subjectively by an individual alone, then it is 'against reason' for the second party to fulfill the agreement. Seen solely in terms of the 'individual reason' of an abstract individual, it is always beneficial for the individual *not* to keep an agreement. He who performs first has betrayed himself to his enemy, to the second (non)performer. However, this particular example is concerned with someone in the state of nature who, in order to protect himself more securely, has entered into a defensive agreement with others. Now, I have argued that the existence of social relationships of any kind is problematic in the state of nature. Let us suppose, however, that an individual has entered into an agreement with some confederates for mutual defence. If, Hobbes argues, this individual now declares that it is reasonable for him not to keep his part of the bargain, he 'cannot be received into any Society, that unite themselves for Peace and Defence, but by the errour of them that receive him'. This is, indeed, now the appropriate conclusion. The hypothesis of the defensive confederation has, in one small area, transformed the anomie and war of the state of nature into social life, and it has, therefore, transformed the problem of performing second.

The keeping of covenants must now be considered from the perspective of individuals in a mutual relationship (the confederation or small society), *not* from the subjective perspective of an isolated individual. The communal or social perspective gives a different answer to the question of what is 'against reason' than the subjective judgement of the single, isolated individual.[11] If there is to be any social life, as I shall show shortly in discussing the laws of nature, individuals must understand that, generally, agreements should be kept, and that it is 'against reason' to insist to the contrary. In the state of nature there is no peace, and cannot be, because each individual reasons purely subjectively; hence there can be no limitations on what is, or is not, 'against reason'. Individuals have the right to all things and so, strictly speaking, the idea of something being 'against reason' makes no sense. This is why Hobbes' hypothesis of a confederation is an improbable one. In the state of nature confederations are unlikely to form because each individual will judge it beneficial to break agreements when they have (foolishly) been trusted by others—and all will learn from experience.

There is, however, another way in which the confederation can come into being: through what I shall call an enforced covenant. Our understanding of the 'acts of our own' that give rise to obligations is that they must be free and voluntary. Usually, if I have been forced under threats to say 'I promise', my promise will not be regarded as valid; it is not a 'real' promise. However, Hobbes treats as 'voluntary' even those acts performed under threat of violence or death. Fear and liberty are compatible, and thus Hobbes argues that covenants 'entered into by fear in the condition of meer Nature, are obligatory' (XIV; 198). If, therefore, a confederation is formed because one individual is able to terrorize others into joining with him, their 'obligation' to perform their part of the agreement is, according to Hobbes, just as valid as if they had all willingly banded together. He also argues that if you have agreed to pay an armed robber a ransom in return for your life, then you must pay when the time comes. The reasonableness of 'performing second' in this case, if one may safely refuse to do so, can well be questioned. More importantly, Hobbes' notion of an enforced covenant is central to his conception of obligation and 'consent'.

In Chapter 1, I drew a distinction between the two forms of self-assumed obligation: self-assumed obligation as the free creation of obligations, and self-assumed obligation as consent. Initially, Hobbes' discussion of obligation appears to focus on the first form; obligations are created when individuals freely say certain words. Hobbes' radical individualism means that he must begin with this form of self-assumed obligation. Nevertheless, his argument is actually based on self-assumed obligation as consent—and the 'consent' in question is that involved in an enforced covenant. Hobbes' theory provides a particularly clear example of the way in which voluntarism can be transformed into the most empty form of hypothetical voluntarism. If a robber makes a demand backed by the threat of death then, Hobbes argues, the individual will always 'consent' to the demand to save his or her life. The individual's submission can *always* be interpreted as 'consent'; 'obligation' can always be inferred from forced submission. Hobbes uses 'consent' in the same sense when he refers to the relation between parent and child, between conqueror and subject, and, as I shall show later, between Leviathan and the individuals who authorize his rule. Hobbes states that 'the Rights and Consequences of both Paternall and Despoticall Dominion, are the very same with those of a Soveraign by institution; and for the same reasons' (XX; 256). The reason is that they are all based on 'consent'. An individual, whether a victim facing a robber's gun, a prisoner facing a conqueror's sword, or a child facing a parent who can expose it, will always 'consent' to be ruled rather than forfeit his or her life. It is not the power or force that is exercised that is relevant to the subsequent right to rule, but the 'consent' that can always be inferred from the individual's submission. Hobbes is a completely consistent—and completely hypothetical—conventionalist. All authority, he argues, whether that of a parent over a child, or the conqueror over defeated subjects, is based on 'consent': 'command alone has no more significance in Hobbes than power alone'.[12]

The only 'obligations', arising from covenants, likely to be found in the state of nature are those implied by the 'consent' to enforced covenants. But, based on threats and force, these covenants cannot be accepted as constituting valid obligations. What then of contracts? There are no special problems about contracts in the Hobbesian state of nature, providing that the mutual transfer of right takes place simultaneously between individuals. If the contract takes the form where both parties agree to perform together at a future date, all the problems about trust and keeping faith, already discussed, arise once more. The major difficulty about contracts is whether they constitute anything that can properly be called 'obligation'. As Hobbes is well aware, a relationship of 'obligation' is one based on keeping faith; to have assumed an obligation *is* to have committed oneself in a relationship of trust. In introducing the notion of a contract Hobbes refers to economic exchanges and transactions (XIV; 193). Hobbesian contracts are nothing more than simultaneous exchanges by possessive individuals, in which each individual independently judges that the exchange will be advantageous. Contracts do not provide an example of obligation in the state of nature. Their significance lies in what they reveal about the form and character of (uncoerced) social relationships that can be derived from a radically abstract individualism; 'social life' can be seen only as a series of discrete exchanges between individuals.[13] Not all theorists draw Hobbes' absolutist conclusions from this reductionist view of social relationships. In Chapter 7 I shall consider Godwin's philosophical anarchist alternative to the rule of Leviathan.

One further comment needs to be made about Hobbes' treatment of these topics. Individuals can threaten others, but they can also give them things; Hobbes says that where an individual makes an offer unilaterally to gain friends, or enhance reputation, this is not a contract or covenant but a 'GIFT, FREE-GIFT, GRACE: which words signifie one and the same thing' (XIV; 193). It is worth digressing slightly at this point because many present-day theorists insist that obligations, including political obligations, can arise from the receipt of benefits, or 'grace' (an argument that I criticize in Chapter 6). Hobbes says that 'benefits oblige' and that gratitude, or cheerful acceptance, is due to a superior who bestows a benefit (XI; 162–3). However, this cannot, as he implies, be the case in the state of nature; the benefit would merely be seized with no question of 'gratitude' arising. Later, Hobbes discusses gratitude in the context of the laws of nature, and he says that individuals must 'Endeavour that he which giveth [a benefit] have no reasonable cause to repent him of his good will' (XV; 209). But this, as I shall show in the next section, does not involve an obligation but, rather, that individuals who desire peace ought to act in this way.

The Laws of Nature

I have so far said nothing about the place of the laws of nature in Hobbes' discussion of covenants, contracts and the natural condition. The status and role of the laws of nature has given rise to a major controversy in recent studies of Hobbes' political theory. A great variety of interpretations is to be found, ranging from Watkins' characterization of the laws of nature as 'assertoric hypothetical imperatives', to McNeilly's view that they are a purely formal statement of the necessary means to peace, and Warrender's much discussed argument that Hobbes' laws of nature are laws of nature in the traditional, pre-modern, sense of God's law in the world, and that they are binding on individuals for that reason.[14]

I have argued that we can make sense of Hobbes' state of nature only because certain social qualities and relationships are implicitly presupposed; these include the relationships summed up in the laws of nature. Once the abstractly individualist character of the natural condition has been established, it can be seen that the laws of nature provide an essential social background, necessary if the transition to civil society is to be possible. The laws of nature provide the necessary conceptual and empirical minimal conditions for a moral and social order, for a 'society', to exist. Or, to make the point in a different way, in terms of the distinction I drew in Chapter 2, Hobbes' laws of nature provide a background of 'oughts' against which 'obligations' can be freely assumed. In the state of nature the keeping of agreements is always a 'problem'; indeed, to say that they *ought* to be kept is meaningless, because there is a right to all things, and nothing that generally ought to be done or not done. On the other hand, as I noted earlier, individuals in the natural condition have a capacity for understanding what moral words would mean in a situation of social peace. If it is possible for an individual in Hobbes' state of nature meaningfully to say 'I covenant' or 'I promise', then it is being taken for granted that the individual understands the nature of the relationships involved in a covenant, and understands that commitments *ought* to be carried out. In short, it presupposes an understanding of the social practice of covenanting, or presupposes Hobbes' third law of nature, 'that men performe their Covenants made'. And this, according to Hobbes, means that we are presupposing some notion of justice. In the third law of nature 'consisteth the Fountain and Originall of JUSTICE. ... the definition of INJUSTICE, is no other than the not Performance of Covenant' (XV; 202).

Hobbes tells us that his individuals are not doomed to remain in the natural condition. Both their passions and their reason enable them to create a peaceful civil society, the overriding passion being, of course, the fear of premature death. The passions are aided by reason which 'suggesteth convenient Articles of Peace, upon which men may be drawn to agreement. These Articles, are they, which otherwise are called the Lawes of Nature' (XIII; 188). A few sentences later, Hobbes states that a law of nature 'is a Precept, or generall Rule, found out by Reason, by which a man is forbidden to do, that, which is destructive of his life'. But which sense of 'reason' is this? As the preceding discussion suggests, it is not the 'individual reason' of the inhabitants of the state of nature. The 'reason' that is capable of discovering and understanding the laws of nature and their social purpose is the reason of individuals who live socially with others. Because we, Hobbes' readers, are able to imagine ourselves independent of all social relationships we can also imagine a purely private, subjective, judgement or reason. But 'individual reason', in this sense, can play its part in Hobbes' state of nature only because it is an imaginative abstraction from a conception of reason and rational action that is inherently social.

The first three laws of nature cited by Hobbes are the crucially important ones. The first law states that individuals must 'endeavour' peace where there is hope that it is possible. The second prescribes that each individual should be willing, when others are too, to give up the right to all things in exchange for limited, but mutually equal, rights and freedoms (XIV; 189–90). The third, as stated, underwrites the social practice of covenanting. The laws thus prescribe what individuals *ought* to do if they desire to live socially and at peace with one another. Social life and peace require mutual, equal forbearance, and some general rules to regulate individual judgement and action. The laws of nature provide a statement of the fundamental conceptual requirements for a coherent notion of 'social life'; in that sense they are formally or logically necessary. However, they are not only conceptual necessities. The laws of nature are also empirically necessary. If there actually is no mutual trust (justice), mutual aid, and forbearance, then, as Hobbes' account of the state of nature shows so graphically, social life falls apart into a war between arbitrarily acting individuals.

These basic relationships are moral as well as social. Hobbes states that the science of the laws of nature 'is the true and onely Moral Philosophy' (XV; 215–6), but it is a major source of disagreement among his students whether there is a proper moral philosophy to be found in *Leviathan*. The presentation of the characteristics of possessive individuals as 'natural' human features tends to mislead Hobbes' commentators here (the more so since these individuals are abstracted from a form of social life that has been greatly consolidated and enlarged since Hobbes wrote). Hobbes contends that all voluntary actions are self-interested, and it seems to many theorists that a theory resting entirely on the claims of self-interest cannot contain a properly moral philosophy. However, Hobbes' contention follows logically from the theoretical perspective of abstract individualism, and should not be confused with his general argument about the laws of nature. The laws provide the necessary basis for moral relationships to exist. Without an understanding by individuals of the 'meaning' of the laws of nature no morality would be possible at all. Individuals understand that the laws of nature are in their 'interest' because without them they would have no security and small hope of achieving their desires and needs and wants. This general moral 'interest' of individuals seen socially, not severally, must not be confused with the specific, self-interested 'natural morality' with which Hobbes equips his individuals.

It is often assumed that if Hobbes' laws of nature are moral laws, then they must be 'laws of nature' in the traditional sense, and so impose obligations on the inhabitants of the state of nature. By calling his rules 'laws of nature' Hobbes has contributed to the confusion. His conception of the rules is a modern one; it has nothing in common, except the name, with the long tradition of political argument that called upon God's natural law of the universe. The traditional conception of natural law was of a Divine Law that stood above civil laws, which could be used to evaluate them, placing a limitation upon the scope of the powers of temporal rulers. This idea of a higher law was anathema to Hobbes; nevertheless, he writes of the 'laws of nature' because he

> has not fully emancipated himself from the medieval conception of natural law. He is not fully aware of his own originality ... Hobbes's label, law of nature, misleads in containing 'law'. But only we, who are the beneficiaries of the revolution in moral and political concepts which Hobbes, among others, initiated, are in a position to draw clearly the conceptual lines with which Hobbes struggled.[15]

As I shall show in more detail later, it is a cornerstone of Hobbes' political theory that the sovereign must be the sole lawful interpreter of God's word. God Himself appears in Hobbes' political theory only as mediated through the commands of the sovereign. It is only when God's commands are also the commands of the sovereign that they are, properly, laws. The Word of God, supreme commander of humanity, is traditionally called 'law'. But, Hobbes states, law 'properly is the word of him, that by right hath command over others' (XV; 216). Only an absolute sovereign has both the right to command and can exercise *effective* command. God's commands have to be carried out by people, and, in their natural condition, they are unable to act as God would have them act. God's commands are *called* laws, but they are not properly laws because in the state of nature they will not, and cannot, be acted upon or enforced:

> For the Lawes of Nature, ... in the condition of meer Nature ... are not properly Lawes, but qualities that dispose men to peace, and to obedience. When a Common-wealth is once settled, then are they actually Lawes, and not before; ... For it is the Soveraign Power that obliges men to obey them (XXVI; 314: also 322–3).

The laws of nature are, then, principles of reason that enable men to live peacefully or socially. They are a statement of what individuals necessarily ought to do to this end. Hobbes does, however, sometimes imply that they are more than this, but on these occasions he is, like many present-day theorists, using 'obligation' or 'oblige' as shorthand for all those actions which we ought to perform. I drew attention, earlier, to one instance of this when Hobbes is discussing gratitude. Another example occurs in Hobbes' statement that 'The Lawes of Nature oblige *in foro interno*; ... but *in foro externo*; that is, to the putting them in act, not alwayes'. The laws ought to be followed, but, in the state of nature, they will invariably be ignored. If the individual tries to follow them 'where no man els should do so, he should but make himselfe a prey to others, and procure his own certain ruine' (XV; 215). There has been no covenant or contract to follow the laws, and could not be with God because he cannot be covenanted with, so they cannot, according to Hobbes' own definition, constitute 'obligations' (XIV; 197).

This has been denied by some commentators who argue, to use Warrender's words, that 'Hobbes's theory of obligation is based upon natural law and not upon promise-keeping as such'.[16] There are two important points to make about this argument. The first is that Warrender discusses Hobbes' theory in terms of the 'validating conditions' for obligations which render them 'operative' or 'inoperative'. This, however, is begging the question about the existence of obligations in Hobbes' state of nature, for the formulation assumes that they do exist and that what matters is whether they are 'operative'. Secondly, to assume that obligations exist means that individuals can only consent to the obligations; they cannot freely create them for themselves. Warrender ignores the radically voluntarist character of Hobbes' theory. He claims that God's commands are proper laws and obligatory because of God's omnipotence, and so assimilates 'obligation' to enforced covenants. It is fear of God's irresistible power that 'validates' the obligation, just as fear of the robber's threats gives rise to an enforced covenant through 'consent' to his demands.[17]

To fill Hobbes' state of nature with Divinely sanctioned relationships of obligation is to rob it of its originality, and also to fail to see why it is a condition so dreadful that Leviathan's absolute rule is the only alternative. Hobbes' political argument depends upon the fact that, no matter how strongly it is held that the laws of nature *ought* to be obeyed, when all individuals' actions are based on individual subjective judgement, it will always be 'unreasonable' actually to obey them. Warrender interprets Hobbes to mean not that there is no obligation to obey the laws of nature, but that the reference to '*in foro interno*' implies that the laws *oblige* in conscience;

'*all* the obligations of men in the State of Nature could be described as obligations in conscience'.[18] To talk of 'obligations in conscience' begs the vital question whether, in the state of nature, 'conscience' can refer to anything other than the absolute right of individual judgement or the right to all things. The last thing that Hobbes would want is that 'conscience' in the conventional sense should be enshrined at the heart of his political argument; he makes it very clear that conscience has no politically relevant place in civil society.

To allow that individuals have conscientious obligations placed upon them by God would enable them to question the rightness and justice of Leviathan's rule in the name of God. This is precisely what Hobbes wishes to avoid in civil society. Any such questioning is, in his eyes, a return to the state of nature and the ideological conflict that he saw as the cause of the English Civil War. When Leviathan's word and sword replace the traditional Word of God—and who exactly could rightfully wield His sword?—it is impossible for any limitation to be placed on Leviathan's rule if peace is to be secured.

The Social Contract and the Authorization of the Sovereign

Before turning to Hobbes' account of the social contract and the institution of Leviathan, I want to say something about the general significance of liberal social contract theory. The idea of the social contract supplies a voluntarist explanation of how 'in the beginning' free and equal individuals could legitimately be governed. The transition from the state of nature to civil society is accomplished through the medium of the liberal social contract. The contract brings a new political association into being and it also establishes a new political status for individuals. During the social contract, individuals exchange their 'natural' freedom and equality for the status of civil subject with civil freedom and equality; they 'put to the act' Hobbes' second law of nature. By entering the social contract, individuals, through their own actions, institute a new political status and the rules which govern it. They become formally equal subjects whose freedom is equally protected through the impartially administered rule of civil law. It should be emphasized that the new political status exists independently of any differences between individuals; all individuals are formally equal as political subjects no matter what social inequalities may divide them. All this is, however, only part of the liberal social contract. The contract, conceptually, is a two-stage process; in Hobbes' version the two stages are simultaneous, but in Locke's theory, which is discussed in the next chapter, the two parts are more easily discerned. In the second part of the liberal contract individuals agree to alienate to a government of representatives the right to make political decisions. It is thus the second stage that is crucial for liberal voluntarist arguments about political obligation; individuals take upon themselves the obligation to let representatives decide upon the content of their political obligation.

Contemporary writers on political obligation implicitly assume that the second stage of the contract is indispensable. The question they are concerned with is how individuals can be said to consent to this arrangement, or voluntarily oblige themselves. I am arguing that, taken seriously as a political ideal, self-assumed obligation undermines this assumption and requires that very different questions are asked. In *The Political Theory of Possessive Individualism*, Macpherson reaches an apparently similar conclusion; he states that it is 'impossible' today 'to derive a valid theory of obligation from the assumptions [of possessive individualism]'.[19] However, Macpherson's interpretation of Hobbes and Locke takes no account of the social contract or of liberal voluntarist arguments about political obligation. He argues that, if individuals are to acknowledge a morally binding political obligation that is not based on God's will, or the purposes of nature, they must be capable 'of seeing themselves as equal in some respect more important than all the respects in which they are unequal'.[20] In the seventeenth century the relevant equality was derived from the equal subordination of each individual to the laws of the market. This subordination was regarded as inevitable, and it thus provided individuals with a reason for recognizing an obligation to the political authority that maintained social order in a market society. In the twentieth century, Macpherson argues, this reason no longer holds good. With the development of workers' political consciousness and organizations the laws of the market are no longer seen as an inevitable or natural feature of the world. It is, therefore, no longer accepted that the requisite equality exists, and political obligation has lost its seventeenth-century justification.

One problem with this argument is that, notwithstanding the achievement of the labour movement in the liberal democracies, it is questionable how far it has brought the legitimacy of the liberal democratic state into question. Indeed, it could be argued that it has helped consolidate that legitimacy. It is true that the capitalist market and its inequalities are often criticized by workers' organizations, but by concentrating on the market at the expense of the specifically political aspects of the development of liberal democracy, Macpherson has failed to take into account the extent to which criticism of the market is insulated from criticism of the political institutions that developed with it.

I have emphasized that the development of liberal individualism was an integral part of the development of liberal society, of the capitalist market economy and the constitutional state. 'Free and equal individuals' are necessary for a market economy to operate and, conversely, without the emergence of the market these creatures would not have inhabited the state of nature. However, this is not to say that there is no need to look further than the market for a justification of political obligation. Macpherson gives no explanation of why the social contract and consent are central to Hobbes' and Locke's theories. His argument shows why 'naturally' equal individuals should recognize the need for regulation of the competitive interaction of possessive individuals in the market. But it fails to take into account that 'naturally' free individuals also have voluntarily to agree to institute a political authority to govern them. To ignore the social contract is to ignore that the agreement sets up, in civil society, an equality of exactly the kind that Macpherson argues is needed for justifying political obligation; a formal equality that exists over and above the inequalities of the market or the private sphere.

To ignore the social contract is also to overlook that it stands at the beginning of the long process through which the political sphere has come to be seen as separate from the rest of social life. This helps explain why criticism of the market and the economy can be insulated from criticism of liberal democratic political institutions. The conception of a separate political sphere is also important if the actual development of liberal democracies, rather than the logic of the social contract, is considered. By the mid-twentieth century, with the introduction of universal suffrage and the institutionalization of civil liberties, the formal political status of individuals had been consolidated and extended as the formal political equality of citizenship. Macpherson argues that universal suffrage has undermined another aspect of the seventeenth-century justification of political obligation: the cohesion of self-interest among those, the propertied classes, who chose the representatives.[21] However, universal suffrage and the formal political equality of citizenship has given all individuals a political 'interest' in common. Contemporary liberal voluntarist arguments about voting and consent cannot be fully understood unless the continuity between the liberal social contract story and arguments about universal suffrage is appreciated. It is assumed that all individuals have a reason to enter the contract because it ensures protection of their interests. Similarly, contemporary liberal theory, as I shall show in Chapter 5, argues that universal suffrage ensures the protection of all citizens' interests irrespective of their substantive social position— hence it is reasonable to infer that consent is given through voting.

Furthermore, without an examination of the political implications of the idea of self-assumed obligation and the role of the second stage of the social contract, the liberal democratic form of political authority remains unquestioned. Macpherson argues that this form can no longer be justified in traditional liberal terms, but he says nothing about the form itself. He argues that in the late twentieth century a justification for obligation can be derived from the equality of insecurity brought about by the development of nuclear weaponry. Although he states that this will look beyond 'a single national state alone', he appears to assume that the liberal democratic form of authority will remain.[22] But by appealing to global insecurity all links to liberalism and self-assumed obligation have been cut. There is little reason, as Hobbes' theory shows, to suppose that an appeal to survival alone will lead to democratic conclusions.

Hobbes concludes from his appeal to self-preservation that an absolute ruler is required, but Leviathan obtains his authority from the consent of his subjects, *not* directly from considerations of security. The principal desire of Hobbes' individuals is protection, but, as 'naturally' free and equal individuals, they must voluntarily enter a contract together to obtain the security of Leviathan's sword. Hobbes' version of the social contract, in one sense, gives expression to the ideal of self-assumed obligation, but its effect is completely to sweep away and transform political 'obligation' into an unconditional political obedience.

> Every man should say to every man, I Authorise and give up my Right of Governing my selfe, to this Man, or to this Assembly of men, on this condition, that thou give up thy Right to him, and Authorise all his Actions in like manner (XVII; 227).

It is by saying these words to each other that Hobbes' individuals leave the state of nature and enter civil society. The words create a society and institute a ruler to enforce order. It should be noted that the social contract is a contract, and not a covenant, and so possible in Hobbes' state of nature. Individuals simultaneously exchange certain words and, in so doing, mutually give up their right to all things to the sovereign. The contract is, however, a somewhat magical event. In the short time that it takes for the words to be spoken, a collection of warring individuals is transformed into a peaceful community with Leviathan at their head; a unified body politic is brought into being and individuals become political subjects.

Hobbes' notion of the unity of the new political community is a peculiar one. In the state of nature individuals have no sustained relations with each other; in civil society they are unified through the figure of Leviathan himself who becomes the 'bearer' of their persons and the 'author' of their acts. For political purposes Leviathan and his subjects are one; 'it is a reall Unitie of them all, in one and the same Person' (XVII; 227). Once instituted as sovereign, or representative, Leviathan makes 'A Multitude of men into One Person, ... For it is the Unity of the Representer, not the Unity of the Represented, that maketh the Person One' (XVI; 220). The actions and decisions of the sovereign are henceforth to be seen as if they were those of the subjects themselves; they are 'author' of what he does. Leviathan personifies his subjects and, quite literally, according to Hobbes, acts for them.

The two stages of the liberal contract take place simultaneously in Hobbes' version of the contract story. The same words bring individuals into a political association and place Leviathan in authority over them. Given Hobbes' conception of the state of nature, the contract must take place in this way, and the sovereign himself can take no part in it; before the words are spoken there is neither an 'all' to contract together, nor a 'sovereign'.[23] The fact that individuals contract between themselves and not with Leviathan is a crucial element in Hobbes' argument. It can never be claimed that Leviathan has broken his part of the agreement, 'consequently none of his Subjects, by any pretence of forfeiture, can be freed from his Subjection' (XVIII; 230).

Through the contract Hobbes' individuals bring an absolute political obedience into being. They give the sovereign the right to do everything necessary to secure their protection, and, having willed this end, it is 'absurd' for them to hinder the sovereign. I argued above that Hobbes' conception of a contract does not give rise to an 'obligation', but is a simultaneous exchange. During the social contract individuals exchange one status for another; but do they also exchange a condition where obligations would not exist for a condition of political obligation? In one sense the contract gives expression to the principle of self-assumed obligation, for individuals freely say the words. On the other hand, a meaningful sense of 'obligation' disappears as soon as the words have been spoken. At that instant the individuals become subjects, and their relationship to Leviathan and his sword becomes analogous to that between a victim and a robber demanding a ransom in return for life. As the contracting individuals turn themselves into political subjects they also 'consent' to Leviathan's rule, or make an enforced covenant to obey him. Hobbes' equation of 'consent' with enforced covenants is perhaps most clearly revealed in the majority version of the social contract. He states that those that dissent 'must now consent with the rest; that is, be contented to avow all the actions he [the sovereign] shall do, or else justly be destroyed by the rest'. Merely by taking part in the contract, Hobbes declares, the individual has tacitly agreed to accept the majority verdict, so would be acting unjustly not to consent. The minority now stand in relation to the majority like the individual to the conqueror; they must 'consent' or be killed. Hobbes goes even further and argues that anyone who comes within the ambit of the new political society, whether their consent has been asked or not, must submit to the sovereign or otherwise remain in a state of war, and can 'without injustice be destroyed by any man whatsoever' (XVIII; 232).

In Hobbes' theory 'consent' is as much a political fiction as the social contract. In civil society all authority relationships, even between parent and child, are alleged to be based on 'consent', yet the question of how consent might actually be given never arises at any point. Hobbes argues that 'consent' and obedience must last as long as a ruler provides protection. If protection fails then subjects must submit or 'consent' to a new sovereign or face the state of nature. Hobbes' voluntarism is completely hypothetical—and meaningless. His theory contains nothing that can properly be called political 'obligation'. This is not, as is frequently suggested, because of his appeals to self-interest, but because 'obligation' implies free individual judgement, choice and decision that Hobbes ruthlessly eliminates from civil society. The price of leaving the state of nature is absolute and unquestioning political obedience.

Hobbes' absolutist political conclusions follow from the extreme individualism of his state of nature. His theoretical perspective leads to a conception of civil society as a completely artificial condition. Social and moral relationships spring into being all of a piece together with Leviathan and his sword, and their stability and continuity depend upon the strength of that sword alone. Humans do not change in the dramatic passage to civil society. It is because of their fear of Leviathan's sword that they are able to make use of their (implicit) capacities and understanding of what social life would be like, and enter into stable relationships with each other in civil society. But the bonds of civil life rest on the sword, not on individuals' social capacities. The unity of this curious community is appropriately symbolized in the 'person' who sits at its head. Leviathan's presence is so fundamental and far-reaching that it is he who turns words into a meaningful moral language, it is he who legislates a stable understanding of 'good' and 'wrong' into existence: 'Hobbes's ethical scepticism and ethical authoritarianism went hand in hand ... there must be one Humpty-Dumpty who really is Master and who determines what moral words shall denote'.[24]

Hobbes' Humpty-Dumpty is also a political authoritarian because the artificial civil union is inherently extraordinarily fragile. Social life and an unconditional and unquestioning obedience stand and fall together. Any individual who attempts to question Leviathan's commands is allowing the chaos of the clash of subjective, private judgements to enter civil society. However small the intrusion, it constitutes a shattering of part of the artificial bonds that individuals have created. Hobbes' theoretical perspective has no room for any intermediate state between a peaceful unconditional political obedience and a war between a collection of arbitrarily acting individuals.

Hobbes' discussion of civil society is similar to his picture of the state of nature. The state of nature can be peopled with abstract, isolated individuals only because we already know that individuals live together in society, and because we implicitly invest the 'natural' individuals with some social capacities and characteristics. Similarly, we can imagine a form of civil life held together by the power of Leviathan's sword, because we implicitly envisage its force at work against a background of everyday social life and relationships that do not depend on that sword for their continuity and cohesion. Hobbes is theoretically consistent enough to argue that the family in civil society provides an example of an artificial community in miniature, held together by the consent of its individual members to the jurisdiction of its 'representative person'. On the other hand, he also, unavoidably, writes of the family as if its bonds developed from, and rested upon, the continuing mutual relationships and sympathies of individuals who form a 'natural' community.

When discussing the natural rather than the artificial family Hobbes drops his attack on the patriarchalists and, inconsistently with his radical individualism and conventionalism, allows that the father, as the 'naturally' stronger and more active, will exercise authority within the family.[25] The natural, rather than the artificial, family is seen by Hobbes as an important additional source of political stability and order. Parents can teach their children appropriate political ideas and teach them the necessity of political obedience. Hobbes writes that the necessity of the absolute powers of the sovereign must be 'diligently, and truly taught; because they cannot be maintained by ... terrour of legal punishment' (XXX; 377). Hobbes' grasp of the importance of what today would be called political socialization in the maintenance of political obedience and political authority runs counter to his 'demonstration' of the mutual exclusiveness of social order and limited government. If political socialization can supplement, or even, to an extent, provide an alternative to the sword, then such an awesome embodiment of political authority as the sovereign Leviathan may no longer be required. In other words, a less extreme individualism than Hobbes' opens the way to less stark alternatives than posed in his theory. Nevertheless, less extreme, or more conventionally liberal, theorists still have to find a solution to the problems of self-assumed obligation if they are to preserve intact the authority of the liberal state.

The absolute rule of Leviathan is a long way removed from the liberal, constitutional state but, nevertheless, Hobbes' arguments do share some important features with liberal theory. Leviathan is not an arbitrary ruler. The civil status of subject implies certain liberties (and I shall comment on these in the next section) and also equality before the law. Individuals in civil society share an equal subjection and owe an equal obedience like servants before a master (XVIII; 238). In return for giving up the unlimited natural right to all things, they gain equal protection and security within a framework of publicly known and impartially enforced laws. If there is to be security there can be no distinction between rich and poor under the law; the rich 'may have no greater hope of impunity' from legal sanctions than the poorest subject (XXX; 385).

Secondly, Hobbes' theory shares a basic structural feature with liberal theory, namely the separation of the political sphere from the rest of social life. Hobbes' theory illustrates this, as so much else, in a singular and graphic fashion. In entering the social contract Hobbes' individuals take their first, and last, political action. The result of the contract is the total alienation to the ruler of their political rights. In Hobbes' civil society there is only one political actor—Leviathan himself. His actions are those of his subjects; they act vicariously through their 'person'. The political status of subject is thus purely formal and completely subsumed in political obedience. Hobbes' theory establishes an unbridgeable gulf between the everyday life and political obedience of the 'consenting' subjects, and the political sphere, symbolized in the figure of Leviathan and his sword.

Ironically, Hobbes has reintroduced individual judgement in all its arbitrariness at another level. It is true that he allows for the possibility of a sovereign assembly but, for good reason, he prefers an absolute monarch. In an assembly clashes of opinion could endanger peace. To avoid conflict Hobbes also argues that the sovereign should name his successor. Interestingly, he argues, too, that although parents are equal, only one can be the 'representative person' in the (artificial) family because children cannot 'obey two Masters' (XX; 253). The logic of Hobbes' theory requires a single-person Leviathan; security in civil society still depends on the judgement of a sovereign individual.

Political Obedience and the Right of Refusal

In Chapter 29 of *Leviathan* Hobbes discusses 'internall diseases', or seditious doctrines, that may strike a commonwealth, threatening political authority and raising the spectre of the war of the state of nature. The character of these diseases is overlooked by the commentators who wish to treat Hobbes as a traditional natural law theorist and to enshrine the claims of individual conscience at the heart of his political theory. Hobbes explicitly states that, in civil society, to proclaim that it is sinful for a man to act against his conscience is to spread a seditious doctrine. In a civil society the command of the sovereign, 'is the publique Conscience', and individuals cease to have the right to judge whether or not actions demanded of them are good or bad (XXIX; 365–6).

Hobbes rules out all possibility of disobedience by individuals acting on the basis of their own conscientious judgement, whether that judgement is secular or supernaturally inspired. If an individual claims that God has spoken in a personal revelation, although authoritative for the individual concerned, it cannot be taken as God's divine law and thus binding on others. There is no way in which such individual inspiration can be clearly distinguished from dreams, madness, other fancies, or from false testimony made from ambition. If God's Word rests only on individual revelation then 'it were impossible that any Divine Law should be acknowledged' (XXXIII; 426).

Faith is an entirely private, inward matter for the individual, and public religious declarations must be guided by what the sovereign commands: 'Profession with the tongue is but an externall thing, and no more than any other gesture whereby we signifie our obedience' (XLII; 527–8). Political obedience must always come first because the requirements of social order take precedence in this world. Every individual, including the sovereign, must answer to God in the next world; in civil society it is professions that count, even if these constitute a denial of conscientious convictions. Hobbes is ruthlessly consistent in his argument that faith or conscience must never encroach into political life. It is the sovereign, not religious authorities, who must have the final say in matters of religious doctrine. This is central to Hobbes' argument against another 'disease' of the commonwealth, the claim that sovereign power can be divided. There must be no competing voices raised against the sovereign or subjects will be no better off than in the state of nature, with its lack of authoritative interpretation of 'right' and 'just'.

The purpose of Hobbes' very long discussion of religious matters in *Leviathan* is to subordinate the traditional claims of the church to the commands of the sovereign. Hobbes reduces the status of churches to that of any other association or organization, or 'private system', in civil society, and their priests and vicars are required to submit to the decision of the sovereign in doctrinal matters. If peace is to be maintained there can be no religious power on a par with the sovereign, able to sit in judgement on what he commands. A divided sovereign power of this kind serves only to confuse subjects and opens the way to disobedience. 'Temporall and Spirituall Government, are but two words brought into the world, to make men see double, and mistake their Lawfull Soveraign' (XXXIX; 498); there must be no 'Ghostly Authority' to challenge the civil power. If the sovereign 'give away the government of Doctrines', Hobbes caustically remarks, 'men will be frighted into rebellion with the feare of Spirits' (XVIII; 236).

The threat of divided sovereignty is also raised by the seditious doctrine that the sovereign is subject to civil laws. Unless the sovereign stands outside the law his commands can be questioned in the name of the law itself, which is tantamount to setting up another sovereign ... and there would be no end to the chaos that would ensue. Similarly, although a major function of the civil law is to protect each individual's property, Hobbes regards it as seditious to argue that the individual's right to his property 'excludeth the Right of the Soveraign' (XXXIX; 367). Individuals, in entering the social contract, gave the sovereign the right to do everything necessary to maintain peace and security, so they cannot exclude the possibility that Leviathan may judge it necessary that they give up some of their property.

Hobbes closes all avenues through which challenges can be made to the authority of the sovereign. He excludes traditional religiously-based questioning, and subjects cannot challenge Leviathan on the grounds that he has broken the social contract or acted unlawfully. Subjects are the authors of their sovereign's commands so they cannot claim to have been injured by them; 'to do injury to ones selfe, is impossible' (XVIII; 232). Moreover, in civil society it is the sovereign who brings a definitive interpretation of 'unjust' and 'wrong' into existence through his commands; 'Hobbes' system excludes the very *possibility* of a wrong or unjust law'.[26]

Yet is this the end of the matter? Hobbes devotes a chapter of *Leviathan* to the topic of the liberty of subjects and, more importantly, he has argued that one right, the right of self-preservation, is inalienable. If Hobbes' theory really calls for unquestioning and unconditional political obedience, how could there be 'surprising parallels between Hobbes's arguments and the arguments of recent proponents of civil disobedience'?[27]

The surprising point about these parallels, insofar as they exist, is what they reveal about citizenship in the liberal democratic state rather than about Hobbes' theory. Hobbes never admits that individuals have the right of *political* action, or the *political* right to question the commands of the sovereign; the rights and liberties he allows Leviathan's subjects lie outside political life. In a Hobbesian order, civil disobedience could be seen only as sedition; as a virulent, and probably fatal, disease of the commonwealth. Civil disobedients make precisely the kind of political claims that Hobbes wishes to eliminate. For Hobbes they are engaging in an act of war; they are subjects who 'deliberately deny the Authority of the Common-wealth established', and to whom 'vengeance is lawfully extended, not onely to the Fathers, but also to the third and fourth generation not yet in being ... because the nature of this offence, consisteth in the renouncing of subjection' (XXVIII; 360). Hobbes' account of the liberty of subjects is concerned only with the liberty they have in their *private* lives. It is in private, everyday life that free individual judgement and choice, and the principle of self-assumed obligation find their place. Where the law is silent, or where the law allows individuals to act, then they can order their lives as they see fit. In civil society individuals have the:

> Liberty to buy, and sell, and otherwise contract with one another; to choose their own aboad, their own diet, their own trade of life, and institute their children as they themselves think fit; & the like (XXI; 264).

Providing that individuals' liberty remains a private matter then, like conscientious religious faith, it can pose no threat to peace and good order.

The sovereign retains the right to regulate any of these matters if security requires it, as Hobbes' comments on the right to private property illustrate, but individuals have an inalienable right to act as they see fit if their self-preservation is at stake. Hobbes introduces this right in the following way: he asks, 'what are the things, which though commanded by the soveraign, [the subjects] may neverthelesse, without injustice, refuse to do' (XXI; 268)? It is not 'unjust' to do something if the right to do it has not been contracted away. Therefore, because the right of self-preservation is inalienable, subjects can legitimately refuse to do things which will endanger their lives. A subject may refuse a command to become a soldier if an adequate substitute can be found, and can 'without injustice' refuse to confess to crimes, or refuse to let himself be assaulted.

Nevertheless, the sovereign has commanded the subject to perform the actions, and his commands are binding and must be enforced. There is no requirement upon the sovereign to allow subjects successfully to exercise a refusal to obey if he has judged that it will put security in danger. A murderer may 'justly' refust to confess, but he can rightfully be executed, and if the survival of the commonwealth demands that all able-bodied men must fight then they must be compelled to do so. 'The end of Obedience is Protection' (XXI; 272); no one has the right to help another refuse a command of the sovereign even though all have the right of self-defence. If disobedience threatens protection and order, then the 'right' of refusal must be defeated by Leviathan's sword, aided by obedient subjects who must each do what is required to 'protect his Protection' by ensuring the punishment even of 'just' refusers (XXIX; 375).

It is on the question of punishment that Hobbes appears to anticipate recent discussions of civil disobedience.[28] It is typically argued that, if political disobedience is to be 'civil' disobedience, participants must willingly accept the legal penalties for their breach of the law. In accepting punishment they are distinguishing themselves from revolutionaries and criminals, and affirming that they are acting in good political faith out of a sincerely held conviction that serious injustice exists. At the same time, they are demonstrating that, although they have broken the law for a political reason, they are still allegiant citizens who wish to uphold, not undermine, the rule of law. It is thus tempting for theorists who wish to establish a case for conditional political obligation to look to Hobbes' argument about just refusal and the right of Leviathan to exact a penalty. Hobbes would regard a disobedient as subversive, no matter how willingly he or she embraced punishment or how 'civil' the action was, but the comparison between Hobbes' argument and discussions of civil disobedience is interesting. It raises the question why contemporary writers are so insistent that punishment 'is the natural and proper culmination of [the] disobedient act',[29] when civil disobedients are not seen as subversive but as allegiant citizens.

The orthodox account of civil disobedience, as it has been developed in the academic literature over the past decade or so, has been drawn exceedingly narrowly.[30] For most writers, the idea of civil disobedience is acceptable only to the extent that it can be reduced to an essentially symbolic activity that, in itself, makes no impact on the law or policy at issue. It is seen as a way of showing intensity of feeling, or drawing attention to injustice, rather than as a potentially effective form of political action. This is illustrated in Rawls' discussion, in which civil disobedience is compared to public speech with the aim of appealing to the sense of justice of fellow citizens. This view of civil disobedience reduces it to little more than the 'all-purpose threat' of the little girl in the English children's stories: 'if you don't do it I'll scream and scream until I make myself sick'.[31] The argument that civil disobedients should willingly accept punishment for engaging in what is little more than an exercise of free speech follows the same line of reasoning as Hobbes' argument that the just refuser's action should be rendered ineffective by Leviathan's sword; punishment is necessary if the authority of the state is to remain inviolable. The orthodox account of civil disobedience, like *Leviathan*, is written from the perspective of what the state may tolerate if the political obligation of citizens is to remain unquestioned. In one sense, the insistence on punishment as a sign of acceptance of political obligation is more essential for contemporary writers than it is for Hobbes. Civil disobedience is based on moral and political evaluations of laws and policies, not, except indirectly, on self-preservation, and thus it contains a critical political dimension that is entirely absent from a Hobbesian polity.

This raises the broader, and more fundamental, question of whether Hobbes is not right about the character of political action open to citizens if political obligation is to remain unquestioned. This would be strongly contested by almost all present-day theorists; they argue for conditional political obligation, even though they insist that political obligation generally is unproblematic. I have argued that Hobbes' absolutism is a consequence of his extreme individualism. It might be thought that this argument in itself shows that Hobbes cannot possibly be right. A theory based on a more sociologically and anthropologically adequate individualism would have no need to subsume the political life of individuals in unconditional obedience and allow only the right of self-defence. It could encompass a liberal, constitutional form of limited government, based on conditional political obligation. Institutional recognition could be given to such political rights of citizens as voting and free speech—and, perhaps, a right to disobey. Locke's less radically individualist contract theory is often taken to give support to this claim, and the import of the critics of the very narrow, orthodox account of civil disobedience is that citizens do, or should, have such a right. For instance, attention has been drawn to the inconsistency of arguing, simultaneously, that civil disobedience is morally justified and that it must be punished.[32]

The claim that citizens in the liberal democratic state do, or should, have a right to disobey is a claim about a moral not a legal right. If a 'law' exists then, logically, there can be no right to disobey it (legal exemptions, or conscientious objector status, can be granted, but that is a different matter). It has been suggested that a legal defence of 'conscientiousness', rather like self-defence, or insanity, should be recognized by the courts, but if a legal defence of civil disobedience is successful, however that defence may be formulated, then the apparent illegality was not what it seemed.[33] However, to argue that citizens have a moral right to disobey has implications that are unpalatable to most theorists of political obligation. If it is morally justified to exercise this right, if civil disobedience is justified in certain circumstances, then to claim that the disobedient must be punished is to reduce the notion of a 'right' to virtual meaninglessness. But punishment, as we have seen, is held to be necessary because it constitutes a recognition of the authority of the liberal state. Thus to admit a right to disobey, at least in any genuine sense of a 'right', is to pose a threat to the authority of the state.

Furthermore, 'the right to disobey' implies that citizens have a right to decide for themselves whether or not they ought to consent to the demands, or prohibitions, of the liberal democratic state. This leaves open the possibility that consent may be refused or withdrawn, and so takes seriously the idea of self-assumed obligation as consent. Such a notion of 'consent' is very different from Hobbes' identification of consent and submission under threat of violence; it also differs from the hypothetical voluntarism that infers 'consent' from various actions of citizens, whether or not they themselves interpret the actions in this way. In short, if the right to disobey is seen as more than an extension of free speech for which punishment must be inflicted, difficult questions about the basis of political obligation and its general justification begin to be raised. In particular, the question has to be faced whether political obligation can be placed on the secure footing demanded by many present-day theorists if Hobbesian absolutism and unconditional obligation is eschewed.

If theorists stop short of the limits of hypothetical voluntarism represented by Hobbes' theory, then, as Hobbes foresaw, there is always scope for potentially embarrassing questions about the justification and character of political obligation.

Discussions of civil disobedience illustrate this point very well; the more narrowly that 'civil' disobedience is defined, the more it invites criticism. As the criticism becomes more radical, so the problem of political obligation in the liberal democratic state is increasingly clearly revealed. Today, it is less easy for theorists to be quite so ruthless as Hobbes in his attempt to rid voluntarism and consent of their radical implications. Nevertheless, the very fact that recent arguments are more typically liberal makes it impossible for the problem of political obligation to be completely suppressed, since it is a problem inherent in liberal voluntarism itself.

Chapter 4

'No Expressions of it at All'

All the pleasing illusions, which made power gentle, and obedience liberal, which harmonized the different shades of life, and which, by a bland assimilation, incorporated into politics the sentiments which beautify and soften private society, are to be dissolved by this new conquering empire of light and reason.

E. Burke, *Reflections on the Revolution in France*.

The shade of John Locke hangs heavily over most recent discussions of political obligation. Arguments about consent invariably contain some reference to Locke's notions of express and tacit consent, and his theory also provides an attractive source of support for writers on political disobedience. In Chapter 1, I introduced the term 'hypothetical voluntarism' by using Locke's argument about tacit consent as my example. I deliberately chose Locke because most contemporary arguments are little more than a modernization of, and variations upon, Locke's hypothetical voluntarist concept of consent. His theory appears so 'moderate and sensible'[1] today precisely because it anticipates much of the argument of liberal democratic theorists about political obligation and, more generally, about the character of liberal democracy.

When Locke produced his theory of limited, constitutional government in reply to the advocates of absolute monarchy, the divine right of kings and patriarchy, he was justifying a new form of political authority and, through his account of the state of nature, justifying socio-economic relationships that were in their first stage of development. One of the reasons why theorists can presently claim that it is nonsensical to raise general questions about political obligation in the liberal democratic state, or assume that any problems are easily resolved, is because Locke's justification of the liberal state and the relationships of a market society was so successful. His argument was at once revolutionary in the context of the prevailing theories of his time, and yet showed the way in which a liberal theory could defuse the subversive implications of the ideals of 'natural' freedom and equality and self-assumed obligation. Locke's theory has served liberal democratic theorists of political obligation so well because it is 'fully as much a defense against radical democracy as an attack on traditionalism'.[2] It has also served them well because it is based on an individualism that, while still abstract, is more moderate, and consequently more sociologically adequate, than Hobbes' radical individualism. The character of Locke's individualism also owes a great deal to the fact that in one vital respect his theory is completely traditional. Locke's 'natural' society is a community of Christian believers and he sees the law of nature in traditional terms as part of God's Divine Law of the universe. This enables Locke to distinguish, as Hobbes could not, between the overthrow of a government and the destruction of social life itself, and to argue for limited political obligation.

Commentators on Locke's political theory frequently discuss only half of his argument about consent. To appreciate the ingenuity of his hypothetically voluntarist arguments it is essential to consider his discussion of consent in the state of nature as well as consent in civil society. Locke's state of nature is a social state that not only contains money and a flourishing, capitalist economy, but it also contains government. In Locke's theory self-assumed obligation always takes the form of consent. The legitimacy of specific forms of government is established—a father–ruler in the state of nature, the liberal state in civil society—and then the hypothesis of continuing consent to these forms is advanced. Locke's theory thus involves a subtle, but important and influential shift in the way that the problem of political obligation is conceived. The emergence of the idea that individuals are 'naturally' free and equal gave rise to the general problem of justifying political authority and placed the conception of political 'obligation' at the centre of liberalism. Like the other social contract theorists, Locke takes this problem as his starting point, but he passes over it very rapidly and in a purely formal fashion. The question with which he is concerned, and to which his successors have directed their attention, is how it can plausibly be maintained that individuals consent to a form of political authority that is already assumed to be justified.

The greater sociological realism of Locke's state of nature gives rise to problems that are completely by-passed by Hobbes' extreme abstract individualism. Hobbes' conception of social life as a completely artificial condition, held together by the power of Leviathan's sword, has no room for any mechanism through which consent, even hypothetically, might be given; 'consent' is merely identified with forced submission. Locke has no theoretical reason to take his hypothetical voluntarism to this limit, although he does come near it when he refers to the relation between master and servant in which 'the Subjection of the Needy Beggar began not from the Possession of the Lord, but the Consent of the poor Man'.[3] But Locke distinguishes this 'consent' from the despotical power that a master (justifiably Locke thinks) exercises over a conquered slave. Locke bases his hypothesis, that individuals can be said to consent to the authority of the liberal state, on the claim that various voluntary activities constitute that consent. Locke thus leaves himself open to arguments about what does, and does not, count as consent and how consent can, properly, be given. Moreover, because of the form of Locke's hypothetical voluntarism the roots of the problem of differential political obligation also lie in his social contract theory.

The Lockean State of Nature

Locke's picture of the state of nature is much less original than Hobbes'; he begins with individuals as God made them living together in a form of society which is familiar to us. There has, even so, been a good deal of controversy about the character of Locke's natural condition, and particularly about the significance and role of the state of war. It is often overlooked that Locke's discussion of the state of nature consists of two distinct, but related, parts: a formal definition, and a conjectural history of the development of the state of nature.[4] The existence of the state of war, and the reasons why individuals enter the social contract, can be fully understood only in the light of the conjectural history, and not merely on the basis of Locke's definitions of the 'state of nature', the 'state of war' and 'civil society'.

Locke begins his formal account of the state of nature with the statement that individuals are all 'by nature' free and equal to each other. Individuals are free to 'order their Actions, and dispose of their Possessions, and Persons as they think fit' (S4),[5] and because individuals are also equal to each other, in the state of nature, 'naturally there is no superiority or jurisdiction of one, over another' (S7). The state of nature 'properly', Locke writes, is a condition of 'Men living together according to reason, without a common Superior on Earth, with Authority to judge between them' (S19). God has given individuals reason in order that they can know how to live peaceably together. This is not the purely subjective, 'individual reason' of Hobbes' state of nature, but the reason of individuals who live socially and who can 'consult', understand and follow the rules embodied in the law of nature that God has provided to regulate their interactions with each other. God's law provides a general constraint upon the judgement and action of individuals; it tells them what they ought to do in their life together. In Locke's state of nature individuals see that it is reasonable to act as the laws of nature prescribe that they ought, and they usually do so:

> Locke's account of the state of nature and his differences with Hobbes on this point are thus grounded in the theological conviction that God cannot have issued rules for men to obey and then have created beings who, in their most natural state, are necessarily unable to follow those rules.[6]

Individuals are God's property and must not destroy themselves. The law of nature 'willeth the Peace and Preservation of all Mankind' and tells individuals what they ought to do to protect and preserve each other. The law is concerned with individuals collectively, not singularly, and it states that 'being all equal and independent, no one ought to harm another in his Life, Health, Liberty, or Possessions' (S6). The law of nature thus establishes the basic rules of mutual aid and forbearance that are fundamental to social life. It prescribes mutually equal but limited rights and freedoms necessary for peaceful social life. It is possible to see this aspect of Locke's discussion in terms of the conceptual argument, referred to in Chapter 2, which stresses that such basic rules, and notions such as 'rights', are a necessary implication of a coherent conception of 'social life'. To see Locke's argument in this light can, however, obscure an important point about his conception of the individual and the relationship between individuals and the law of nature.

Locke's formal definition of the state of nature may suggest that his is a social rather than an abstract individualism, but its social character is more apparent than real. Locke does not specifically state that the law of nature enjoins individuals to keep faith with each other, but this is implied in his references to 'promises', 'contracts' and 'bargains' in the natural condition. He also states that the 'keeping of

Faith belongs to Men, as Men, and not as Members of Society' (S14). Locke may mean 'not as members of civil society' because he is not completely consistent in his terminology but it is more likely that 'Men as Men' refers to individuals as God's creation. The 'natural' attributes of Locke's individuals are those that God has given to each of them. He has created them with freedom, equality and the capacity to keep faith with each other. These attributes belong to each individual as a separate entity (they are his property) and owe nothing to society. The abstractly individualist character of Locke's argument is also demonstrated by the relationship between individuals and the law of nature and the necessity of religious faith.

The law which individuals consult is God's law; it is given to individuals and exists independently of them. They have not chosen the rules which the law embodies, although they have the choice whether to recognize and follow them; the rules will exist no matter what individuals think or do. The question can thus be asked why individuals should choose to follow the law of nature (compare, why should individuals choose to observe the 'rule of promising'?). Locke's answer is that God has made individuals so that they usually will so choose, but their choice depends upon religious faith. Individual reason is not sufficient to ensure that individuals will usually follow the law of nature. In *A Letter Concerning Toleration*, the arguments of which are closely related to those of the *Second Treatise*, Locke wrote that 'promises, covenants, and oaths, which are the bonds of human society, can have no hold upon an atheist. The taking away of God, though but even in thought, dissolves all'.[7] The law of nature is not a 'law' for atheists. They inhabit a radically individualist state of nature where there are no rules to constrain them and where the keeping of promises is always a 'problem'. Locke avoids the difficulties of a Hobbesian radically abstract individualism only by relying on religious faith and a traditional conception of natural law.

The formal account of the state of nature establishes why the Lockean natural condition has many 'inconveniences'. God has created individuals so that, with faith, they are able to observe His natural law. But He has also created them with moral failings and other human weaknesses and these are the source of the 'inconveniences'. In the state of nature each individual has the right to interpret and execute the law of nature, including the right to punish and exact reparations from offenders against the law. Locke calls this a 'strange Doctrine' (S9), and he notes that the objection will be made that individuals would be partial to themselves and their relations and friends and go too far in their punishments. Partiality is a major cause of 'inconveniences', and other moral failings, such as laziness and weakness of will, reinforce this. Some individuals will not bother to consult the law of nature, and there will be many disputes about interpretation and execution where there is no authoritative means of deciding between conflicting individual judgements. However, such 'inconveniences' must not be confused with the state of war.

Locke distinguishes the 'passionate and hasty' actions of individuals from those that quite deliberately go beyond the constraints of natural law. There is a difference between the problems that arise from moral failings and those consequent upon calculated flouting of morality. A distinction can thus be made between the force that may lawfully be used against an offender (even though passion may lead to excessive punishment) and 'force without right' arbitrarily used to put one individual in another's power.[8] This unlawful use of force based on a 'sedate setled Design upon another Mans Life' (S16), whether in the state of nature or civil society, constitutes the state of war, to avoid which individuals agree to enter the social contract (S21). However, this does not explain why the state of war becomes so pressing that individuals leave the state of nature. The latter might be a tolerable place, even with its inconveniences, if the state of war occurred infrequently. It is necessary to turn to Locke's conjectural history of the state of nature to discover why individuals freely give up their right of individual judgement and action and authorize a few representatives to make decisions for them.

Locke's conjectural history provides an excellent illustration of the integral relationship between political concepts and specific forms of social life. The character of the historical state of nature and the relationships of its inhabitants, justified by Locke in terms of the law of nature, closely resemble those of a developing capitalist market economy. The conjectural history is of particular importance for arguments about political obligation because of the key role played by consent in the development of the state of nature, and the continuity between Locke's discussion of consent in the conjectural history and the argument about consent in civil society. Moreover, consent, in the state of nature, is given to a ruler. The historical state of nature is not bereft of an authority to judge between individuals. Government, Locke states, is an institution that God has appointed and it is 'hardly to be avoided amongst Men' that live together'; nor do they avoid it in the natural condition (S105). This is not, however, to say that Locke's state of nature is seen *by him* as a political state. Locke distinguishes between government in general, the government of one man, and a properly political or civil authority. This distinction may seem odd but it is not unique to Locke.[9] *Political* authority, according to Locke, does not exist in the state of nature; it becomes necessary only at a certain stage of socio-economic development.

Historically, the 'inconveniences' of the state of nature arise not, as the formal account suggests, because all individuals judge for themselves, but because government is in the hands of one man, and hence open to all the failings of individual judgement. Locke's account of the origins of government largely follows that of the patriarchalist Filmer, even though much of the argument of the *Second Treatise* is directed against him. Locke agrees with Filmer that fathers were the first rulers, but he rejects the argument that their authority derives from the fact of fatherhood. The patriarchalists denied that individuals could be seen as naturally free and equal; they are born under the subjection of their fathers who are their natural superiors. Locke's reply to this claim is both simple and ingenious. He *reinterprets* the patriarchal argument in terms of consent.

Locke, in contrast to the patriarchalists and Hobbes, makes a sharp distinction between parental or paternal authority and the political authority of a ruler. Parents exercise a natural authority over children while they are in their nonage (although this does not give parents the political right of life and death over their children (S65)), but parental authority ceases when children become mature: 'we are born Free, as we are born Rational; ... Age that brings one, brings with it the other too' (S61). Once mature, children, or rather, male children, are as free as, and equal to, their fathers. In practice, however, the authority of fathers does not cease—at the maturity of children it is transformed into the political authority of a monarch. Locke argues that by 'an insensible change' fathers become political rulers; through a 'tacit and scarce avoidable consent' children grant political authority to their fathers (S76; 75). Historically, the political right of judgement and action that, formally, individuals have as inhabitants of the state of nature is always given up to a monarch. The 'strange Doctrine' has no writ in practice; as soon as the 'first children' become adult the natural obedience they owe to their parents is, voluntarily, transformed into political obedience to their father–ruler.

But what kind of 'consent' is it that is 'scarce avoidable'? Locke could not put forward his formal definition of the state of nature without resting legitimate political authority on consent, but he also had to counter the patriarchal charge that 'consent' was subversive of political authority. His conception of 'consent' allows him to do this. In the state of nature, just as much as in civil society, consent is, as Pitkin has argued, always hypothetical consent.[10] Locke has no quarrel with the argument that fathers are suitable rulers; they are 'fit umpires' and so mature children ought to consent to their authority—and can be said to have done so. It can always safely be hypothesized that consent is given to a legitimate ruler. In his care for his children during their nonage, the father has shown them that he is the 'fittest to be trusted' with authority (S105): the mature children understand that 'the Rule of one Man, ... where it was exercised with Care and Skill, with Affection and Love to those under it, it was sufficient to procure and preserve to Men all the Political Happiness they sought for' (S107). The father–ruler, with his family's interests at stake, is likely to rule justly and well, and hence the 'consent' of the children can always reasonably be inferred or assumed. However, the argument of the *Second Treatise* is also an argument that absolute monarchical rule is no longer justified. To see why the hypothesis of consent to father–monarchs has become unreasonable, it is necessary to turn to another aspect of Locke's conjectural history: his theory of property.

The development of property (in the material sense) in the state of nature falls into two broad historical stages. The rule of the father–monarch is suited to the 'Innocence of the first Ages', to the 'Golden Age' of the first stage of the conjectural history where individuals' property-holdings are equal (S94; 111). Locke argues that God gave the world to everyone in common to use to their advantage but, if all were to benefit, individuals must be able to appropriate the fruits of the earth for private use. Property becomes the individual's own when labour is mixed with the land and its bounty through an extension of the 'property' that each individual has in his or her person. The law of nature places a limitation on individual appropriation; no more must be taken from the common stock than an individual can use, there must be 'enough, and as good left', and nothing must be wasted or spoiled (S33; 31). This limitation ensures that 'there could be no doubt of Right, no room for quarrel' because each individual would own roughly the same amount of property as the others: 'What reason', Locke asks, 'could any one have ... to enlarge his Possessions beyond the use of his Family?' (S39; 48).

All this is changed by the invention of money, which ushers in the second stage of historical development and provides the second example of, or hypothesis of, consent in the historical state of nature.[11] Locke argues that by 'tacit Agreement' or 'Consent' individuals 'put a value' on money (S36). This consent has momentous consequences. The introduction of money sweeps away the limitations on individual accumulation, because money does not spoil or waste if it is hoarded, and it can be exchanged for other things. Locke also links the invention of money to an expansion in individuals' desires so that they now begin to expand their property (S49).

Before the introduction of money there is land for all in the historical state of nature, but with the expansion of individual property-holdings this will eventually cease to be the case. What then is the position of those who can no longer appropriate land? These individuals still have some 'property': namely, the property they possess in their person, their liberty and their labour. In the pre-monetary stage Locke allows that individuals can contract to become servants and he argues that the labour of a servant enhances the property, not of the servant, but of the master (S28). After 'consent' to money many individuals will be able to protect their 'property' in their lives only by selling their labour through wage-contracts. The consequence of the 'consent' to money is, therefore, the development of social and economic inequality and the emergence of two classes in the state of nature: those who accumulate material possessions of land, capital and other goods and who buy the labour of others, and those who own only their person and their labour and who sell the latter.[12] Yet none of this, according to Locke, transgresses the law of nature: 'it is plain, that Men have agreed to disproportionate and unequal Possession of the Earth, they having by a tacit and voluntary consent found out a way, how a man may fairly possess more land than he himself can use the product of' (S50). The reason why it is plausible to infer that 'consent' has been given to money and its consequences is that *all* individuals benefit from this development. Although property is now very unequally distributed, great wealth has been generated and the poorest day-labourer is better off than a king among the American Indians (S41).

At this stage of socio-economic development the state of war becomes pressing and monarchical rule becomes illegitimate. There is now plenty of 'room for quarrel' about property ownership. It is plausible, although this is largely implicit in Locke's discussion, that inequality would lead to an increase in partiality and moral lapses, thus 'inconveniences' would multiply, and with the justification of unlimited accumulation, that some individuals would use force or 'war' to try to improve or safeguard their position. Insecurity, particularly for those with large amounts of property, would increase and would be aggravated because government is in the hands of one man and the protection of property depends on his individual, and partial, judgement. In the pre-monetary stage the 'Honesty and Prudence' of the father–ruler could be relied upon, but now it has become impossible to trust the monarch to use his authority for the 'publick good'. Rulers like their subjects, have become infected with ambition and they have developed 'distinct and separate Interests from their People', and have even begun to claim that they rule by divine right (S111-2). When rulers are at war with their subjects, and the subjects with each other, the time has arrived for a new form of government to be instituted that will securely protect individuals' property.

Locke's conjectural history of the state of nature thus provides the explanation why individuals agree to enter the social contract and establish civil government. Locke notes that 'at best an Argument from what has been, to what should of right be, has no great force', but the history of the state of nature shows that, once the development of the capitalist, market economy is underway, an 'Absolute Monarchy, ... is indeed inconsistent with Civil Society', even if once it sufficed (S103; 90). A new form of government must be set up which is worthy of individuals' 'consent' or to which their 'trust' can be given. Locke's conjectural history, therefore, is neither 'a descriptive and politically neutral anthropology',[13] nor merely 'polemical' rather than 'logically essential' to his argument as a whole.[14] It forms a vital bridge between the formal definition of the state of nature and the justification of a particular form of political authority; it is the basis from which Locke can argue that, given the social relationships of the market economy, there is only one legitimate form of political authority, that of the liberal constitutional state.

Because Locke argues that so much follows from consent to money it might be supposed that agreement to the political authority necessary to protect the new form of social life can be inferred also from the original consent. Such an argument would be compatible with Macpherson's claim, discussed in Chapter 3, that Hobbes and Locke derived a justification for political obligation directly from the market. In addition to the objections that I have already offered to this argument, it cannot account for the fact that Locke himself regards none of the relationships in the state of nature as political. Consent in the state of nature is not sufficient to set up a properly political authority; a specifically *political* agreement, namely the social contract, is required to do that.

One further comment is needed before I turn to Locke's account of the social contract. Locke states that 'no rational Creature can be supposed to change his condition with an intention to be worse' (S131). The change from the state of nature to civil society is, according to Locke, a change for the better because it ensures the protection of property (in both senses). It is also, however, a change that maintains and consolidates the unequal social relationships that have developed in the state of nature. Those who own estates and material property and buy labour will not enter civil society if they become worse off. Those who own only the property in their person and labour are, Locke argues, better off in civil society because their lives and liberty are more secure under a limited, representative government. The latter, though, can have no expectation of any change in their material condition if such change is to be brought about only at the expense of the propertied; at most they can expect further advance through the economic development begun in the historical state of nature. The Lockean, liberal social contract thus gives further justification to, and is expressly designed to preserve, the social inequalities of the capitalist market economy.

The Lockean Social Contract

Locke's formal definition of civil society follows from his formal definition of the state of nature: 'civil society' exists where there is a 'common superior', a 'Judge on Earth', or 'Umpire' to make authoritative decisions binding on all members of the society. It should be noted that the formal contrast between the two conditions says nothing about the specific form of political authority required in 'civil society'. To understand why a liberal, representative and limited government is needed, reference has to be made to the conjectural history of the state of nature, not the formal definitions. An 'umpire' has existed throughout the history of the state of nature, but that is not sufficient to sweep away the distinction between a political or civil society and the state of nature. It is only at a certain stage of socio-economic development that a *political* society and the liberal state—in short, 'civil society'—become necessary, and it is then that the social contract is entered into.

The Lockean social contract provides an excellent illustration of the two conceptually distinct stages of the liberal social contract. In the first stage a new political association or political society is formed; in the second stage a liberal government is established. In Hobbes' version of the social contract the two parts must be entered into simultaneously; a society has to be brought into being together with a political association—and no society is possible without Leviathan's sword. Locke's less radical individualism allows the two stages to be seen consecutively, or, more accurately, they are consecutive in terms of the formal logic of the contract. In discussing Locke's state of nature it is essential to distinguish the formal and the historical accounts, but also to consider them in relation to each other. If the conceptually distinct stages of the contract are considered in the context of the development of the historical state of nature, it becomes clear that while the second stage, the establishment of the liberal state, is necessary because of historical development, the first stage remains as a purely conceptual or formal necessity.

The first stage of the social contract follows logically from Locke's formal definition of the state of nature. In the state of nature individuals are 'naturally' free and equal so that Locke is faced with the problem of how these creatures can justifiably be governed. The first stage of the contract provides the answer; individuals voluntarily agree to form a new political community and institute a political authority and so commit themselves to a bond of political obligation. When the contract is made, Locke argues, each individual gives up the right of interpreting and executing the law of nature and 'resign'd it up into the hands of the Community' and the new community itself becomes the 'Umpire' (S87). Each individual 'puts himself under an Obligation to every one of that Society' (S97). That is to say, the members of the community are to act as their own political authority, freely assuming the obligation to each other to maintain this new political relationship. In his critique of liberal social contract theory, Rousseau, as I shall show in Chapter 7, argued that a contract of this type was the only contract to which free and equal individuals could justifiably commit themselves. Locke, however, drew no such substantive conclusions about the first stage of the social contract; for Locke it is no more than a logically necessary, but purely formal and abstract, preliminary to the all-important second stage. Nevertheless, the fact that the liberal social contract cannot do without its first stage poses a problem for liberal theory.

The conception of political obligation that emerges from the first stage of the contract is of a horizontal relationship between the members of the political community. On the other hand, the result of the second stage, and the traditional liberal view of political obligation, is of a vertical relationship between each individual and the liberal state. How are the two conceptions reconciled? It should be noted that Hobbes' version of the contract contains the same tension, but this is glossed over because, although the contract is made between individuals and not with Leviathan, the formation of a vertical relationship is presupposed if the contract is not immediately to be void. This feature of the liberal contract and the difficulty to which it gives rise is interesting because contemporary theorists are now running into the very same problem. In the 'Introduction' I drew attention to the currently popular argument that political obligation is owed primarily to fellow citizens rather than to the state, and noted the difficulty of linking this horizontal relationship between citizens to their vertical relationship to the state. Locke's theory, for very good reason, offers no help in making this connection. If one turns from the formal definition of the state of nature to the conjectural history, the need to form a new political community no longer exists and the first stage of the contract is irrelevant.

The inhabitants of the historical state of nature make the transition from absolute monarchy to liberal government, or, as Locke sees it, from a government only to a properly political form of authority. Formally, the second stage of the contract follows the first; historically, the second stage is all that matters. In logical terms, the new community agrees to give up political authority to a few representatives; in historical terms, the members of the existing society consent to a different form of government. The first stage of the contract plays no substantive role in Locke's theory. In effect, the liberal social contract immediately gives rise to a vertical conception of political obligation. Individuals exchange their 'natural' freedom and equality for civil freedom protected by the civil law and the status of formally equal political subject. This status is independent of the social and economic inequalities that divide individuals so that, as political subjects, they can be regarded as having an equal political obligation constituting a discrete vertical bond between each subject and the liberal state.

Locke's discussion is not always as clear as it might be; at one point, for example, he says that the individual 'authorizes the Society, or which is all one, the legislative thereof' (S89), but his argument for a limit to political obligation depends precisely on the legislative and society not being 'all one'. He is quite clear that 'civil society' requires a very specific form of political authority: 'the People', he writes, could never 'think themselves in Civil Society, till the Legislature was placed in collective Bodies of Men, call them Senate, Parliament, or what you please' (S94). In civil society the exercise of political authority is no longer dependent upon the fallible and partial judgement of one man: 'all private judgement of every particular Member [is] excluded' (S87). Representatives use their 'political' judgement and legislate in the public interest to protect the property or interests of all individuals. Locke's metaphor of the representative legislature as an 'umpire' conveys this very well. The liberal state is indifferent between the competing interests of the economic or private sphere, and impartially enforces the law on rich and poor alike; like an umpire the state stands apart from the game that is being played in the market society. The separation between Locke's 'umpire' and liberal society is not so complete and unbridgeable as between Leviathan and his subjects, but, like Leviathan, Locke's liberal state, or the political sphere, stands over and above, and external to, the world of everyday life. In many respects, Locke's 'umpire' anticipates Schumpeter's influential conception of liberal democracy as an impartial procedure or 'political method' for regulating and protecting competing private interests. The major difference between the two is that Schumpeter's method is seen as unrelated to any specific political values or principles; it is purely a procedural device.[15] Locke's 'umpire' is constrained by the law of nature, which provides representatives, and their subjects, with criteria to evaluate political decisions. Contemporary liberalism has only the procedure to fall back on.

My emphasis on the social contract might seem mistaken for it has been argued that Locke's theory is based on trust rather than on contract.[16] Locke does frequently refer to trust, but this is part of, rather than an alternative to, his version of the social contract and his theory of consent. As my discussion of promising and of Hobbes' covenants has illustrated, 'trust' is implied in these social practices. A person who makes a promise is trusted to fulfill the obligation; similarly, individuals who consent to the exercise of political authority by representatives trust them to use that authority to protect their property. The significance of Locke's use of 'trust' is, firstly, that it tempers voluntarism and suggests that liberal political authority resembles that of the first father—monarchs; subjects can 'trust' the liberal government to use its authority properly just as children can trust a father. Secondly, it is significant for what it reveals about the 'majority' and those whom I shall call the politically relevant members of society. Locke argues that individuals who agree to form a political community also agree to majority rule. The obligation that they assume includes the obligation 'to submit to the determination of the majority, and to be concluded by it' (S97). Locke's argument for majority rule is an empirical one. The community could not survive a unanimity requirement; business affairs and ill-health would make it impossible for all to be present to make decisions, and differences of opinion and interest (likely in the developing capitalist economy) make unanimous agreement very unlikely. It has sometimes been claimed that Locke argues that whatever the majority decides is right, but this makes nonsense of the role of natural law and the right of the people to resist a government that sets itself at war with its subjects. More importantly, Locke's argument says nothing about the character of the 'majority'.

All individuals who enter the social contract are members of the political community, but only the males who own substantial amounts of material property are politically relevant members of society. Although Locke attacked absolute monarchy, he was uncritical of other aspects of the political arrangements of his time, and he took for granted the fact that politically the bulk of the population 'were in but not of civil society'.[17] Locke inferred the 'trust' or tacit consent of the mass of the people because the property they had in their persons was protected by civil law. 'Trust' between the propertied, politically relevant members of society and representatives is, however, based on more than an hypothesis or inference. They can trust each other because, like the original father—rulers and their adult offspring, they have strong ties of mutual interest. They also understand that they have come into civil society to stabilize and, if possible, improve their position. Locke argues that he who enjoys the protection of government must contribute to its cost 'out of his Estate'—if he has 'an estate'. Taxation deprives individuals of part of their property so cannot be imposed without their consent. If it were not for the trust between the propertied and their representatives Locke would not be able, in the same sentence, to equate individual consent with consent of a majority of representatives (S140). The 'majority' thus turns out to be the majority of the representatives, and the latter are chosen by the propertied.

Consent in Civil Society

In his conjectural history of the state of nature Locke used hypothetically voluntarist arguments to reinterpret the patriarchal relationships between father–monarchs and their sons. Similar arguments also enable him to meet the patriarchal objection that, in civil society, political arrangements made by fathers, i.e. the social contract, could not be binding on sons, if the latter were also born free and equal, and to contain the radical implications of his reply. Locke says that no one has any doubt that an individual's 'express consent' makes him a 'perfect member' of a society and subject to its government. The difficulty, Locke goes on, is:

> what ought to be look'd upon as a tacit Consent, and how far it binds, i.e. how far any one shall be looked on to have consented, and thereby submitted to any Government, where he has made no Expressions of it at all (S119).

Locke easily meets this difficulty but, in his 'murky statements' about consent, he fails to give an explicit account of what constitutes express consent.[18] The only equivalent to leaving the state of nature and consenting to put one's (material) property under the authority of civil government is inheriting property within the jurisdiction of the liberal state: 'any person who enjoyed property rights, ... was placed on the same footing with the original covenanters'.[19] Therefore, the inheritance of property, which is an explicit act, can be seen as an example of express consent. A son can securely enjoy his father's property only because it is protected by civil government and its laws, so that it is plausible to infer that inheritance is express consent to political obligation: 'if they will enjoy the inheritance of their Ancestors, they must take it on the same terms their Ancestors had it, ... By this Power indeed Fathers oblige their Children ... to this or that Political Power' (S73). Locke calls those who expressly consent 'perfect members' of the society and he indicates that such consent precludes the right of emigration (S121-2).

Those who make no expression of their consent, the individuals who have no property except that in their persons, their liberty and their labour and resident aliens and visitors, are covered by Locke's famous notion of tacit consent. Tacit consent can be inferred from the the fact that people are going peacefully about their everyday lives. The protection of civil government makes it possible for an individual to 'travel freely on the highway', so it is a reasonable hypothesis that in so doing any individual is 'consenting' to the authority of the government and to his political obligation. In the historical state of nature it could be inferred that male children, at maturity, gave a 'scarce avoidable' consent to the father's authority as monarch. Similarly, in civil society, the tacit consent of subjects can be assumed to have been given if they elect to remain in their political community at their majority. When discussing inheritance, Locke states that individuals give their consent separately as each comes of age and so 'People take no notice of it' (S117).

It might be argued that choosing to remain within one's country of birth when reaching adulthood is a more plausible basis for inferring tacit consent than activities such as walking the highway; a specific act, or example of inaction, is involved, rather like accepting an inheritance. However, as Hume pointed out long ago, this is rarely a genuine choice for most people:

> Can we seriously say that a poor peasant or artisan has a free choice to leave his country when he knows no foreign language or manners and lives from day to day by the small wages which he acquires?[20]

One reason why 'people take no notice' of the hypothesized giving of consent is that few people would connect consent to the performance of their everyday activities, or to remaining where they were when they came of age. In most critical discussions of Locke's arguments the point is made that individuals do not interpret their everyday lives in this way. The difficulty with this response is that it quickly begins to undermine Locke's hypothetical voluntarism. It suggests, quite rightly, that 'consent' is meaningless if people do not know that to perform a certain act is to consent. However, if they do know this, then the possibility is there that consent may be refused; people may deliberately refrain from performing the action. Locke wished to rule out this possibility, except as a last resort when a government had already ceased to protect property or had already ceased to be a properly liberal government. Usually, there is no question about political obligation and consent because there is no question that the authority of the liberal state is justified. The task of the theorist then becomes that of showing how individuals can be said to give the consent that ought to be given. Unless hypothetically voluntarist arguments, however implausible, are accepted, problems about political obligation are opened up that Locke, and his successors, regard as closed.

In view of all the well-known difficulties of providing a satisfactory theory of consent in the liberal democratic state, it is hardly surprising that writers on political obligation now often present voluntarist arguments that avoid the term 'consent'. I shall discuss in detail whether they thereby also avoid the problems associated with consent in Chapter 6. As a preliminary to that discussion I want to raise the question here of the relationship of such arguments to voluntarism couched in terms of tacit consent. It is significant that it is relatively easy to reinterpret Locke's hypothetical voluntarism to eliminate all reference to consent; indeed, some commentators would claim that this is how he should be read.[21] For example, Locke can be interpreted as arguing that civil government provides many benefits or 'enjoyments' which individuals voluntarily accept, and that in return for these benefits they have an obligation to obey the government that makes them possible: alternatively, Locke can be read as arguing that when individuals participate in, for example, the social practice of inheritance, they are voluntarily assuming an obligation to obey the rules that make inheritance possible and to obey the government that impartially enforces the rules. That Locke, a classic consent theorist, can plausibly be interpreted in voluntarist terms without reference to 'consent' poses the interesting question whether recent voluntarist arguments are not merely tacit consent in a new guise. They appear to be making exactly the same inferences about obligation as Locke and merely reformulating the language of tacit consent.

Another contemporary problem about political obligation foreshadowed in Locke's arguments is that of differential obligation. I have argued that, as a result of the social contract, individuals share a formally equal status in civil society as political subjects and so can be seen as sharing an equal (and vertical) political obligation. Locke's arguments about consent and obligation focus not on individuals as subjects and formal equals, but on individuals in their daily lives. In this context they are not equal but divided into two unequal classes. Each individual has a good reason to exchange 'natural' freedom and equality for the protection of the civil laws and the status of political subject because this gives security to property. However, some individuals have estates, capital and other material possessions to protect as well as their lives, liberty and labour, and they gain more from the exchange than the propertyless. If inferences about political obligation are to be drawn from everyday activities then it does not seem unreasonable to suggest that some individuals have a greater obligation or owe more to the government than others. Locke hints at such a conclusion when he suggests that the 'perfect members', who give express consent, also give up the right of emigration and thus have a greater obligation than those who consent only tacitly. Present-day theorists have the advantage over Locke that the political status of subject has now been transformed into that of citizen; liberal democratic citizenship includes the right to vote and it is frequently claimed that to vote is to consent. Thus contemporary writers can focus on a formally equal status and a specific political act which gives plausibility to the assumption that political obligation is shared equally. However, the theorists mentioned earlier who avoid the term 'consent' also tend to follow in Locke's footsteps and cast their net of hypothetical voluntarism much more widely than the franchise. They too tend to look to everyday activities, not citizenship, in their inferences about obligation, and so raise the same question about differential obligation as Locke's arguments about express and tacit consent.

Locke suggests that the political obligation of the propertied and the propertyless may differ, but neither Locke nor present-day writers trouble to consider whether the political obligation of men and women can be the same, in view of beliefs about the proper or 'natural' social role of women that have been widely accepted for the last three hundred years (and longer). The question of women and political obligation remains virtually unexplored and Locke's arguments make a useful starting point. It is also worth noting that Hobbes, despite his absolutism, was a much more vigorous opponent of patriarchalism than Locke, arguing that the authority of parents over children was conventional, and that women were the equals of men in strength and prudence in the state of nature. It will be recalled that Hobbes argues that in civil society only one parent can exercise authority within the family; he remains silent about the status of the other parent or, at least, he does so when discussing the family conceived as an artificial unit.[22] When his theoretical consistency lapses and he refers to the natural family, Hobbes too capitulates to the patriarchalists and argues that the father will 'naturally' rule in the family, for men are stronger and more active than women.

In contrast, Locke's attack on the patriarchal theorists was confined to the relationship between fathers and sons. In his hypothesis of the father's transformation into a monarch in the state of nature he does not mention the position of the wife and mother. It is merely taken for granted that she too consents to this change in the role of her husband. Yet, given the 'natural' freedom and equality of individuals, it would be logical for the two parents to be joint rulers, or for either the father or the mother to rule (queens as well as kings exist). Locke takes it for granted that a father rules over a mother as well as over mature sons because, in the *First Treatise*, he had already agreed with Filmer that a wife's subjection to her husband has a 'Foundation in Nature'.[23] He assumes that a marriage contract will always place a female individual under the authority of a male individual. In the *Second Treatise* he argues that authority over children in the family in civil society is 'parental' and not just 'paternal', but he also takes care to point out that this is as far as the mother's authority runs. The wills of the wife and husband can clash, and so in the family (as in society) there must be a 'last Determination'; this role, Locke states, 'naturally falls to the Man's share, as he is the abler and the stronger'. The wife has her own 'peculiar Right' because the husband does not have the political right of power over her life. Nevertheless, the wife must bow to her husband's decisions in the family about 'their common Interest and Property' (S82). In the *First Treatise* Locke had established to his own satisfaction that the father and husband 'as Proprietor of the Goods and Land' of the family must have 'his Will take place before that of his wife in all things of their common Concernment'.[24]

Perhaps the most controversial aspect of Macpherson's interpretation of Locke is his claim that the propertied and propertyless differ even in their rationality.[25] As my argument illustrates, it is possible to benefit greatly from Macpherson's work without accepting this point. All individuals are equally rational when they enter the contract (or they could not see its advantage) and all sons are assumed to be rational at maturity when they consent to their father's rule, or remain within the commonwealth; age brings freedom and rationality. Moreover, all males are assumed to be rational enough to govern their families. If anyone is deficient in rationality in Locke's eyes (apart from lunatics and children) it is women: they are naturally fitted for subordination. Neither in his discussion of the state of nature, nor civil society, does Locke indicate that women are included among 'naturally' free and equal 'individuals'. In Locke's theory, 'individuals' are males. In this usage too he has been faithfully followed by liberal theorists, right down to our own day. Who, then, are the 'individuals' who enter the social contract? A person fitted only for subordination seems an unlikely candidate for this task, and, in the seventeenth century, it was widely assumed that the 'individuals' in question were fathers of families.[26] Women, as Locke's friend Tyrrell argued, were 'concluded by their Husbands'.[27]

Once the social contract has been made Locke's inference about tacit consent is all-encompassing enough to embrace women too, but this merely glosses over the basic problem of whether women are seen as 'naturally' capable of assuming their political obligation for themselves. If they are indeed 'naturally' fitted only for subordination, the logical conclusion is that women's 'obligation' should be differentiated from men's; perhaps they might be held to have a natural duty of obedience that is acknowledged in public through the actions of their fathers or husbands when the latter voluntarily assume their political obligation. The fact that women are now accorded most of the rights of liberal democratic citizenship, and are seen (more or less) as formal political equals, does not answer the problem of sexually differentiated 'consent' any more than Locke's hypothesis about tacit consent. The same beliefs about women's 'natural' subordination and 'natural' capacities and social place are still widely held. To cite the formal equality of citizenship in response merely draws attention to a contradiction of liberalism. For three hundred years liberalism has reconciled itself to, and transformed and consolidated, the patriarchal conception of women's 'natural' place, even though liberal theorists once attacked patriarchalism on other grounds. If it is to continue to be claimed that men and women have an equal political 'obligation', which implies that both sexes are free and equal individuals, then liberal theorists—and liberal democratic practice—must shed their patriarchal inheritance.

The Limit of Political Obligation and the Right of Resistance

Locke argues that government is instituted for certain ends which are prescribed by the law of nature and can be summed up as the protection of property. When a government is pursuing this end it will always be reasonable to infer that subjects are giving their consent or trust to it. However, there can be no guarantee that governments will always act as they ought; if a government acts in an arbitrary manner the hypothesis of consent is undermined, for the security of property is threatened: 'whenever the Legislators endeavour to take away, and destroy the Property of the People, ... they are thereupon absolved from any farther Obedience' (S222). The people are absolved from obedience because the government has forfeited its title to authority. Locke's conception of natural law enabled him to make the traditional distinction between a government that acted within the bounds of natural law and one that went outside these constraints and became a tyranny. A tyrannical government can legitimately be overthrown. Locke's theoretical perspective enabled him to distinguish, as Hobbes could not, between the 'dissolution' of a government and the destruction of a community. A community can be destroyed if, for example, it is mangled 'to pieces' by an invader, but this should not be confused with the exercise of the right of the people 'to resume their original Liberty, and, by the Establishment of a new Legislative ... provide for their own Safety and Security' (S211; 222).

At times Locke seems to suggest that a single individual has the right to resist arbitrary and unjust treatment from his government, but he usually refers to the right of the majority to do so. It is not really clear whether Locke here means the 'majority' of all those who enter the social contract, or the 'majority' of the politically relevant members of the community. It may be that the most appropriate place 'to appeal to the people ... is the two Houses of Parliament', but it is the actions of the legislative that are in question.[28] Parliamentary representatives are chosen by the propertied not the whole population, and the propertied, as 'majority', have strong ties of mutual interest to impel them to mutually advantageous political action. Locke is aware that (however the 'majority' is interpreted) the objection will be made to his argument that 'no Government will be able long to subsist, if the People may set up a new Legislative, whenever they take offence at the old one' (S223). He meets this objection by appealing to the fact that most people remain unmoved by oppression if it affects only a few unfortunate individuals: governments will not be disturbed by a 'heady Male-content' if the majority are untouched (S208). Subjects will always know when a government is acting for their good, just as children know this about their father, and it takes a great deal to rouse them to action; the majority will not exercise their right of resistance unless there is 'a long train of Abuses, Prevarications, and Artifices, all tending the same way' (S225). The right of individual action is thus rather like Hobbes' right of just refusal; it exists but it will be ineffective if used. People will put up with the 'inconveniences' of mistakes and hasty actions of a government that affect only a few individuals but, as in the state of nature, inconvenience is not the same as war; if the government is clearly designing to use unlawful force against the majority of its subjects it puts itself at war with them, and so action will be taken. Rather than 'laying a perpetual foundation for Disorder', Locke's argument is for a right that will be exercised only as a last resort when political obligation can no longer be justified.

Locke agrees with Hobbes that obedience lasts only as long as protection. His individuals are able to take action themselves to remedy their political lot, and not merely make another enforced covenant, but this does not mean, as is often assumed, that Locke's theory gives direct support to present-day arguments for a right of civil disobedience. For Locke, in the *Second Treatise*, the limits of liberal political obligation lie outside the state. His theory allows for two alternatives only: either people go peacefully about their daily affairs under the protection of a liberal, constitutional government, or they are in revolt against a government which has ceased to be 'liberal' and has become arbitrary and tyrannical, so forfeiting its right to obedience. When 'consent' can no longer be inferred, nor can the government properly be called 'civil'. In order to see the relevance of Locke's arguments for contemporary discussions of conditional obligation and civil disobedience, it is necessary to consider the *Second Treatise* together with Locke's support for religious toleration and the right of disobedience on purely religious or conscientious grounds.

In his earliest political writings Locke took an almost Hobbesian view of the political dangers of the individual conscience. In his *Tracts on Government* he argued that unless the magistrate had the absolute right to legislate as he saw fit about religiously indifferent things the entire basis of law would be undermined: 'do but once arm their consciences against the magistrate and their hands will not be long idle or innocent'.[29] By the 1680s Locke took a quite different view and argued that when conscience was outraged individuals might be justified in disobeying. This new argument was possible not because Locke had ceased to believe that 'If private man's judgements were the mould wherein laws were to be cast 'tis a question whether we should have any at all', but because he had by then arrived at his conception of civil government as an umpire between competing private interests.[30] This enabled Locke to take a modern view of religious belief as a purely private matter for the individual (which also meant the end of religiously indifferent things).[31] Hobbes saw religion in the same way, but his radical individualism led him to argue that Leviathan must legislate about public doctrine, whereas Locke is able to treat faith and conscience as part of the individual's private property or interests which the government protects, but also tolerates or treats impartially.[32] Or, at least, it tolerates those beliefs and churches that do not pose a direct threat to public order; Locke argues that Catholics cannot be tolerated for they owe allegiance to a foreign prince, and nor, for a different reason, touched on above, can atheists.

Even if faith is seen as a private matter for individuals in the liberal state, conflict between the demands of government and the demands of conscience cannot be ruled out. Locke distinguishes two cases of such conflict, the first of which corresponds to the limits of obligation already considered. If a magistrate exceeds his authority and rules, for example, that subjects join a specific church, claiming that this is for the public good, 'men are not in these cases obliged by that law, against their consciences'. Locke counsels caution, however; individuals are concerned for their salvation but peace and security are also important: 'there are very few will think it peace ... where they see all laid waste'. The second case is of more interest for present-day arguments, for this concerns the ruler who acts lawfully but also offends consciences. Locke argues that the individual may 'abstain from the action' demanded but, because the law is validly enacted and so obliges subjects, 'he is to undergo the punishment'.[33] At this point Locke's right of religious or conscientious disobedience and Hobbes' self-defensive right of just refusal converge. I shall not repeat the discussion of Chapter 3 about the reasons for the emphasis on the acceptance of punishment in discussions of civil disobedience, but turn to the relation between the orthodox account of civil disobedience and Locke's arguments.

It must always be kept in mind that Locke's argument for limited political obligation was aimed at absolute monarchy. When a monarch ruled arbitrarily and acted like a tyrant the 'people' had a right to bring his rule to an end and institute a properly political form of government. In this context it is a revolutionary doctrine, but once the liberal state is established Locke's theory looks rather different, although it is often taken to support a right of revolution. Locke argues that the people have a right to set up 'a new Legislative, differing from the other, by the change of Persons, or Form' (S220), but any new government must be suited to the prevailing socio-economic conditions. 'Revolution' today usually implies more than a change in government (or a *coup d'état*); revolutionaries attempt to bring about a change in wider social, especially property, relationships. Locke's civil government, however, is established precisely to preserve the property relationships of the developing capitalist market economy, not to disturb them. If a liberal government were 'dissolved', the new form of legislature must provide security for the existing distribution of property between the two classes of civil society; only then is it worthy of consent. It is entirely unreasonable to infer the consent of the descendants of the participants in the liberal social contract to anything that changes their material condition for the worse.

If a liberal government were ever to forfeit the 'trust' of its subjects, their political obligation would be suspended rather than abolished; it would be, so to speak, waiting to be renewed as before. The aim of overthrowing the government is to enable consent to be given once more; Locke's political theory 'aimed to restore a previous political health; not to initiate but to revert'.[34] It is in this sense that Locke's arguments foreshadow the orthodox theory of civil disobedience. The justification of the authority of the liberal state is now taken for granted, and the aim of civil disobedience is to restore the political obligation of citizens that has been 'suspended' in a specific area by the action or inaction of government. The limited form of action set out in the orthodox account of civil disobedience is little more than a modernization of Locke's right of religious refusal, although disobedience is no longer confined to purely religious matters.[35] Locke transformed the religious conscience into part of the individual's private property or interests and, from this conception of conscience, it is a relatively easy path to a secular notion of conscientiously undertaken civil disobedience, with acceptance of punishment as a sign of good conscience. If Locke allowed disobedience only by the individual as religious believer, contemporary theorists often argue that civil disobedience must only be undertaken by the individual in an attempt to remedy some flagrant breach of the formal equality of liberal democratic citizenship, such as the denial of the right to vote, or use of public facilities, to certain sections of the population. Rawls, for example, argues that civil disobedience is not an appropriate action in cases of wider social injustice because these matters are too difficult to evaluate.[36] Another way of looking at this claim is that the liberal democratic state, as 'umpire', upholds and regulates the inequalities of the capitalist economy and liberal society. If these inequalities are seen as 'injustices' for which civil disobedience may offer a remedy, then civil disobedients begin to offer a challenge to, and not, as the orthodox account demands, a recognition of, the political authority of the liberal democratic state.

Locke's 'umpire' government is constrained by the law of nature, which provides principles of political right or morality against which the actions of government can be judged. The development of the conception of liberal democracy as no more than a political method or procedure for regulating conflicting private interests is part of the secularization of liberalism. Liberal democracy can be evaluated only in terms of the procedure and its requirements, such as the formal equality of citizenship or universal suffrage. It is thus not surprising that the orthodox account of civil disobedience tries to confine this form of political action to breaches of the procedure; by what criteria could civil disobedience be justified in other areas? I noted above that Locke's traditional view of natural law provided individuals with an external standard which they could recognize, but which they did not voluntarily choose to order their political life. Similarly, the political method of liberal democracy provides a procedure to which individuals are said to consent, but which they do not themselves choose. Part of Rousseau's critique of liberal contract theory is that it does not and cannot give expression to the ideal of social life as a voluntary scheme based on self-assumed obligation, because it cannot find a place for substantive principles of political right that are freely chosen and adhered to by citizens themselves. I shall return to this point in Chapter 7. Most contemporary theorists of political obligation ignore Rousseau's critique, and in the next two chapters I shall look in detail at recent voluntarist justifications of political obligation in the liberal democratic state.

Chapter 5

Contemporary Consent Theory

> One of the standard embarrassments of consent and contractarian
> theories of political obligation is that accepting them seems to lead to
> the conclusion that very few people have or have ever had political
> obligations.
>
> R. E. Flathman, *Political Obligation*.

The 'consent of the governed' is frequently presented by political scientists and
political theorists as a central, if not the major, distinguishing feature of liberal
democracy, and consent is an idea that has wide popular currency. Nevertheless,
there are surprisingly few thorough examinations of the meaning of 'consent', or the
manner in which it is, or can be said to be, given, in the recent academic literature on
the subject, and there are even fewer genuinely critical discussions. Theorists who
frame voluntarist justifications of political obligation in terms of consent usually take
it for granted 'that there is a sense in which [liberal] democratic states *are*
characterized by the consent of the governed, and that this is consent in some
significant sense',[1] and one of their main concerns is to avoid the 'standard
embarrassments' of consent theory referred to in the epigraph to this chapter.

Consent theorists adopt two basic strategies to deal with this embarrassment, one
of which raises doubts about the importance, or even the relevance, of consent; the
second, far from identifying a 'significant sense' of consent, empties it of most or all
of its genuine content. An example of the first approach is provided by Plamenatz's
statement in *Consent, Freedom and Political Obligation* that,

> consent is not the sole basis of the duty of the governed to obey their rulers or else … there
> exists in every state, however democratic, a large number of persons under no obligation
> to obey its laws. The latter conclusion is suspect from the start, …[2]

Most liberal writers on political obligation share Plamenatz's suspicion of this
conclusion, but they can be reduced to some very odd arguments to avoid it. I have
already referred to Tussman's claim that liberal democracies are inhabited by
numbers of 'child-bride' citizens, whose political obligation is not based on consent
and 'who have a status they do not understand'.[3] These arguments invite the
question of why any reference need be made to consent; few consent theorists ask
why consent is important or how their theories would differ without it.

Nor do theorists who adopt the second strategy usually ask this question. They get
round the 'embarrassment' by claiming that all citizens do, or can be said to, consent.
The claim is rarely backed up with a critical look at relevant empirical evidence
about consent; 'consent' is frequently identified with the mere existence of certain

82

social or political practices. This approach to consent provides a very good illustration of the extent to which discussions of political obligation rest on the ideological assumption that liberal democratic theory and practice coincide. There is no longer any recognition that the voluntarist claim about consent meets a problem about political obligation. Today, most of the intellectual and political depth of the classic social contract and consent theorists has vanished and all that is left to underpin 'consent' are some notions about individual free choice. Some theorists frankly reduce consent to a useful political fiction (useful that is for political rulers and theorists of the liberal democratic state):

> the question why, or under what conditions, are we obliged to obey the state is not now usually regarded by political philosophers as a profitable way of approaching an examination of the nature of the state. But the idea of 'consent' has survived rather as a constituent element of democratic ideology: as a specification of an essential characteristic of democratic regimes which distinguish them from the non-democratic.[4]

The logical conclusion of this approach is to see 'consent' as no more than a political myth which reinforces a 'widespread popular belief in the government's moral right to rule'. To propagate the myth of consent 'is not to delude the people, but to convey the essence of democracy to them in the most efficient manner'.[5]

In the final section of this chapter I shall discuss Walzer's *Obligations*, which forms a notable exception to the typical approach to consent. However, because Walzer explores the implications of consent as an actual and explicit act of commitment, his essays (rather despite themselves) reveal the magnitude of the problem of justifying political obligation in the liberal democratic state. Most consent theorists are content with the emptier forms of hypothetical voluntarism and uncritically accept the institutions of the liberal democratic state, seeing no difficulties in the claim that these are based on 'consent' and political 'obligation'. One consequence of this view of the state is that their arguments tend to oscillate between the two theoretical extremes referred to in Chapter 2. On the one hand, 'consent' is seen from an abstractly individualist perspective and the problem of arbitrariness tends to loom large. The individual is seen as 'the guardian of his (*sic*) own consent'[6] and, given this possessive 'guardian', the problem immediately arises that there seems 'nothing in the notion of consent which requires that ... reasons for consenting be good reasons in the sense of showing that the action is justifiable, ...'.[7] It appears (in Hobbesian fashion) that 'merely by refusing to consent, for whatever reason, [the individual] can render inapplicable the entire apparatus of concepts and justification that is part of the practice of political obligation'.[8] On the other hand, consent is also treated as unproblematic by means of all-embracing inferences from, or assertions about, the existence of certain political practices, which ignore individuals' intentions or their own interpretations of their actions.

Another consequence of taking the liberal democratic state for granted is that consent theorists subsume political obligation under consent; there is no appreciation that consent to obligations is only one form of self-assumed obligation. Theorists are thus unable to offer a satisfactory account of political obligation in a direct or participatory form of democracy and also have difficulty in distinguishing consent from promising. For example, in *Consent, Freedom and Political Obligation*, one of the best-known and most frequently cited discussions of consent, Plamenatz argues that 'consent' takes the following form: A gives B permission to act or the right to act in a certain way; A thus authorizes B's actions and is indirectly responsible for them. Plamenatz also suggests that if A makes a promise 'he' might be said to consent, but in the different sense of consenting to himself doing something, or 'merely creating an obligation'.[9] Oddly enough, despite the title of the book, Plamenatz does not explicitly discuss the connection between A giving B permission to act and A then having, or consenting to, obligations consequent upon B's acting; he concentrates on the right to act granted to B. The example he discusses (consent theorists are fond of patriarchal examples and metaphors) is that of a father consenting to his daughter's marriage and the right this gives the daughter to act.[10] However, this is not a very good example, for the father's permission does not make his daughter his agent or create an authority relationship. When Plamenatz turns to representative and direct or, as he calls it, pure democracy, the problems are multiplied. Having argued, quite rightly, that individuals do not consent to their own acts, he then has to claim that individuals in a direct democracy cannot be said to consent to their own legislative actions—but he is left with no means of explaining on what basis their political obligation rests. In a representative system the right of the government to legislate rests upon consent, but usually only upon the consent of a minority (its size depending upon the electoral system): 'It follows from this that consent cannot be taken to be the only basis of political obligation'.[11] Again the question remains of the grounds of the obligation of the rest of the population, and Plamenatz argues that they are obligated because they receive the benefit of the protection of the liberal democratic state.

Plamenatz takes it for granted that consent, when present, in liberal democracies is given through liberal democratic voting and most consent theorists assume that this is the case. I now want to examine this widespread assumption.

Consent and Liberal Democratic Voting

The main reason why it may appear obvious that consent is given through liberal democratic voting is because, as I argued in Chapter 1, there is a general conceptual connection between voting and self-assumed political obligation. This is not, as I also argued, to say that liberal democratic voting gives actual expression to this relationship; there is good reason why promising, which exemplifies self-assumed obligation in everyday life, and political obligation in the liberal democratic state always seem to differ. Unlike promising, liberal democratic voting, for example, allows citizens to vote only at times, and on matters, chosen by others, and in voting, citizens choose representatives who will then determine the content of their political obligation.[12] Consent theorists do not, however, usually examine the concept of 'self-assumed obligation', nor do they ask what form of political institutions are required for such a practice to exist. It is taken for granted that 'political obligation' can and does exist in the liberal democratic state, constituted by 'consent' arising from liberal democratic voting.

The general theoretical reasons for rejecting the alleged relationship between political obligation and liberal democratic voting undercut much of the contemporary discussion of consent. However, because so many theorists treat the liberal democratic state as if it were a natural feature of the world, dismiss out of hand any suggestions that 'democracy' and 'voting' could mean anything other than liberal democracy and its electoral procedure, and disregard the history of 'obligation', 'consent' and voluntarist arguments, I shall temporarily set aside the theoretical objection of Chapter 1. Instead, I shall take consent a good deal more seriously than is usually the case and look at some of the empirical evidence about liberal democratic voting to see how far it is possible for citizens to consent, and how plausible is the inference that they do.

To call the claim about consent an example of hypothetical voluntarism is rather generous, since many writers merely identify consent with the existence of the liberal democratic electoral mechanism. Any problems and embarrassments about consent are thus quickly and neatly defined out of existence. For example, it is asserted that:

> the means by which consent is given have been institutionalized in the case of voting ... consenting now becomes a definite and decisive affair, represented by an accepted social practice.[13]

Or Schumpeter's liberal democratic political method is merely restated in terms of consent; 'the method of consent' is said to consist in a procedure that 'leaves open to every sane, non-criminal adult the opportunity to discuss, criticize, and vote for or against the government'.[14] This approach makes it possible to include all citizens, whether or not they exercise their right to vote, within the scope of consent. Plamenatz's modification of his early definition of consent is interesting in this context. In the 'Postscript' to the second edition of *Consent, Freedom and Political Obligation* he states that he has come to believe that the stress on permission, in the definition I referred to above, is mistaken; consent is, rather, 'to do or to take part in doing something which the doer knows, or is presumed to know, creates in another a right he would not otherwise have'.[15] The change in emphasis from permission is, however, largely verbal; both definitions treat consent as authorization. The real effect of Plamenatz's widening of his definition, and the important difference between his original argument, the 'Postscript', and the discussion of consent in *Man and Society*, is to make consent all-inclusive. In the latter work, Plamenatz distinguishes between direct consent, which 'grants authority or establishes or alters a system of government', and indirect or tacit consent[16] All those who take part in an election directly consent to the government which takes office, because they voluntarily took part in knowledge of the consequences of an election. Those who abstain from voting give tacit consent to the political system as a whole. Abstainers have the opportunity to vote, and their failure to use it counts as consent 'when it is abstention from voting or from legal opposition to the system when such opposition is safe and easy and might be effective'.[17] Another theorist goes further and places all citizens on the same footing whether they vote or not; the meaning of consent is that 'one can participate if one chooses to do so', and, therefore, 'the individual is obligated ... whether he personally utilizes his opportunity or not ...'.[18]

I commented earlier that the exact status and importance of 'consent' in many discussions is far from clear. It is worth noting at this point that just as it is possible to reinterpret Locke's tacit consent argument in voluntarist terms without using 'consent', so with these arguments about voting: it can be argued that the act of participation in elections gives rise to political obligation, although this is not based on consent, or it can be claimed that because citizens accept the benefits deriving from the practice of liberal democratic elections they are politically obliged for that reason. I shall discuss these formulations in the following chapter but I mention them here to illustrate that it is not self-evident that voting and liberal democratic elections should be interpreted in terms of 'consent'. More generally, the appropriate interpretation or meaning of voting and electoral abstention in liberal democracies is a controversial matter. Empirical investigators of voting behaviour in the post-war period have typically drawn very comforting conclusions from their data, particularly about the functions of political apathy and electoral abstention, and one of the most striking features of the inference about consent and voting is its close resemblance to these conclusions. To appreciate the full significance of this similarity it is necessary to consider the role of voting in the liberal democratic state.

It will be recalled that Locke's individuals had good reason to leave the natural condition and enter the social contract because it ensured protection of their property or private interests. It is then possible to infer the continuing consent of subjects to the liberal state because, no matter what their social position, their interests continue to be protected. With the introduction of universal suffrage this protection is placed on an even more secure footing; if representatives do not legislate in the public interest (or impartially protect all interests) they will be held to account and subject to the sanction of loss of office: voting has an instrumental function. Consent theorists, in one aspect of their argument, implicitly rely on the ideological assumption that the instrumental function of voting works in practice as it is held to in theory. This is an assumption they share with the empirical investigators who praise political apathy. It is suggested by the latter that the liberal democratic political method works so well that it is often rational for citizens not to vote; the fact that they can do so if the need arises is sufficient to ensure that representatives act in their interest.[19] Thus, not only can complacent claims be made about the positive functions of political apathy but, because it is assumed that all citizens' interests are in fact protected, it can also be claimed that it is reasonable to infer the consent even of electoral abstainers.

The preceding argument lies at one of the two theoretical extremes of consent theory; it is an argument (or assertion) about the alleged necessary consequences of the existence of a certain political practice. On the other hand, if consent theorists focus not on the practice of liberal democratic voting but on the individuals who consent, the instrumental function of voting fades into the background and, as Plamenatz's definition of consent illustrates, it is voting as authorization that becomes crucial. Voters know that elections give authority to the representatives whom they choose to act for them and, whether or not they make use of their electoral opportunities, they can be said to consent to this arrangement. However, in either case, an examination of the empirical evidence about voting and elections undermines the claims about consent and consent theorists' basic ideological assumptions.

One preliminary point that should be made is that the theory of liberal democratic voting, and the inference that it constitutes political 'obligation', implies that citizens are free to choose whether or not to vote in a particular election. Yet in Australia, for example, many inhabitants are legally required to attend at the polling station and accept a ballot paper, and can incur a fine if they fail to do so.[20] It is impossible to see how either voters or abstainers have an 'obligation' where legal compulsion exists; but it is equally as implausible to claim that electoral abstainers consent where voting is voluntary. One group of abstainers who are usually not mentioned in discussions of consent are the anarchists who deliberately do not vote, and encourage others to follow them, because they see voting as a contrivance that keeps the working class more tightly bound into the system through which they are exploited.

The claim about consent and non-voting rests on the implicit argument that the formally equal status of citizenship, shared by all adult individuals, gives them all good reason to use their vote or to abstain if they choose to do so; no matter what their substantive social postion, their interests are protected through the liberal democratic electoral mechanism. A reasonable conclusion to be drawn from this argument is that electoral abstainers should be drawn equally from all sections of the population. Any citizen could decide, on a given occasion, and for the same reason, not to exercise the franchise. In fact, electoral abstainers (like the politically inactive in a broader sense) are far from constituting a random cross-section of the population; they tend to be drawn from lower socio-economic backgrounds and to be disproportionately female. Neither the empirical investigators of voting behaviour, nor the consent theorists, have seen this as a fact worthy of special note, but the systematic social differentiation of political participation on sex and class lines cannot be regarded as an unsurprising or 'natural' fact about liberal democracies.[21]

The 'explanation' offered by political scientists and political sociologists, and implicitly accepted by consent theorists, for the 'rationality' of abstention is merely a way of treating this social fact as unremarkable. The empirical evidence itself suggests a very different explanation. The reason for the division of the citizenry into the more and less politically active along class and sex lines is because the inactive and electoral abstainers do not see political participation as worthwhile. Their abstention is rational because they do not perceive the vote as instrumentally effective and they do not believe that liberal democratic voting operates as it is claimed to. Answers to survey questions such as, 'Whoever you vote for, things go on pretty much the same', or, 'The way people vote is the main thing that decides how things are run in this country', are usually interpreted as showing something about the psychology of respondents (do they feel politically efficacious, for example) or about their commitment to 'democratic norms'. But they can also be interpreted as an indication of the respondents' evaluation of the liberal democratic electoral mechanism, as telling us something about the way in which liberal democracy is perceived by many of its inhabitants, especially the working class, who tend not to give the 'correct' answers.[22] Similarly the poor tend to feel cheated:[23] 'Elections come and go, and the life of poverty goes on pretty much as before, neither dramatically better nor dramatically worse'.[24] That such beliefs and doubts about the operation of liberal democratic elections are quite rational is supported by the findings of one of the most recent large-scale empirical studies, *Participation in America*; the major conclusion of this study is that political participation, including voting, '*helps those who are already better off*'.[25] It is hardly plausible to interpret electoral abstention as consent, even indirect or tacit consent, to a voting system that helps reinforce social inequality and the disadvantaged position of the abstainers themselves, when it is seen by them as doing so.

A similar explanation can be offered for the tendency of women not to use their vote. Feminist political scientists have now begun to re-examine the typical claims about female voters found in voting studies.[26] It has been taken for granted in the standard discussions of the empirical evidence (invariably by male writers) that it is 'natural' for women to be less politically active and interested than men because of the alleged 'natural' differences in the characters and social roles of men and women. However, the social and economic position of women, and the fact that they are always told that political life is not for them, suggests a very different explanation: 'What reasons do women have ... to participate in politics?'; the answer is very few indeed. Political life is conventionally seen in terms that have little or no relevance to women, nor do they have the social and economic 'stake' in politics that makes participation worthwhile for men (or some of them at least).[27]

If it is therefore implausible to insist that electoral abstention by women is consent, there is no better reason to interpret the votes of women as constituting consent. I have referred in previous chapters to the difficulties caused by beliefs about women for arguments about political obligation. The liberal view of the instrumentally functional role of voting depends also upon a specific conception of the motivation of the voter. In voting the citizen is acting to protect private interests; but, according to many political scientists, only male voters act with this intention. My analysis of the role allotted to women in Locke's theory, and the reasons he gives for this, shows how, for liberal contract theorists, it is males alone who are equipped with the 'natural morality' of the possessive individual, a morality necessary for the individuals who are to pursue their interests (in which the interests of their families are subsumed) in the market. The strength and persistence of this assumption is graphically illustrated by the contemporary argument that it is only males who vote out of self-interest. A woman's vote is 'qualitatively different from the male's vote', and reflects not self-interest but 'a kind of bloodless love of the good'.[28] Such a love of the good (attenuated though it may be) is a more secure basis for the practice of self-assumed obligation than pure self-interest but, nevertheless, it is impossible to see how a female vote can be, at the same time, both 'qualitatively different' from a male vote and have the same meaning of consent.

This leaves the problem whether males' votes can plausibly be interpreted as giving rise to consent. An obvious objection to regarding all male votes in this way is that some citizens vote for revolutionary candidates who are pledged to change the liberal democratic system, or who state that they will not proceed to parliament if elected and are only using their candidature as a platform to reach the people. Plamenatz argues that these voters consent because 'you make use of the system in order to change it'.[29] But this is like saying that to vote in an election where tyranny is a possible outcome commits one to the authority of a tyrant if elected.[30] Plamenatz claims that it is the fact of voting that matters and not the individual's intention, but to discount the intention of voters is to treat their vote as a meaningless gesture to which the theorist can attribute any content whatsoever. While this accords with the doubts often expressed by political scientists and political sociologists about the rationality of voters, it places the hypothesis of consent on shaky ground. There is no good reason to suppose that votes for revolutionary parties are not cast intentionally and deliberately, and so, as in the case of electoral abstention, there is no good reason why 'consent' should be inferred.

More generally, there are features of the liberal democratic electoral method that undermine the simplistic identification of elections and consent. If consent is to exist in 'some significant sense' then, at a minimum, there are two conditions necessary. First, consent has to be seen as something that arises from the acts of citizens. Now it is frequently regarded as a matter for governmental manipulation; 'consent' is something that governments can (and should) 'manufacture', 'enlist', 'forge', 'generate', 'arouse' or 'maximize'. This view of consent is so well established that it can confidently be pronounced that 'no one' will doubt that the 'process whereby public opinion is prepared for policies and measures governments are in due course enabled or encouraged to embark on ... is consent'.[31] I need hardly labour the point that there is very great room for doubt that this constitutes 'consent'. Secondly, if citizens are to consent then, as in the social practice of promising, they must be able to ascertain what kind of commitment they are undertaking and whether good reasons exist for them to do so. It is virtually impossible for them to do this in liberal democratic elections since the consequences of voting are so difficult to determine. This is not merely a matter of the often large discrepancies between what is stated by parties and candidates before the election and what is done afterwards, or of the secrecy about many important matters, but of the wider context in which the vote is cast. Citizens 'consent' in an electoral system where 'issues' on which they vote are largely arrived at by a process of 'non-decision making',[32] and in which parties and candidates are 'sold' to the electorate like commodities, not for their political worth but for their commercial 'image'. Moreover, citizens may also have to try to see their way through corruption, deceit and criminal activity by their representatives (which may generally be summarized under the heading 'Watergate') and to cope with attempts by officials to bring about a 'defactualized' political world.[33]

Even if these difficulties could be overcome, other problems concerning the nature of liberal democratic voting and its connection to political obligation remain. From liberal social contract theory onwards, liberal theorists have seen individuals as interested mainly in the pursuit of private interest in daily, especially economic, life. They are content to let representatives act for them in the political realm, becoming political actors only periodically on the special occasions when, acting as citizens, they have the opportunity to exercise the franchise. Voting is widely seen as *the* political act of the liberal democratic citizen, and one reason why it seems so reasonable to equate consent with voting is that voting is a political act which therefore has a direct relationship to political obligation. But in what sense is liberal democratic voting a 'political' act? To many people this will seem an absurd question to ask, but to take the character of liberal democratic voting for granted is to overlook how paradoxical it is.[34] When citizens cast their ballot, they do so in defence of their private interests; as Schumpeter stated, in liberal democratic voting, 'the social [political] function is fulfilled, as it were, incidentally—in the same sense as production is incidental to the making of profits'.[35] Formally, individuals act as citizens or political actors when they vote; substantively, they are still concerned with private affairs. At election time individuals put on what Marx called their 'political lion skin' of citizenship, but underneath they act as before.[36] This is why liberal democratic voting is held to be instrumentally effective and why liberal democratic theorists can claim that it is often rational for individuals to pursue courses other than voting in defence of their interests. If voting, as an unambiguous political act, is to be directly connected to political obligation, then it would seem that attention must be directed away from its substantive content and instrumental function, to its formal character and its formal function of authorization.

The liberal democratic vote can be given a constant, political meaning or interpretation as authorization if each individual voter is seen singularly in his or her formal status as citizen. Indeed, if one begins from an abstractly individualist consideration of the 'consent' of each particular individual, then 'consent' will appear as nothing other than authorization (recall Hobbes' radically abstract individualist theory of consent). The individual act of voting by each citizen can be interpreted as 'consent' because, as Plamenatz argues, each citizen knows, or is presumed to know, that to vote is to create 'in another a right he would not otherwise have', so the voter 'consents' to the existence of this right. The voter thus consents to the determination by representatives of the content of his or her political obligation. By focusing on the formal aspects of the act of voting, the political theorist can both reaffirm voluntarism—the individual freely chooses to vote—and emphasize the difference between promising, or obligation in everyday life, and political obligation. In authorizing representatives to take office (or consent), the content of political obligation, unlike that of a promise, seems necessarily to involve the subordination of the judgement of individuals to that of others.

To see voting purely as authorization is, in many ways, a realistic view of liberal democratic voting, although it is not without its problems for arguments about consent. The evidence already cited illustrates that 'the electors and the elected can share a belief in the legitimacy of the political hierarchy because votes are cast and counted, without that same counting of ballots necessarily leading to accountability'; to the extent that 'volunteerism', or the movement of representatives in and out of office through a process of self-selection and elimination, not electoral challenge, is widespread, then electoral accountability is missing.[37] At one point in his discussion Plamenatz refers to the liberal democratic vote as a deliberate 'symbolic gesture' that has a particular consequence, namely authorization.[38] It has also been argued that liberal democratic elections are nothing more than ritual legitimations of governments.[39] Although this is far removed from the liberal theory of elections, it does accord with the way in which a large number of citizens see their votes. The evidence indicates that many citizens vote not from any expectations of instrumental effectiveness but because they regard voting as a duty of citizenship. It has been commented that:

the duty to vote, through a process of socialization, becomes a response to an internal compulsion. ... voting is not so much behaviour freely undertaken by an individual seeking to initiate or advance interests, but rather a more-or-less passive response ... to continuing social pressures ...[40]

If this is an accurate characterization of liberal democratic voting, if it is no more than a symbolic gesture of authorization, or a performance of a duty which ritually affirms a government in office, then the identification of voting and consent is untenable even if explicitly reduced to an aspect of liberal ideology that serves to distinguish the liberal democratic state from other political systems. These other systems are usually also based on universal suffrage today because it is an eminently 'modern' way of legitimizing the power of rulers of all kinds. If liberal democratic voting and consent are to be interpreted merely as authorization then, even as ideology, liberal theory is unsuccessful, since the consequences of liberal democratic voting cannot be distinguished from those of voting in other existing political systems.

The objection might be made that, even if my arguments were acceptable, the preceding discussion does not show that consent cannot be given through liberal democratic elections. Electoral reforms might be introduced that, for example, increased the accountability of representatives, and attempts might be made to develop a more general understanding that to vote is to consent. The difficulty with such suggestions is that they open the Pandora's box of empirical and conceptual problems that liberal theorists wish to keep firmly closed. In particular, they draw attention to the possibility that consent might not be given, and to the position of 'child-bride' citizens and all those who might refuse or withdraw consent. Contemporary consent theory is firmly in the Lockean tradition, offering only the alternatives of all-embracing consent or revolution. It is argued that all those who make use of the electoral 'method of consent', and all those who refrain from illegal political activity, are consenting. The established legal channels of liberal democratic political life have to bear a great deal of weight. Plamenatz goes so far as to argue that 'consent' requires that legal opportunities exist for 'changing the political system'.[41] He does not elaborate on the meaning of this but, even if it is interpreted to mean 'making radical changes within the liberal democratic system', the implications are unacceptable to liberal theorists and, as recent events have indicated, such changes are unlikely to be so easily obtainable in practice. I have shown how Locke's consent theory is formulated to preserve, not to make radical changes within, the liberal state and the inequitable social relationships of its capitalist economy; the identification of consent with voting and legal abstention once more follows Locke's lead. The practical limitations of liberal democratic voting as a means of bringing about substantive social and political changes are starkly revealed by the exceptionally brutal and bloody overthrow of the elected Allende government in Chile and, less dramatically, by the 'dismissal' from office in 1975 of the moderately reformist Labor government by the Governor General of Australia.

Contemporary consent theorists who identify consent and voting leave themselves no alternative but to treat all dissent that falls outside the 'method of consent' as revolutionary activity. Again, this blurs the distinction between other existing regimes and the liberal democratic state with its 'consenting' citizens, and it also means that consent theorists are, for example, unable to distinguish urban guerillas from non-violent civil disobedients because both engage in illegal activities. Consent theory offers a crude and simplistic perspective on political life which can take no account of the complexities of political action and inaction, or give any help in evaluating different forms of political activity. Contemporary consent theorists are left with nothing consistent to say about citizens who participate in civil disobedience *and* vote; they cannot agree that the form of action taken by civil disobedients is such that it demonstrates the citizen's general adherence to the liberal democratic system, but they have to admit that the very same citizens are also consenting. Consent theorists face an insoluble dilemma: either they reduce 'consent' to a political myth that bolsters the claim to authority of the liberal democratic state, and so preserve the claim that political obligation is unproblematic; or they can continue to insist that 'consent' in a genuine sense is possible within the liberal democratic state and so expose the gap between the liberal voluntarist ideal and the realities of the liberal democratic state. In other words, they begin to expose the gulf between liberal democratic voting and the practice of self-assumed political obligation.

Consent and Pluralism

Not all consent theorists identify consent and voting. Consent is sometimes seen as an outcome of liberal democratic pluralism, or a result of the existence of a multiplicity of organizations and institutions within the liberal democratic state, and the inter-electoral process of 'consultation and negotiation'.[42] The claim about voting and consent is little more than a restatement of some of the conclusions drawn from empirical studies of voting behaviour, and similarly, the pluralist variant of the consent hypothesis sometimes rests on no more than a restatement of some other now-familiar conclusions of empirical political science; and it is thus open to all the equally familiar criticisms. Such criticisms do not necessarily deter consent theorists. Partridge, for example, noting the conventional objections that not everyone is an organizational member, that not all organizations are equally influential, and that leaders are often remote from rank-and-file members, still rejects the argument that a plausible account of consent requires a more participatory pluralist process; lack of participation is part of the 'logic of ... pluralism' and we 'cannot speak as if non-participation were a somehow curable sickness ...'.[43] In view of this excellent example of the tendency for liberal theorists to treat the institutions of liberal democracy as if they were natural facts about the world, it is hardly surprising to find that Partridge regards the distinction between voluntary and involuntary action as largely irrelevant in political life, and sees consent in the liberal democratic state as a 'form of acquiescence which closely resembles habitual or customary following of established practice'.[44] Organizational leaders and the politically influential can, however, be said to consent in a different sense, but Partridge does not pursue the implications of this differential consent for liberal democratic ideology.

'Pluralism' is a term that, like 'democracy', has now become almost completely subsumed under 'liberal democracy', but earlier in this century a group of 'pluralist' theorists interpreted the concept very differently, so that it did not coincide with the theory and practice of the liberal state. This earlier conception is recalled by Walzer's *Obligations*; indeed, he refers to one of these pluralists, G. D. H. Cole. Walzer's essays provide a very welcome relief from discussions of consent based either on an abstractly individualist account of consent, or the complacent identification of consent and voting or pluralism (or both). Nevertheless, although Walzer provides many insights into consent and obligation in the liberal democratic state his argument is ultimately deeply ambiguous. It remains uncertain whether Walzer's pluralism is another defence and redescription of liberal democracy or radically subversive of it. In short, *Obligations* provides a clear illustration of the difficulty of trying to combine a genuine sense of 'consent' with the assumption that political obligation is justified within the liberal democratic state.

Walzer begins his discussion by stating that he is following Hobbes' definition of obligation. Consent must arise from an individual's own action and the 'paradigm form of consent theory is simply, I have committed myself (consented): I am committed (obligated)' (p. viii).[45] The consenting individual is autonomous and responsible, leading an aware and self-conscious moral life, so that consent can always be reconsidered and, if necessary, withdrawn. Walzer argues that consent is much more than authorization; it can, for example, signify a whole variety of commitments, a readiness to stand by a principle and the sense of the self as a citizen. Consent is a social relationship and obligations are assumed within groups: 'Obligation, ... begins with membership' (p. 7). However, obligation does not rest merely upon the fact of being born into and socialized within a certain group, as so many consent theorists insist, but arises from 'willful membership', from deliberate and conscious commitments. Walzer also implicitly distinguishes his account of consent from the hypothetical consent of Locke's theory in which, because the government is legitimate, subjects can be said to consent. Walzer argues that in consent theory:

> we do not say that the government is just, therefore the citizens are obligated, but rather that the citizens have committed themselves, therefore the government is just (p. x).

The difficulty with this formulation is that it invites the charge that consent is an arbitrary basis for political life. It will be argued that citizens can commit themselves (or not) to anything they wish, and so 'justice' is anything they decide it is. This is one illustration of the uncertain relation between Walzer's argument and liberal individualist theory. Walzer says that consent theory 'suggests a procedural rather than a substantive ethics' (p. viii), but his essays are illuminating and helpful because they have moved away from the conventional treatment of consent as little more than an aspect of the liberal democratic political method or decision-making procedure. All that Walzer says about consent, membership and commitment presupposes substantive principles of political morality.

The conclusions that Walzer draws from his analysis of consent are in striking contrast to the usual claims of consent theorists. Walzer is one of the theorists to whom I referred in the 'Introduction', who argue that political obligation is owed first and foremost to fellow members or fellow citizens: 'we commit ourselves to our representatives in very limited ways indeed compared to the commitments we simultaneously make to our fellow voters' (p. xi). Not only is the citizen's relationship to the state a limited one but the state 'is not the only or necessarily the most important arena of our moral (or even of our political) life' (p. xiv). There are no practical alternatives to membership of the liberal democratic state for most citizens so, therefore, 'the willfulness of that membership seems to have only minimal moral significance' (p. 18). Walzer has some harsh things to say about the liberal conception and practice of citizenship. It is based on an impoverished view of the citizen as no more than an individual in receipt of protection from the state and has nothing to say about the moral and political dimensions of citizenship. There is no suggestion of any relationship between citizens but, instead, a series of singular relations between each citizen and the state, 'a pattern that might best be symbolized by a series of vertical lines' (p. 207). Genuine consent is irrelevant to an understanding of liberal democratic citizenship, rather 'a key' is provided by the silence, inaction and passivity that 'may be construed' as tacit consent (p. 100). Walzer sees tacit consent as the mark of a resident who is as an alien, receiving the protection of the state but nothing more; many citizens might even be seen as 'a kind of moral proletariat whose members have nothing to give to the state—neither advice nor consent—except their lives' (p. 111).

This characterization of liberal democratic citizenship and the contrast that Walzer draws with the ideal of a pluralist citizenship resting on morally self-conscious group membership, explicit commitments and participation, leads one to suppose that he will comment upon the difficulty of justifying political obligation in the liberal democratic state. Such expectations are heightened when he argues that:

> However useful we may be or want to be, our usefulness is not organized or given expression within the political community. Now these facts are clearly a reflection on the moral quality of the modern state. They may well constitute an entirely sufficient argument for its radical reconstruction (pp. 186–7).

In the end, however, these expectations are disappointed.

Walzer's distinction between genuine consent and the tacit consent that is inferred from silence and passivity is not so clear cut as it appears at first sight. He comments that express and tacit consent produce 'different degrees of obligation' (p. 117). He discusses these degrees throughout the essays (members of oppressed minorities having no obligations at all), but, nevertheless, despite the sensitive fashion in which Walzer deals with these questions, he still sees tacit consent as giving rise to a genuine political obligation; the 'moral proletariat' are not as sharply differentiated from the rest of the population as this graphic phrase would suggest. Walzer offers several different arguments to explain how citizens are justifiably obligated in the liberal democratic state. He suggests that this is because of the 'expectations aroused among one's fellow residents' in the activities of daily life (p. 28). But such expectations are concerned rather with the actions we 'ought' to perform in our daily lives than with political 'obligation'; like many other theorists Walzer does not distinguish between these two concepts. The argument about mutual expectations, and some of his other comments about 'membership' and 'participation', closely resemble the conceptual argument about political obligation that I shall discuss in detail in Chapter 6, so I shall leave these aside. Plamenatz solves the problem posed by non-consenting citizens in the liberal democratic state by arguing that their obligation arises from the benefit of protection that they receive from the state; it is 'no more than a special case of the general obligation to help persons who benefit us'.[46] Similarly, Walzer claims that citizens, irrespective of consent, are justifiably obligated by virtue of the benefits they accept from the state (p. 28). However, since Walzer also equates this claim with the liberal conception of citizenship it is doubtful if it should be given much weight in the general argument of *Obligations*.

Walzer also argues that political participation is the 'best' expression of consent. I have already noted a reference to the commitments that fellow voters make to each other, and he argues that citizens commonly pledge to one another to uphold the liberal democratic system during elections. To be sure, he adds that this participation must be meaningful; no obligation can be incurred through actions 'about whose effectiveness and significance [the citizen] is deceived' (p. 111). But Walzer does not examine liberal democratic voting to see whether it meets the criteria for obligation, although some of his comments about liberal democratic citizenship reveal doubts that this is the case. For example, he comments that the ideal of pluralist citizenship now often serves an ideological role. We are told (how often by political theorists!) that we are citizens and political obligation is inferred from this, and the citizen may accept this ideology and participate, but 'he' does so in 'trivial' ways: 'If the state stands over him as an alien force, he does not know it; he thinks it is his own' (p. 227). Walzer's treatment of voting is indicative of a major problem in his argument as a whole. He introduces the essays by stating that he will not assume that consent exists 'without looking for evidence that it has actually been given' (p. viii). Unfortunately, Walzer does not actually do this, and it never becomes clear whether or not he regards genuine consent as present, or possible, within the framework of liberal democratic institutions.

Walzer argues that 'the force of contradictions' of citizenship in the liberal democratic state is reduced once it is admitted that citizens do not, as liberalism maintains, face the state as single individuals (p. 218). Their relationship to the state is mediated through groups and associations: 'Self-determination is an indirect process made possible by the participatory politics of church members, union members, party members, and so on' (p. 219). But do these associations allow or require genuine consent? Walzer notes, for example, that the membership of voluntary associations, like political participation, is related to social class, but he does not pursue the implications of this for his conception of a moral proletariat. Nor does he discuss in any detail the authority structures of associations and the nature of membership within them. Few voluntary associations are organized on participatory democratic lines and Walzer states that consent and willful membership is most likely in religious sects and ideological parties and movements: 'Rotarians cannot sell out' (p. 11). Most industrial and commercial associations and, to a lesser extent, trade unions and churches, are not democratically structured, and Walzer rejects the conventional argument that because people voluntarily enter these organizations they therefore oblige themselves to obey their rules and officials; this tacit consent establishes no greater degree of obligation than tacit consent to a non-democratic state.

Membership of associations can, like voting, be 'trivial' either because the affairs of the association are of no great moment or because participation has only a trivial place within the association. In either case, 'pluralist mediation loses its moral and political value; it becomes, ... an ideology—not a comfort but an illusion of comfort' (p. 221). However, associations that are not trivial, in either sense, like sects and political movements, are likely to come into conflict with the state. The ambiguity in Walzer's argument comes to the fore here; he argues that 'only if the possible legitimacy of countergroups with limited claims is recognised and admitted can the state be regarded as a group of consenting citizens' (p. 19), and an important theme of *Obligations* is that such countergroups may have a duty to disobey the state. Yet if the authority of the liberal democratic state is not to be brought into question it must be the state that judges legitimacy. The orthodox theory of civil disobedience is claiming precisely that the state can tolerate groups that engage in this form of political activity and need not declare them totally illegitimate. Groups that do not go outside this very narrow limit can, in this sense, be seen as at one remove from the associations about which, in practice, there is no problem of legitimacy. These are the established interest groups that, today, have been incorporated into the state apparatus, and those that concern themselves with 'trivial' non-political affairs. The unspoken problem that lies at the heart of Walzer's essays is whether the liberal democratic state can ever be seen as 'a group of consenting citizens'. He does not face up to the question whether genuine consent and *participatory pluralism* is compatible with the authority of, and political obligation within, the liberal democratic state.

I have noted that Walzer refers to the earlier pluralists, but he does not take sufficient account of the fact that Cole argued that the 'principle of social obligation' required not 'the recognition of associations by the State, but a demand that the State itself should be regarded only as an association'.[47] Cole argued that this involved the 'radical reconstruction' of the state of which Walzer speaks in one mood of *Obligations*. In another essay Walzer seems to doubt that participatory pluralism can be reconciled with the liberal democratic state. He argues that radical social change 'would require that the state embody [popular] willfulness, inviting its new members to choose their own limits and measurements. This it does not, perhaps cannot, do'.[48] It is difficult to avoid the conclusion that, in *Obligations*, Walzer tends to take refuge in the 'great comfort' that liberal pluralism provides (p. 218). He expresses deep doubts about the possibility of realizing the ideal of pluralist or participatory citizenship, and the final essay in the book is a critique of participatory democracy based on Oscar Wilde's observation that socialism would take too many evenings. All that Walzer says about the commitment of membership and genuine consent assumes that this critique is not valid and that it is possible to 'recapture a sense of common life', but rather than showing how 'the debilitating aspects' of liberal democracy can be remedied he 'implicitly demands courage to live with what we have wrought'.[49]

A major thread of Walzer's argument suggests that pluralism, or membership of (at least some) associations, provides a substitute for what is lacking in membership of the liberal democratic state. The state cannot be encompassed within the liberal ideal of social life as a voluntary scheme, so citizens should concentrate on associations within the state to find genuine membership, consent and obligation. But Walzer also hints that the state itself can, or might, be seen as a group of consenting citizens. Although Walzer's approach to consent is very different from most contemporary consent theorists his arguments reveal the same ambiguity about voluntarism that I commented upon in Chapter 1; the liberal democratic state both is (or can be), and is not, part of the voluntarist ideal. One apparent way out of this difficulty is to argue that it is the involuntary nature of membership in the state that is valuable and, at the same time, to claim that self-assumed political obligation exists. It is easy, it can be argued, to leave voluntary associations, so membership in them is of little significance; to see the liberal democratic state as a voluntary association means that 'the problem of political obligation tends to evaporate' because 'the exit option trivializes membership'. Membership in the state is involuntary, but members also voluntarily 'recognize' their membership and the political 'obligation' that comes with it; they should thus 'make the best of it by ... political participation ...'.[50] Walzer does not go this far in trying to have the cake of liberal voluntarism and eat it. Nor does he share the odd belief that membership in voluntary organizations is trivial, not because of their structure or concerns, but because it is possible to leave. Leaving (or expulsion from) some voluntary associations, such as churches or political parties, can be a major and devastating step in an individual's life and, in the case of economic organizations, might lead to virtual destitution.

To pretend that involuntary membership preserves the essence of voluntarism and self-assumed obligation solves nothing. But despite Walzer's insights into membership, and comradeship and solidarity in (some) voluntary associations, and the conflicts of integrity and honour to which they can give rise, he skirts round the question whether such membership is possible in the liberal democratic state. Most consent theorists implicitly follow Locke, and assume that all adults who remain in their country of birth have voluntarily taken up the opportunity of membership (and political obligation), so that what remains for the theorist is to indicate through which of their voluntary actions they continue to give consent. Walzer's conception of consent bars him from taking this course, but he does not consider any alternatives, such as the argument that genuine content can be given to the idea of voluntary membership and political 'obligation' in the liberal state through special membership ceremonies and provision of special areas to which those who reject membership may move.[51] The problem here, as with all arguments about consent that do more than infer or assert that it exists, is that the justification of political obligation in the liberal democratic state here and now is placed in question. Moreover, the fancifulness of these ideas in the context of the liberal democratic state indicates that 'willful membership' is not easily provided for. More serious consideration must be given to Walzer's claim that the moral emptiness of liberal citizenship can be remedied only by the radical reconstruction of the state—by its transformation into a participatory pluralist, or self-managing, non-statist form of democracy.[52]

Another important problem about political obligation in the liberal democratic state is also embedded in Walzer's discussion. The question of how far the horizontal relationship between fellow citizens and the vertical relationship between each citizen and the state are connected to each other was touched upon, in a fairly abstract fashion, in my analysis of Locke's version of the liberal social contract story in the previous chapter. Walzer's pluralist account of consent provides a concrete illustration of how this problem arises. If it is argued that genuine consent can be given, and a significant moral and social life lived by individuals, only in the context of groups and associations within the state, and attention is focused on the obligations between individuals in these associations, then the question presents itself of why the admittedly impoverished relationship that each individual still has with the state should be of any consequence whatsoever. Furthermore, an even more fundamental problem is buried within the question of how the vertical and horizontal conceptions of political obligation are to be reconciled with each other. If associations and groups are, as Walzer argues, the most important arena of moral *and political* life, then what exactly counts as 'political' obligation and where, as it were, is it located?

I have shown how liberal social contract theory stands at the beginning of the long tradition of political thought and practice in which the political sphere is seen as separate from the rest of social life. Liberal theorists have been able to distinguish 'political' obligation from other obligations precisely because it is owed to the state, or concerned with the political sphere and not everyday life. The liberal vertical conception of political obligation may be sadly empty of moral and political content but it does give a clear answer to the question of what counts as political obligation. As I have shown earlier, although it may have to fall back on an abstractly individualist view of the formal status of citizenship, and reduce voting to authorization, it also gives an account of how political obligation is constituted through a voluntary and 'political' act of each individual. When theorists argue that political obligation is owed to fellow citizens and turn to the everyday life of individuals in voluntary associations in their arguments about consent, the long tradition of liberal theory is being challenged. It is directly challenged by Walzer when he argues that the state is a less important area for moral and political life than voluntary associations, although he does not appear to see the full significance of this. In the essay in *Obligations* on corporate authority, Walzer states that he is treating the corporation as a 'political community', but he does not comment upon the fact that this runs counter to the liberal democratic insistence that corporations are *not* political but part of the private, economic sphere of social life; they are outside the scope of citizenship and voting. Nor does Walzer have anything to say about the implications of his view of corporations for arguments about political obligation. If corporations, and perhaps other organizations, are political bodies, then the obligations of their members, which run horizontally between them, are political obligations. They are not merely related to political obligation, or more meaningful substitutes for it, but are *part of it*. Once more, Walzer's participatory pluralist conception of consent and political obligation cannot be confined within the bounds of liberal theory and practice. It also shows how the idea and practice of self-assumed obligation can point the way to a new, democratic conception of political life and political obligation.

Walzer is distinguished from most other recent writers on consent by his critical approach to liberal democracy and political obligation, by his appreciation of the complexities of obligation and political action, and by his recognition that the comfort provided by liberal democratic pluralism may be illusory. But in one respect he shares a major failing of contemporary consent theory as a whole, a failing that helps explain the profound ambiguity of the essays. Walzer, unlike most other consent theorists, begins from Hobbes' starting point of consent that arises from an act of the individual's own, rather than from an all-inclusive hypothetical voluntarism. However, like other writers, Walzer fails to explore the concept of self-assumed obligation in terms other than consent, even though his criticism of citizenship in the liberal democratic state, and his conception of participatory pluralism, make possible an examination of the free creation of political obligation by members of participatory democratic associations. Walzer emphasizes the idea of membership based on explicit commitments, but he does not investigate how that commitment can be politically renewed, criticized, kept alive or, if necessary, reconstituted. Nor does he examine promising and obligation in everyday life—and so never poses the question of what is the political analogue of promising. Walzer's essays expose much of the political emptiness and theoretical bankruptcy of contemporary consent theory, but they also show that, if consent theory is to be put onto a theoretically sound footing, the theorist has to be willing to question the justification of political obligation in the liberal democratic state and to take seriously the conceptual and practical implications of 'obligation' itself. A new approach to consent is required but it will not be forthcoming until it is appreciated that consent is only part of, instead of the whole of, the legacy of the political ideals of obligation, and social life as a voluntary scheme, bequeathed to us by liberal individualism.

A Postscript on 'Consent' in the Pre-Modern Period

I noted earlier in my argument that political obligation as a central category of political thought, and contract and consent theories as general theories of political life, are modern phenomena. In pre-modern times political life was 'conceived as a problem of moral and intellectual virtue, ... [not] as a problem of obligation and legitimacy'.[1] 'Obligation' and 'consent' are, however, frequently discussed as if they were timeless, and as if present-day theories were merely minor variations on ancient themes. The interesting question is why, in arguments about consent, the vast conceptual and social distance that separates us from ancient and medieval times can often be disregarded and, in particular, why the emergence of a general problem about the relationship of individuals to political authority can so often be ignored.

Socrates and the *Crito*, for instance, are often discussed as if Socrates was the first civil disobedient and his arguments, as presented in Plato's 'magic doll's house', those of a contemporary liberal democrat.[2] This approach overlooks the obvious fact that Socrates did not, like a civil disobedient, deliberately set out to break the law for a political end, and that the *Crito* is concerned with acceptance of the verdict of a court, not political law-breaking as such. Moreover, it was necessary for Socrates to argue this point in such detail, because in ancient Athens there was no special opprobrium attached to avoidance of legal punishment. His fellow Athenians would have found it hard to appreciate the orthodox theory of civil disobedience and the idea of punishment as a sign of sincerity and conscientiousness.

More generally, to treat Socrates as if his reference to 'agreements' is like that of a contemporary liberal democratic theorist's reference to 'consent' is to ignore the social, conceptual and ethical gulf that separates us from the ancient world. Socrates lived in the Athenian *polis*, in a participatory not a representative democracy. Although citizenship was confined to free, adult, male Athenians it was based on the radical premise that all citizens were equally capable of fully participating in political decision-making. The political relationships of Athenian citizens were very different from citizens of liberal democracies; political obedience was not owed to the state but to fellow citizens, who *were* the *polis*. This distinctive political order was partly constituted by an equally distinctive conceptual and ethical perspective. The idea of individuals as moral beings irrespective of their specific social relationships was, as Adkins has shown, largely foreign to the ancient view of the social world.[3] Problems of political obedience arose not from individual, conscientious moral and political convictions and beliefs, but, as the example of Antigone demonstrates, from clashes of political loyalty with the demands of individual honour and familial reputation and allegiance.[4] It is possible to offer a rather convincing interpretation of Socrates' trial and death in these terms. Socrates can be seen as an heroic figure defending his honour. He threw his fellow citizens an heroic challenge—unconditional acquittal or death—and his death is thus 'the payment of a debt of honor, the payment of a gentleman who has lost a wager and who pays because he cannot otherwise live with himself'.[5]

However, at the time of Socrates' death, these values were being challenged by the teachings of the Sophists—and by Socrates himself. And they raised questions very similar to those that emerged centuries later with the development of modern individualism. To see Socrates as motivated by honour alone cannot account for the fact that he does not speak in heroic terms, or explain his unconventional behaviour in court, and his rejection of all consideration of the shame falling upon his friends if they do not help him escape; he 'avoids in a remarkable way the entire question of the justice of friends helping friends'.[6] Furthermore, Socrates stood aside from the political life of the *polis* and saw himself as 'different from the common run of mankind'.[7] He was a shamanistic figure, given a mission by the oracle, and following the voice of his *daimon*, or god, which forbade him to enter political life. Socrates had a low opinion of his fellow citizens and regarded their view of his actions as irrelevant; what mattered was the judgement of 'the expert in right and wrong', that is to say, of Socrates himself.[8] He can now be seen as similar to a modern individual who, like all his fellows, is an 'expert' in these matters in that he must make his own moral judgements.

It is significant that Crito soon disappears from the dialogue and Socrates, in effect, talks to himself by personifying 'the Laws' of Athens and attributing arguments to them. This also helps explain why Socrates can appear so modern. Most contemporary writers on political obligation also like to argue in the voice of 'the Laws' but, more importantly, this reification of 'the Laws' means the laws of the *polis* cease to be an aspect of, and consequence of, the collective interactions and judgements of the citizens of a participatory democracy, but appear to stand above and externally to Socrates as the liberal democratic state stands in relation to its citizens. Thus part of Socrates' argument appears as a remarkable anticipation of Locke's theory of tacit consent. 'The Laws' speak of 'the agreement between you and us' and argue that the agreement was made when Socrates reached manhood and chose to remain in the *polis*:

> any Athenian, on attaining to manhood and seeing for himself the political organization of the State and us its Laws, is permitted, if he is not satisfied with us, to take his property and go away wherever he likes.[9]

That political theorists usually seize on this early example of hypothetical voluntarism, and pay no attention to what might be learnt about political 'obligation' and 'consent' (if rather anachronistically) from the actual political organization of the *polis*, serves to emphasize the uncritical way in which 'consent' is usually treated. Moreover, to see Socrates' argument as nothing more than an anticipation of Locke is to ignore the fact that his monologue is not directed at the same problem as liberal contract theories. He was not concerned with the general question of why any individual should be governed, but with the specific question of his own sentence and the escape that was open to him. But if liberal theorists of political obligation were to take these things into account they would have to admit that, today, there *is* a problem about political obligation that is a peculiarly modern problem, and this is precisely what they are so reluctant to do. To see only the hypothetically voluntarist aspects of the *Crito*, and to assimilate medieval ideas of 'consent' to those that came later, has a valuable ideological function.

The establishment of Christianity provided a Master and Father who guaranteed the claims of earthly masters and fathers to obedience. St. Paul's famous statement in *Romans* XIII left no doubt of the proper response of subjects to rulers:

> For there is no power but of God: the powers that be are ordained of God. Whosoever therefore resisteth the power, resisteth the ordinance of God: and they that resist shall receive to themselves damnation.

When rulers were seen as part of God's Divine order in the world, general questions about political authority were, literally, inconceivable. This does not, of course, mean that there were no problems about political obedience. The fact that the subject owed allegiance to spiritual as well as temporal powers meant that the commands of the latter were open to claims that they were impious or sinful. Even the harshest doctrine of political obedience, such as that of St. Augustine, allowed that sinful commands provided an exception to an otherwise absolute obedience. In addition, the conception of God's natural law of the universe placed a constraint on the power of temporal rulers, enabling a distinction to be drawn between the legitimate political ruler and the tyrant, and opening the way for defences of tyrannicide.

It might seem sufficient warrant of authority that rulers were seen as placed in office by God, but the medieval period was full of ideas of contracts and consent to government. One legacy of the Roman Empire was a 'general conception of the state as an association held together by a bond of law (*vinculum juris*), and by consent to law (*juris consensu*)'.[10] However, this 'consent' has to be seen in the context of medieval political relationships, which were inseparable from wider religious and social ties that bound members of communities into an hierarchical web of 'natural' inequality and subordination. It is difficult to bring together accounts of the medieval view of the community as a mystical body, of a universal, law-governed chain of being, of contracts between lords and vassals and of consent in guilds and town councils, with other accounts of children's crusades, mass flagellation and a view of the middle ages as 'a cross between a charnel house and an insane asylum, in which ... cruelty and licence flowered on a scale which has seldom, if ever, been equalled'.[11] Nevertheless, it does seem clear that the medieval view of law was that it 'was the result of usages and practices which by common consent were based on tacit agreement'.[12]

This statement, albeit tautologous, illustrates the import of 'consent' in this period. A society governed by customary usages and practices is such by virtue of the fact that its members see or 'accept' these customs as the right and 'natural' way of doing things. This 'acceptance' can also be seen as 'consent'. St. Thomas Aquinas, for example, says that 'whatever is done frequently would seem to result from a deliberate judgement of reason', and goes on to speak of the 'consent of the whole community in the observance of a certain custom ...'.[13] This sense of 'consent' is no more than an interpretation of unselfconscious and habitual observance of custom as 'consent'; if a community and law exists then 'consent', in this sense, must logically exist too. Nothing is implied about individuals' actions or intentions by such 'consent', although it provides an additional strength and comfort to Divinely ordained rulers.

Religious developments were partly responsible for the disintegration of the world view of the middle ages.[14] Protestantism, with its notion of the equality of individual consciences and the priesthood of believers, and especially Calvinism and the idea of the calling, developed into a full-scale attack on the traditional order and formed an important part of the wider social developments that gave rise to capitalist society and the liberal state. Because the Protestant sects formed communities of the faithful, questions were asked about social and political life as well as religious faith. (This culminated in the flowering of extremely radical ideas and groups during the English Revolution.)[15] In both religious doctrine, and secular, liberal political theory, the conception of a 'natural' hierarchy of authority and inequality had been swept away. The community of the faithful had to be created on the basis of the agreement and voluntary commitment of believers, just as political authority in civil society could now rest on self-assumed political obligation and consent. The Calvinist individual, facing God directly and interpreting His word without intermediaries, is the religious counterpart of the abstract conception of the 'naturally' free and equal individual of the political theorists, and has the same subversive impact. As Walzer has commented, 'conscience, unless bound by an authoritative church, has no rules'.[16]

Calvin provided a theocratic and absolutist constraint upon this conscience, just as Hobbes provided a secular, absolutist answer to the problem of unconstrained individual private judgement.

There could be no sharper contrast than that between the pre-modern notion of consent, and the conception of consent required by religious individualism or the secular liberal theory of the social contract. But the radical implications of the modern conception of consent and the problem to which it provided an answer have now largely been 'forgotten' by political theorists. Locke's transformation of conscience into part of the individual's private interest, and the massive consolidation of the secular liberal democratic state, has enabled the problem of political obligation to fade from liberal theoretical consciousness. The empty hypothetical voluntarism of most consent theorists leaves one with the impression that they would be happy if 'consent', once again, could mean no more than it did in the pre-modern period. Certainly, most consent theorists still offer a great comfort to political authorities. If they no longer call on God as well as consent it is, perhaps, because He is no longer required. The liberal democratic state is now so well established as a 'natural' feature of the world that, according to some political sociologists, it now functions like a religion[17]—and one of the main articles of faith of the theorist of that state is that there is no longer any genuine problem about political obligation.

Chapter 6

Hypothetical Voluntarism and the Conceptual Argument

To ask why I am to submit to the power of the state, is to ask why I am to allow my life to be regulated by that complex of institutions without which I literally should not have a life to call my own.

T. H. Green, *Lectures on the Principles of Political Obligation.*

The abstractly individualist arguments that stand at one extreme of liberal theory have been discussed in earlier chapters, except for philosophical anarchism which I shall examine in Chapter 7. I now want to turn to an argument that lies at the opposite theoretical extreme: the conceptual argument that claims that it is a sign of philosophical disorder even to suggest that there could be general problems about political obligation. An abbreviated version of this argument was briefly discussed in Chapter 2, but it is much more complicated and wide-ranging than was suggested there. Its advocates give no hint that they are following the lead of another theorist who presented a brilliant and elaborate formulation of the conceptual argument— namely Hegel.

One problem about the conceptual argument is that it is far from clear how it should be characterized. While discussing Locke's theory I drew attention to interpretations of his argument about tacit consent that make no reference to 'consent'. Nor do theorists who make use of the conceptual argument talk in terms of 'consent'; they avoid it because, like Hegel, they see consent as part of the abstractly individualist perspective that is at the root of the spurious general problem about political obligation. However, arguments about accepting benefits and participating in liberal institutions, which form part of the conceptual approach to political obligation, can, as the readings of Locke's theory show, be used as alternatives to arguments framed in terms of tacit consent. Although the conceptual argument is part of an attack on consent and abstract individualism, it is, in many respects, little more than a reformulation of familiar tacit consent arguments, and so open to the same objections and difficulties.

In this Chapter I shall discuss Hegel's theory, and I shall also look in some detail at Rawls' arguments about political obligation in *A Theory of Justice.* In part, Rawls provides a contemporary example of a complex use of the conceptual argument; however, the interest of his argument for my study is much wider than this. I have already referred to his discussion of promising in Chapter 2, but the most fascinating aspect of *A Theory of Justice* is that the two extremes of liberal theory coexist within its pages. Not only does Rawls rely upon the conceptual argument, but his 'original position' is an example of the most radical abstract individualism. The tendency for liberal theory to oscillate between the two theoretical extremes could not be better illustrated. Throughout my argument I have used Rawls' reference to liberal democratic society coming 'as close as a society can to being a voluntary scheme' as a convenient summary of the liberal voluntarist tradition of argument, and as an excellent example of its continuing appeal to political theorists. I chose this statement partly because of the reputation of *A Theory of Justice*, but also because it is not without its ironic aspects. One of Rawls' major claims is that most people in liberal democracies have an *involuntary natural duty* of political obedience; only a few owe political *obligation*. Thus Rawls makes explicit the differential relationship between groups of individuals and the state that has been implicit in liberal theory from the outset.

It will be useful to begin by recalling the main points of the abbreviated version of the conceptual argument. Once the 'peculiar picture of man and society' of the liberal contract theorists has been discarded, then, it is argued, it becomes clear that there is no general problem about political obligation.[1] From the perspective of an 'organic' or 'collectivist' theory such problems are meaningless and the conception of political obligation is superfluous.[2] Problems apparently arise only because abstract individualism cannot encompass the internal, conceptual connections between notions such as 'social life', 'being a member', 'rights', 'rules' or 'obligation'. Theorists who use conceptual arguments typically make a direct move from general, abstract points about relationships between concepts to substantive conclusions about social and political relationships. Thus it is argued that:

> 'Why should I (a member) accept the rules of the club?' is an absurd question. Accepting the rules is part of what it *means* to be a member. Similarly, 'Why should I obey the government?' is an absurd question. We have not understood what it *means* to be a member of political society if we suppose that political obligation is something that we might not have had and that therefore needs to be *justified*.[3]

This attempt to provide an unassailable basis for political obligation in the liberal democratic state is stretching some general, conceptual points far beyond their proper limits. Even though one may agree that all 'societies' are necessarily 'political societies' and that, therefore, 'authority' and 'government' are involved, such general conceptual points say nothing about *specific forms* of authority and government and how they are to be justified. The general, abstract conception of 'political society' cannot simply be identified with the actual, present-day institutions of the liberal democratic state and the claim made that it is therefore nonsensical to ask questions about political obligation within these institutions.

Contemporary theorists were preceded in this theoretical move by Hegel. His theory also shows how an insistence on the unproblematic character of political obligation has an unwelcome consequence. Contemporary advocates of the conceptual argument do not wish to argue for unconditional political obligation. They stress that it is meaningful for citizens to have doubts about specific instances of political obligation; they do not wish completely to eliminate individual judgement, choice and decision from political life. But Hegel's theory, like Hobbes' in its very different fashion, shows that the price of absolute security for political authority is unquestioned and unconditional political obedience. Only if it is granted that general questions about political obligation in the liberal democratic state are meaningful, and have their roots in the actual form of social and political organization of liberal society, instead of being merely reflections of the conceptual confusions of abstract individualism, is it possible for theorists to avoid travelling some of the way down the uncongenial path of unconditional political obedience.

Political Obedience in the *Philosophy of Right*

It has often been denied that Hegel's political theory has any place in a discussion of liberal political theory. Although the extreme claims once made about the 'totalitarian' character of his work are no longer accepted, it is true that the specific form of political organization advocated by Hegel is neither clearly liberal nor conservative.[4] However, as in the case of Hobbes' absolutist state, the precise form of Hegel's state derives from general theoretical considerations rather than from his remoteness from liberal ideals and problems; Hegel's 'conceptual apparatus (though not his conclusions) links him ... closely to the great contract theorist ...'.[5] His aim in the *Philosophy of Right* is to show how 'subjective freedom', or the liberal conceptions of individual freedom, individual judgement and will, and self-assumed obligation, can be given their proper place in a modern, constitutional state, while avoiding the threat that such ideas pose for political authority and socio-political order. Hegel does not totally reject liberalism, notwithstanding such notorious statements as 'individuals are related as accidents to substance' to the state (S145).[6] Rather, he argues against abstract individualism and ideas of individual consent which have led to a dangerous misunderstanding of the relationship between individual and state. Hegel argues that the individual must be seen as part of a community or as a member of associations, as part of a structured whole, into which he is bound, not individually, but as a member of specific groupings. Today, Hegel's theory is often characterized as pluralist, and, indeed, it was Hegel who first revealed what a 'comfort' could be derived from a pluralist view of the liberal state.[7]

'(T)he state as such is not so much the result as the beginning' (S256). Hegel's task, as he states in the 'Preface' to the *Philosophy of Right*, is to show how the state, and the citizen's relationship to it, should properly be understood. The state must not be seen as something accidental or contingent, based on the capriciousness and arbitrariness of individual consent, but comprising necessary and rational relationships. Hegel's argument begins in the same place as the contract theorists, with individuals' 'abstract' or 'natural' rights and the exercise of individual subjective judgement or will; but the context of Hegel's starting point is utterly different. Although he discusses the familiar subject-matter of contract theory—rights, freedom, contract, property, the family—Hegel does not base the state, and the justification of its authority, on this foundation. Instead, he discusses these matters in order to show how, taken by themselves, they provide only a partial and dangerous view of the state, which places its authority, and political obligation, on an extremely precarious basis.

Hegel argues that to understand the state as it has developed historically as a rational social order, and to understand the meaning and implications of individualism, it has also to be understood that they presuppose each other. They are two inseparable dimensions of one social and ethical whole. Some problems arising from the attempt to abstract or separate individuals from this whole, discussed by Hegel, have been examined in detail already, especially in Chapter 3 in connection with Hobbes' state of nature. No limitations or constraints can be placed on the will or the freedom of abstractly conceived individuals; taken in isolation, individual moral judgement can only be purely formal (duty for duty's sake) or purely subjective and arbitrary. The state, therefore, 'cannot give recognition to conscience in its private form as subjective knowing' (S137). Hegel is extremely scathing about the tendency to make the individual conscience the criterion of right; the result is that 'crime and the thoughts that lead to it, ... or opinions however wild, are to be regarded as right, ... simply because they issue from men's hearts and enthusiasms' (S126). Furthermore, although property, and the ability to enter into contracts to exchange and alienate it, is essential to the development of individual selfconsciousness and personality, it is madness to base the state—or marriage—on a contract. Hegel regards it as 'shameful' to see marriage as no more than a contractual relationship, and to conceive of the state as a contract is to transfer 'the characteristics of private property into a sphere of a quite different and higher nature' (S75).

Abstract individualism has to be understood for what it is. Each of us has the ability to 'abstract from everything whatever, and in the same way to determine himself, to posit any content in himself by his own effort' (S4). However, Hegel argues that we can do this only *because* we are making an abstraction from taken-for-granted social relationships and practices. The abstract idea of a 'contract' makes sense only because we are presupposing the obligation to keep contracts and the social practice of contracting. (My argument about promising in Chapter 2 owes a good deal to Hegel's insights.) Individuals do not, in fact, act purely arbitrarily. There are substantive, if very general, rules that order social life—the 'laws of nature'—and other rules and laws that are specific to given social practices and associations. Hegel devotes a section of his discussion of 'Ethical Life' to the family, and what would now be called the socialization process, because it is within the family that an individual first is educated to understand and accept the basic rules of social life. The family transcends its contractual origin, and so is part of ethical life, because, within its confines, its members are concerned not with their self-interest, but with the mutual or 'universal' well-being of the family unit as a whole. In the family, and later in other associations, individuals learn to accept the rules that order their mutual interactions as a rational and necessary basis of ethical and social life, instead of seeing them, as they appear from an abstractly individualist perspective, as merely arbitrary barriers to their freedom. 'I am at home in the world when I know it, still more when I have understood it' (AS4). Hegel remarks that the 'only bond' of the state is 'the fundamental sense of order which everybody possesses', a sense which is developed as the individual matures (AS268). The state, properly understood, is based on 'will not force' because individuals learn voluntarily to accept the obligation to obey its laws.

It has been said of Hegel's theory that it is often difficult:

> to be sure how far he thinks he is offering us *a-priori* conceptual truths, how far he is offering us large-scale empirical generalizations, and how far he is pointing out what are characteristics rather than universal connections between concepts.[8]

My reference to the 'state' compounds the ambiguity. The general conceptual point about 'rules' and 'social life' says nothing about specific rules or forms of social institutions. Hegel is making the same move as recent advocates of the conceptual argument, between a general conceptual point and a claim about actual institutions of the modern state. Hegel uses the term 'state' in two senses. The first, the less usual usage, refers to the 'state' as an association, or as an ethical order. It is in this sense that the concepts of abstract individualism are presupposed by the 'state'. Hegel's other sense of the term is the conventional one that refers to actual political institutions of the modern constitutional political order. Now, Hegel, and the writers who use the conceptual argument, assume that the general conceptual point covers the 'state' in this sense too. The specific, historically developed institutions of the 'state' are held to be as much a 'beginning', to be presupposed, in the same way as the 'state' as an ethical association. The state in both senses, it is claimed, must be accepted as rational and necessary and so, therefore, must political obligation. To question the existence of such a general political obligation is to show oneself as conceptually confused. Hegel, and contemporary theorists, are implying that the liberal state is as necessary to its citizens as two internally related concepts are necessary to each other.

In view of this argument it is perhaps not surprising that it can be claimed that, in 'collectivist' theories, the concept of political obligation is unimportant or superfluous. However, even if this were the case, it does not follow that it makes no sense to ask what is the basis of the relationship between individuals and the state in Hegel's theory. Hegel, after all, follows the contract theorists in arguing that voluntarism is the distinguishing feature of the modern constitutional state; individuals 'will' the 'universal' order of the state. I commented above that, for Hegel, individuals voluntarily accepted their political obligation, but this is begging the question whether Hegel's theory has room for 'obligation' in any genuine sense. I argued in Chapter 2 that the conceptual argument, as usually presented, ignores the distinction between 'ought' and 'obligation'. The implication of the argument is that, once a proper appreciation is gained of the character of social and political relationships, individuals will accept that they necessarily *ought* to obey, or that they have a duty to do so. Hegel states that in his theory 'the specific types of ethical life turn up as necessary relationships', but he will not add in each case that 'therefore men have a duty to conform to this institution' (S148). It might seem, therefore, that Hegel's argument is not voluntarist at all.

However, Hegel can also be interpreted as arguing that it can be inferred from various aspects of individuals' interactions that they do voluntarily accept or recognize their duty, otherwise his references to 'willing the universal' seem superfluous. Thus Hegel's theory closely resembles liberal hypothetical voluntarism—but it is hypothetical voluntarism in the weakest sense. Indeed, Hegel's argument is very like Hobbes', except that it lies at the other end of the liberal theoretical spectrum. Hobbes begins with a firm statement about obligation and acts of one's own, and ends with 'consent' as enforced submission: Hegel begins with firm statements about individual will and contract ('obligation') and ends by reducing voluntarism to an hypothesized, implicit 'recognition' of the duty of political obedience. To see how Hegel makes this transformation it is necessary briefly to examine his discussion of social and political institutions. This will also show that, although Hegel apparently places political obedience on a completely secure footing, he is, like the consent theorists, left with two groups who cannot be accounted for: the poor and women.

Hegel adopts the same strategy as the liberal contract theorists towards the problem of political authority and political obligation. He divides social life into two separate spheres, in only one of which, 'civil society', is individual judgement, choice and decision, and the pursuit of private interest, allowed full sway. Hegel removes individual choice and action from the political sphere as decisively as Hobbes, while claiming to give it full recognition.[9] For Hegel, the economic sphere, or civil society, is not merely a collection of self-interested and contracting individuals, but a structured plurality of associations which play a mediating role between the two areas of ethical life, the family and the state. Civil society is a 'system of complete interdependence, wherein the livelihood, happiness, and legal status of one man is interwoven with the livelihood, happiness, and rights of all' (S183). This system of interactions is differentiated into 'particular systems of needs, means, and types of work ... in other words, into class-divisions' (S201). Civil society is made up of the three landed, business, and 'universal' or bureaucratic classes, together with a variety of 'corporations' or voluntary associations. It is only membership in a corporation that can provide the individual with 'evidence that he is a somebody' (S253).

Civil society is not completely self-regulating; it has its 'police', or public authorities, that act like a Lockean 'umpire' arbitrating between conflicting interests. Hegel emphasizes that the fundamental mistake of the liberal contract theorists was that they confused this regulation of civil society and the protection of private property with the role of the state itself (recall Locke's conception of 'civil society'):

> if the state is confused with civil society, and if its specific end is laid down as the security and protection of property and personal freedom, then the interest of the individuals as such becomes the ultimate end of their association, and it follows that membership of the state is something optional.

The contract theorists grounded membership in, and the authority of the state upon, the voluntary agreement of individuals, which meant that it rested on their 'capriciously given express consent'. This provides no foundation for the state at all; it destroys the 'absolutely divine principle of the state, together with its majesty and absolute authority' (S258).

The practical political consequences of an abstractly individualist view of the state were the terror of the French Revolution. Hegel also regards universal (or more accurately manhood) suffrage as an empirical manifestation of the same conceptual wrongheadedness, and as likely to lead to the same dreadful consequences. The demand that the franchise should be exercised by individuals as such is based on a conception of the community as no more than a collection of individuals, or a 'formless mass whose commotion and activity could therefore only be elementary, irrational, barbarous, and frightful' (S303). The franchise must have a functional not an individual basis, reflecting civil society as a plurality of communities, as 'articulated into associations, communities, and Corporations, which although constituted already for other purposes, acquire in this way a connexion with politics' (S308).[10] As members of corporations, individuals are able to make a rational choice of representatives (who embody the 'universal' interest of their associations) since they know the candidates and are able to assess their abilities and experience. Hegel regards the relation between electors and representatives, in Lockean fashion, as a trust; it is not based on individual self-interest but on the common ties and mutual advantages of members of a corporation: 'We have confidence in a man when we take him to be a man of discretion who will manage our affairs conscientiously and to the best of his knowledge, just as if they were his own' (AS309).

Voters elect representatives to the lower or business chamber of the Estates, which mediate between the particular interests of civil society and the universal sphere of the state. Voting gives formal recognition to individual 'subjective freedom' but its actual political impact is extremely limited. The political role of the representatives is to help the bureaucracy anticipate popular criticism; the Estates deal 'only with rather specialized and trifling matters' (S302). The substantive recognition of individuals' political freedom comes from their 'satisfaction' in 'having and expressing their own private judgements, opinions and recommendations on affairs of state' (S316). Even if Hegel's account of public opinion is, as Avineri says, 'such a sophisticated view', this is surely because it is part of an exceptionally sophisticated example of how 'subjective freedom' can be held out on the one hand, and conjured away on the other.[11] In the context of the political institutions of a rationally structured state and, especially, the public debates in the Estates, the principle of free speech, necessary if individual freedom is to find its place in political life, is rendered 'harmless'. The representatives have a 'mature insight' into political affairs, so the 'general public are left with nothing of much importance to say, and above all are deprived of the opinion that what they say is of peculiar importance and efficacy' (S319). Having been expressed, public opinion counts for little because 'in itself it has no criterion of discrimination, ... to be independent of public opinion is the first formal condition of achieving anything great or rational ...' (S318).

Citizens can be confident that the laws and policies determined through Hegel's system of mediation and differentiation are rational, or 'absolutely valid' (S144), because of the role of the bureaucracy. The bureaucracy is completely independent of public opinion and it has, by definition, the good of the whole community, or the universal interest, as its goal. The function of the bureaucracy is an empirical, political counterpart to the conceptual role of the rules of the ethical order. Individuals are constrained by the latter from totally arbitrary and capricious actions, and the bureaucracy ensures that their political wills and their political life are given substantive content, and the necessary constraint of rational laws. Citizens can unquestioningly and unhesitatingly accept, and obey, these laws as 'absolutely valid'. In the end, for Hegel, 'voluntary acceptance' and obedience are one and the same.

This is why 'it is not ... clear how the right to subjectivity is given political expression in any really meaningful form'.[12] Despite all the claims made for individual freedom in the *Philosophy of Right*, its place in political life is purely symbolic; s' mbolized in the 'I will' of the hereditary monarch with whom Hegel literally cro ns his account of the state.[13] Hegel rejects an elected monarch, which 'superficial thinking finds handiest', because to give the people such a choice is to return to contractual notions and the 'whim, opinion and caprice of the Many' (S281). Here again, Hegel's attempt to place the authority of the state on a completely secure footing shows an interesting parallel with Hobbes' theory. Both begin with absolute individual freedom and both attempt to eliminate it from political life— except for the 'I will' of the monarch. Hegel, like Hobbes, claims that only in virtue of the monarch's 'I will' is 'the state *one*' (S279). In Chapter 3 I commented how ironical it was that Hobbes ends by placing arbitrary, individual judgement at the summit of the state. Equally ironically, either Hegel's monarch's 'I will' is a merely formal endorsement of the decisions of the bureaucracy, and so 'absolute self-determination' is a shadow only; or, if it is more than a formality, then the state is crowned by capricious, individual will.

That Hegel is left only with a symbolic place for voluntarism in political life is due to his belief that anything more is a capitulation, theoretically and practically, to abstract individualism. Hegel, as Riley has argued,

> must use the weakest form of voluntarist language— ... not only contract theory, but also most elections, participation, opinion and 'conscience' (conventionally defined) are denigrated—what is left is will as recognition, above all as acceptance of the rationality of the universal.[14]

And 'acceptance' of the rational order of the state necessarily entails obedience. Not to recognize the law for what it is, and to do one's part consequent upon that recognition, is to fail to understand the meaning of 'being a member' of the state. Thus there is a sense in which it might seem odd to talk of 'justifying' political obedience in Hegel's theory; indeed, Hegel states that if the authority of the state 'has anything to do with reasons, these reasons are culled from the forms of law authoritative within it' (S258). But to explain how the state should be understood is not the same as justifying its authority. Hegel implicitly admits this in the attention he pays to liberal voluntarism and contract theory, and there is a justification of political obedience inherent in his theory.

Notwithstanding Hegel's strictures on abstract individualism, it is tempting to suggest that his argument should be read as follows: the peaceful interactions of individuals in the daily life of civil society, and their participation in the system of functional elections, constitute tacit consent to, and thus recognition of, the authority of the state and their duty of political obedience. However, tacit consent arguments, as shown earlier, can be interpreted in other ways, and these provide a more acceptable reading of Hegel's theory, given his rejection of 'consent'. It can be argued that by voluntarily participating in the institutions and associations of civil and political life and of the state, individuals are voluntarily recognizing or accepting their duty to abide by the rules, or the necessity of obeying the rules, that govern social and political life. Alternatively, it can be argued that by voluntarily accepting the benefits of membership in the associations of civil life, and the state itself, individuals are also voluntarily accepting their duty to obey the rules and laws which make the benefits possible. Certainly, Hegel saw the greatest of benefits deriving from membership in the state. This was not merely the external benefit of protection of property, the concern of the contract theorists, but the benefit the individual finds in fulfilling his duty; the 'satisfaction of the depths of his being, the consciousness and feeling of himself as a member of the whole' (S261). I shall discuss the benefits and participation arguments, and their relationship to the conceptual approach to political obligation, in detail shortly; at present I want to look at the question of differential obedience.

The problem of political obligation to which the social contract theorists addressed themselves derived from the liberal individualist postulate of 'natural' freedom and equality. Hegel, like the contract theorists, saw individual equality as expressed in formal equality under the law, but he went beyond the contract theorists in integrating the inequalities, or differentiation, of civil society (which includes 'moral and intellectual attainment' (S200)) into the structure of mediation between civil society and the state. Hegel's aim is to remove the problem of political obligation by presenting an account of the state in which all its members are voluntarily incorporated, in the fashion appropriate to their particular station or social position, in the structure of mediation and differentiation. However, Hegel is unable to integrate the poor and women into this structure, although he claims to do so in the case of women, because of the specific character of their inequality.

Recent commentators on Hegel's political theory, especially Avineri, have drawn attention to Hegel's discussion of poverty—and to the fact that he is unable to deal with it satisfactorily in terms of his theory: 'This is the only time in his system where Hegel raises a problem—and leaves it open'.[15] Hegel sees poverty as an inherent feature of the development of civil society; as wealth, needs and desires expand, so does the class of the poor (recall Locke's conjectural history of the development of the state of nature). The poor are poverty-stricken not only in a material sense. The division of labour creates work which results in 'dependence and distress' for those who perform it, and leads to their inability to 'feel and enjoy the broader freedoms and especially the intellectual benefits of civil society' (S243). The poverty of the proletariat leaves them

> more or less deprived of all the advantages of society, of the opportunity of acquiring skill or education of any kind, as well as of the administration of justice, the public health services, and often even of the consolations of religion, and so forth (S241).

Moreover, the poor can no longer merely accept their position as part of the natural order of things, for it is believed in modern liberal societies that everyone should enjoy a decent standard of life and take some part in public affairs. The poor tend to become what Hegel calls a 'rabble'. They lose the 'sense of right and wrong, of honesty and ... self-respect', they develop 'a disposition of mind, and inner indignation against the rich, against society, against the government'—and they claim a right to subsistence (S244; AS244). Hegel mentions one section of the poor who belong to corporations and who are assisted by them, and who are thus incorporated into the state (S253). But most of the poor, particularly the 'rabble', remain outside the state; they lack property and membership in associations that enable them to be incorporated into its structure or to develop the appropriate selfconsciousness and ethical understanding. 'The poor are seen only as a potential threat to the state, not as its members or its responsibility'; and Hegel's arguments for obedience cannot apply to them.[16] Political obedience, willingly given, implies that individuals have developed a sense of themselves as respected members of an ethical community; the poor lack this sense and will never have the material and social means of developing it. Outside of the corporations they are, quite literally, nobodies.

Hegel's failure to include women within social and political life is rarely regarded as worthy of attention. His male chauvinist prejudices are shared by too many political theorists to make women's exclusion from the state seem at all remarkable. It is based, not on the empirical fact of the history of the economic development of civil society (so the poor may at least be angry at their plight), but on ancient beliefs about female nature. Hegel does not, like Locke for example, merely assert that women are 'naturally' unfitted for political life, but claims that the 'difference in the physical characteristics of the two sexes has a rational basis and consequently acquires an intellectual and ethical significance' (S165). Its significance is that the 'individual' will, freedom, and ethical capacity, of which Hegel makes so much in the *Philosophy of Right*, actually refers only to males. Women are not 'individuals'; they are not capable of the human development and social education which makes possible voluntary obedience in the constitutional state. Women are an example of the 'natural things' which 'remain as they are and have not freed themselves ... in order to make laws for themselves'.[17] Women's 'substantive destiny' lies in the family; a woman cannot follow a man in his 'labour and struggle with the external world and with himself so that it is only out of his diremption that he fights his way to self-subsistent unity with himself' (S166). Hegel even goes so far as to assert that women are like plants; they develop only sufficiently to be governed by 'arbitrary inclinations and opinions', and they are educated 'who knows how?—as it were by breathing in ideas, by living rather than by acquiring knowledge' (AS166). Clearly, such creatures should be kept out of the state; indeed, like the poor, but for different reasons, they pose a threat to it.[18] It is doubtful whether women can even be seen as being incorporated through their fathers and husbands, since they 'naturally' lack, and cannot develop, the 'sense of order' and an understanding of what it would mean voluntarily to be an obedient member of a social whole what is wider than a single family unit.

There is, finally, one further aspect of Hegel's theory that requires some discussion. In Chapter 2 I argued that the import of the conceptual argument was that citizens always ought to 'consent' to their political obligation in the liberal democratic state—or to 'recognize' rules and laws whose rationality and necessity cannot be disputed. It was for this reason that I suggested above that the conceptual argument and the attempt to show that political obligation is totally unproblematic, whether in Hegelian or contemporary versions, leads in the uncongenial direction of unconditional obedience. It has, however, been disputed that this 'somewhat repulsive doctrine' is what Hegel intended.[19] Hegel, according to Pelczynski, 'quite clearly recognizes the right to rebel in certain circumstances', but he is not very helpful about the nature of the circumstances.[20] Hegel's annual toast on the anniversary of the fall of the Bastille tells us nothing about revolution or political disobedience in the modern state. Hegel regarded the *ancien régime* as illegitimate (or historically outmoded), just as Locke saw absolute monarchical rule in the same light, but their applause for revolutions which ushered in the liberal state should not be taken as support for further political action by citizens within that state. For Hegel, any questioning of the 'absolutely valid' laws, let alone a claim by citizens of a 'right to rebel', is based on wrong-headed notions of 'abstract right' that treat membership as something optional and threaten the authority of the state. To be sure, Hegel does say that there 'may be a discrepancy between the content of law and the principles of rightness', but he also says that 'it is the legal which is the source of our knowledge of what is right' (S212). In any case, the only recourse the individual has is to retreat into himself, where he will find in 'the ideal world of the inner life alone the harmony which actuality has lost' (S138).

It might still be argued that I am ignoring the fact that Hegel's theory is concerned with the Idea of the state, not the actual liberal state. It is not, however, unreasonable to interpret Hegel as identifying the two. He writes,

> The state is no ideal work of art; ... bad behaviour may disfigure it in many respects. But the ugliest of men, or a criminal, or an invalid, or a cripple, is still always a living man. The affirmative, life, subsists despite his defects, and it is this affirmative factor which is our theme here (AS258).

Even if the actual state is 'crippled', it is still the 'affirmative factor', or the rationality inherent in the state and its laws, that is all-important. Neither the state of Hegel's time, nor the present liberal democratic state, may exactly match the Idea, but if citizens question their duty of political obedience they reveal that they have failed to grasp the Idea. They show lack of conceptual understanding and an inability to grasp the 'rose in the cross of the present' to which Hegel refers in his 'Preface': the rose of absolute political obedience which transforms the cross of the rational order of the liberal state into the heart of individual freedom.

Rawls on Obligation and Natural Duties

It may seem a long way from the 'rose in the cross of the present' to *A Theory of Justice*, but the aim of Rawls' argument is more akin to Hegel's task in the *Philosophy of Right* than to that of the liberal contract theorists. Rawls states that he is going 'to present a conception of justice which generalizes and carries to a higher level of abstraction the familiar theory of the social contract' (p. 11).[21] However, although it is true that there are some important features in common between Rawls' theory and liberal social contract theory, they differ in one fundamental and decisive respect: Rawls' aim is not to offer a justification of political obligation in the liberal state but, like Hegel, to show why we should accept the state as rational and necessary, and why, therefore, political obligation is entirely unproblematic. There are other interesting parallels between Hegel's theory and Rawls': for instance, Rawls' 'sense of justice' and its development through the socialization process is very similar to, and plays much the same role as, Hegel's 'sense of order'; and the relationship in the *Philosophy of Right* between the actual, 'crippled' state and the Idea of the state is remarkably like that between the existing, 'nearly just' liberal democratic state and the ideal of the just state in *A Theory of Justice*.

Nevertheless, the two theories diverge because Rawls has failed to appreciate the insights and implications of Hegel's attack on abstract individualism. Rawls relies heavily on the conception of a 'social practice', and he presents a pluralist conception of the liberal state as a 'social union of social unions' (p. 107), but he tries to combine these with a radically individualist approach. The state is not shown to be rational, in Hegelian fashion, through conceptual analysis and an investigation of the internal logic and relationships between our ideas of ourselves and our social institutions, but, rather, through the hypothetical choices of abstractly individualist parties in an 'original position'. The argument of *A Theory of Justice* moves continually to and fro between individuals in the original position, totally abstracted from their social relationships and institutions, and the institutions themselves, conceived in an Hegelian fashion. Since Rawls' argument oscillates from one end of the liberal theoretical spectrum to the other (or from Hobbes to Hegel and back again), it is hardly surprising that all the problems about political obligation in the liberal state with which I have been concerned appear in *A Theory of Justice*.

It is perhaps not too great an exaggeration to see *A Theory of Justice* as bringing together, though not coherently as Rawls assumes, three hundred years of theorizing about the liberal state. The extraordinary attention the book has received is understandable; a thorough ideological defence of the liberal democratic state, in the grand manner, marks a notable departure from the prevailing trends in political theory over the past thirty years or more. Rawls' argument about political obligation is one of the least discussed parts of this theory, but, before I turn to it, there is one further general point to be made to put Rawls' relationship to the contract theorists into perspective. His theory has been seen as 'the culmination of the effort, begun by Kant and Hegel, and carried forward by ... the other ... idealists, to adapt Rousseau's theory of the general will to the modern state'.[22] Rawls refers to the contract theories of Locke and Kant (whom he sees as 'definitive of the contract tradition') and to Rousseau (p. 11). There is little to be found of Rousseau's contract theory in the pages of *A Theory of Justice*, and for good reason. Rousseau's theory, as I shall show in the next chapter, is a devastating critique of liberal contract theory, and cannot be 'adapted' to the liberal state; it has nothing hypothetically voluntarist about it. Rawls' argument, like other contemporary discussions of political obligation, follows Locke closely in many respects, but he agrees with Kant, too, that it is improper to regard the liberal state 'as if its right to be obeyed were open to doubt'.[23] Rawls also takes the Kantian view that the importance of the hypothetical choice of the parties in the original position is that it shows what is rational, even though the people 'would probably refuse its consent if it were consulted'. Rawls' theory, like Kant's, differentiates between two classes of citizens. Rawls' division, while perhaps not so extreme as Kant's, is in the same spirit as the Kantian contrast between those who are merely part of the commonwealth and those who are proper members. For Kant, only male property owners, who neither receive orders nor are protected by others, have the 'civil personality' that enables them to become citizens—though all must obey.[24]

Rawls states that his conception of 'the original position of equality corresponds to the state of nature in the traditional theory of the social contract' (p. 12). In fact, it does nothing of the sort; Rawls does not begin in the same place as the social contract theorists, namely with a *problem* about political obligation, so he does not need the original position for the reasons that they need the state of nature. Rawls' parties are free and equal, like the individuals in the state of nature, but the original position differs from the state of nature in two crucial respects. First, Rawls does not intend the original position as an account, even hypothetically, of the origins of the liberal state; this is another way of saying that it is *not* meant to show why the authority of the state is justified. Rather, the original position is a device that enables us to understand, and accept, that the 'two principles' underlying the 'basic structure' of the liberal state provide a procedure or method of justice. It 'is an imaginary foundation which Rawls wishes to insert beneath the real edifice of liberal society in order to justify that society'.[25] The original position is a construct to show why we, as rational beings, if we were in the position of the parties, would choose these specific rules, and so we can be assured that there is no problem about the authority of the state that enforces the two principles. *A Theory of Justice* reveals the extent to which political theorists now accept the liberal state as a necessary feature of the world and treat it as if it were a natural fact that needs no justification.

Second, Rawls' original position is not, in contrast to the contract theorists' state of nature, meant to be a picture of the 'natural' state of human beings. The original position does not, logically or temporally, come 'before' anything. Individuals do not 'leave' the original position, as they do the state of nature, because, given their natures and their social situation, they can agree that the advantages of civil society give them good reason to accept the constraints of civil law and the state. Rawls' theory *presupposes* that this reason exists, that the authority of the liberal state is justified. He starts in the same place as Hegel, with the state as 'the beginning', and uses the original position to provide an ideological rationalization for that beginning, and for the presupposition that the authority of the liberal state is entirely unproblematic. Rawls states that there are 'many possible interpretations of the initial situation' (p. 121). Each social contract theorist, in contrast, would claim that there is only one acceptable interpretation of the state of nature because it is based on an investigation of human nature. Because Rawls does not explicitly discuss the 'natural' characters of the parties in the original position, the initial situation has a very arbitrary air about it. Yet it is not merely coincidence that the parties' choices happen to be those that would be made by possessive individuals.

Rawls arrives at his description of the original position by a purely circular procedure. The aim is to 'get the desired solution' or to ensure that the hypothetical choices of the parties in the original position 'match our considered convictions of justice or ... judgements about the basic structure of society which we now make intuitively and in which we have the greatest confidence; ...' (p. 141; 19). Rawls makes a very great deal of 'our' intuitions and judgements and they provide the only test of the rational character of the two principles. But who are 'we'? 'We' are fewer than Rawls' arguments imply; the suggestion of *A Theory of Justice* is that 'our' judgements are shared by everyone in liberal democracies (if they just reflect a little), because everyone accepts, or should accept, the socio-political system in which they find themselves. This is why the institutions described in the book so closely resemble existing liberal democratic institutions and why the 'nearly just' society is so familiar. But it is far from self-evident that 'our' judgements do coincide so nicely.[26] In Chapter 5 I referred to the evidence from empirical studies of voting and voters that indicates that the working class is far from sharing the judgements about the liberal democratic state of the middle class. Similarly, it cannot merely be assumed that women 'intuitively' share the convictions of males about social relationships and institutions. The past decade provides plenty of evidence to the contrary.

Rawls can ignore all this, and avoid the question of 'natural' characteristics, because of his radically abstract individualist account of the original position and its parties. Rawls even manages to be more radical than Hobbes in this respect. The 'veil of ignorance' which shrouds the parties makes it difficult to conceive of them as human, whereas Hobbes fills his state of nature with recognizable people. The veil of ignorance hides 'certain kinds of particular facts'; none of the parties knows, for example, their class position, their natural talents, their plans of life, their psychology, or anything about the economic and social character of their society (p. 137). We are also presumably meant to think of them as sexless, yet, if they did not think of themselves as male, they are very unlikely to make 'our' choices that correspond to 'our' considered judgements. Rawls does say that 'we may think of the parties as heads of families' (p. 128). Traditionally it was fathers of families who entered the social contract and, conventionally, men have been seen as the only individuals 'naturally' capable of exercising the authority of a family head. But, sexless or not, the parties are held to know 'the general facts about human society'. They are assumed to understand 'the principles of economic theory' (which theory?), 'the basis of social organisation' and 'the laws of human psychology' (formulated by whom?). It is extremely doubtful whether it is thus 'possible to conceive of men as having a hypothetical knowledge of what it means to have interests and desires without having particular interests and particular desires'.[27] Rawls' parties are an exceedingly curious concoction. They are, however, recognizable, in the sense that they are directly descended from the individuals who inhabit the liberal theorists' state of nature; they have the familiar characteristics of individuals who pursue their competing private interests in a market economy. Rawls' parties are possessive; they 'take no interest in one another's interests' and their only concern is to pursue their private 'plans of life' (p. 127). Although Rawls calls the original position 'fair between individuals as moral persons' it is as doubtful if the parties can be called 'moral' as it is whether Hobbes' natural individuals are moral (p. 12). This is not immediately obvious because, of course, we do not think of the parties as Rawls describes them, but implicitly add all the characteristics and abilities he abstracts in order to make them into moral, human persons.

The hypothetical choice of the two principles by the parties in the original position is not an unexpected one. Nor is the role of each of the principles at all novel; they constitute a procedure or political method for regulating a liberal society. Rawls says of the principles that they:

> presuppose that the social structure can be divided into two more or less distinct parts, the first principle applying to the one, the second to the other. They distinguish between those aspects of the social system that define and secure the equal liberties of citizenship and those that specify and establish social and economic inequalities (p. 61).

Rawls thus makes explicit the liberal separation of social life into two spheres, although without tracing the direct link between his two principles and liberal social contract theory.[28] The first principle states that 'each person is to have an equal right to the most extensive total system of equal basic liberties compatible with a similar system of liberty for all' (p. 302). The continuity with the liberal contract theorists' law of nature is obvious. Rawls states that the first principle can be seen as a principle of equal political participation but that it 'does not define an ideal of citizenship' (p. 227). Rawls does not spell out why this is the case but, as will become clear shortly, it is bound up with the relationship of social inequalities to the formal equality of citizenship.

Locke justified the social inequalities of the capitalist, market economy and liberal society through his conjectural history of the state of nature. The social contract then provided further legitimacy for, and stabilized, these relationships. Rawls is able to do the same thing much more neatly and directly through the second principle of justice. The parties hypothetically choose a second rule that contains two parts; it prescribes equality of opportunity, and that social and economic inequalities should be to 'everyone's advantage' (p. 60). Locke argued that civil society and the inequalities between its two classes was to everybody's advantage *compared to* the state of nature. Rawls' conception of 'everybody's advantage' is quite different. It is not an advantage compared to the original position, but in the sense that the 'difference principle' is satisfied, or that the position of the least advantaged citizen is as good as it can be without making anyone else worse off. Thus Rawls assumes that the 'least advantaged' citizen would choose a situation of Pareto optimality—but his or her 'choice' is constrained by the fact that the only alternatives in Rawls' theory are within the existing structure of the two classes in the capitalist market economy.[29]

By separating individuals from their actual social positions and relationships— 'each person holds two relevant positions: that of equal citizenship and that defined by his place in the distribution of income and wealth' (p. 96)—and placing 'parties' into the abstraction of the original position, Rawls is able to claim that the hypothetical choice is rational and necessary because it is to the actual advantage of all; the 'desired solution' is obtained. However, this circular procedure tells us nothing about the relationship of citizens to the liberal democratic state, the state that is to enforce the two principles or the political method. Here Rawls has to forget the original position and look at actual relationships and institutions, although he occasionally falls back on this abstract construction to fill in otherwise awkward lacunae in his tortuous account of political obligation and natural duties of obedience.

'There is, I believe, no political obligation, strictly speaking, for citizens generally' (p. 114). In making this statement Rawls is not implying that there is a problem about political obligation; rather he is arguing that 'obligation' is a largely irrelevant concept. Rawls states that there is 'another sense of *noblesse oblige*: namely, that those who are more privileged are likely to acquire obligations ...' (p. 116). Only some citizens, the 'better-placed members of society', those who 'are best able to gain political office and to take advantage of the opportunities offered by the constitutional system', are bound by a relationship of political obligation (p. 344). The rest of the population do not have the burden (or benefit) of political obligation. They are bound to the state by a natural duty of obedience which 'requires no voluntary acts in order to apply'. Significantly, Rawls also calls the natural duty of obedience the natural duty of justice, notwithstanding the fact that he has offered social life as a voluntary scheme as a political ideal. Rawls seems to see no inconsistency here; nor does he treat the distinction between obligation and natural duty as in any way remarkable, even though he is explicitly institutionalizing the non-voluntarist status of child-bride citizens and the moral proletariat.

Rawls refers at various points in the book to a variety of natural duties, including the duty not to harm others and to help them when in need. Again, duties of this type are familiar from the liberal contract theorists' laws of nature, or the conceptual argument about the necessary requirements for 'social life'; they are actions that we *ought* to perform or refrain from. But the most important natural duty of justice, or obedience, is the duty to 'support and further just institutions'. Everyone must do what is required to maintain just institutions 'irrespective of his voluntary acts, performative or otherwise' (p. 334). The problem with this 'argument' is that it is no more than the statement of a conceptual point. It closely resembles Pitkin's argument about hypothetical consent, which she recognizes rests on a 'point of grammar'.[30] The concept of a 'legitimate government' necessarily implies that citizens ought to consent or ought to obey. Similarly, Rawls' argument could be formulated as: a 'just state' is one that citizens ought (have a natural duty) to obey—or, in the original position, the parties would agree that they ought to consent to it, or would agree to the natural duty of obedience.

This conceptual point is unexceptionable, but the conclusions that can be drawn from it are another matter. To claim that one ought to obey a legitimate or just state leaves entirely open the vital question of how it is known that the state is indeed just; what are the criteria of justice? Rawls' claim that the hypothetical choice of the two principles provides a procedural criterion of justice depends on the *prior* assumption that the existing liberal democratic state is just, or nearly just. The circular and ideological character of Rawls' argument can be seen by considering a different formulation of this point that takes it beyond a purely conceptual proposition. Singer argues that a decision procedure which is a 'fair compromise', in that it requires that 'everyone gives up his own claim to have more than an equal say in deciding issues, but retains his claim to have an equal say', imposes an obligation on everyone to 'support and preserve' that procedure.[31] Singer then examines the operation of the liberal democratic political method to see whether it actually *is* a fair compromise, or if it does give expression, as Rawls assumes, to the first principle of justice. After examining the way in which the party system works, and the influence and composition of pressure groups, he concludes that liberal democracies 'are not fair compromises'.[32] Presumably, Rawls would claim they are, nonetheless, 'nearly just', because he does not advocate any radical changes in the political process, but this is to go far beyond a purely conceptual statement.

Rawls does raise the question whether compliance with just institutions should not be conditional on individuals' voluntary acts; for example, upon their 'having accepted the benefits of these arrangements, or ... having promised ... to abide by them'. He also states that 'offhand' this seems more in keeping with 'the contract idea with its emphasis upon free consent and the protection of liberty'. Rawls evades the question by referring back to the parties in the original position who, he claims, would be willing to give up compliance based on voluntary acts because of the need to ensure the stability of just institutions. The 'easiest and most direct' answer to this problem is to opt for an involuntary duty of obedience. Otherwise, citizens would only be bound to a just institution if 'they have accepted and intend to accept its benefits', and 'a greater reliance on the coercive powers of the sovereign might be necessary to achieve stability' (pp. 335–7). Hence it is simpler for the parties to agree to involuntary obedience—which is a fairly breathtaking argument from a writer who claims to be working within the social contract tradition.

Given Rawls' own characterization of the original position and its veil of ignorance, it is very likely that the parties would *not* accept this natural duty. The parties' knowledge includes the 'basis of social organization'. There seems no good reason, especially in view of Rawls' own conception of social life as a voluntary scheme, why these parties—good liberal parties that they are beneath their veil—should not know that the 'basis of social organization' in question is that of a voluntarist order, grounded in self-assumed obligation. They can all accept that one ought to support just institutions, but also deny there is an involuntary duty to do so. Instead they would argue that in a just institution there is good reason to assume an obligation to do what is necessary to keep the institution in being. In fact, Rawls admits as much, and so realigns himself with contract theory.

Obligations, according to Rawls, arise from individuals' voluntary actions within liberal democratic social institutions. All obligations arise out of the 'principle of fairness'. If a social practice or social institution is (nearly) just, and if we have 'voluntarily accepted the benefits of the arrangement or taken advantage of the opportunities it offers to further one's interests', then the principle of fairness requires that individuals have an obligation to do their share by abiding by the rules that keep the practice or institution in being: 'We are not to gain from the cooperative labors of others without doing our fair share' (p. 112). This is no more than a restatement, in voluntarist terms, of the conceptual point about the natural duty of justice.

Rawls says that, at first sight, the principle of fairness seems redundant. He recognizes that 'we can ... explain what can be called obligations by invoking the duty of justice. It suffices to construe the requisite voluntary acts as acts by which our natural duties are freely extended' (p. 343). But why is it necessary to introduce 'obligations' when it is much more economical to argue in terms of the natural duty of justice or obedience (and more in keeping with the Hegelian character of the enterprise of *A Theory of Justice*)? The answer is that Rawls wishes to cloak his theory in the mantle of the contract theorists, and claim that liberal democracies are 'voluntary schemes' involving 'obligation'. Hence a voluntarist gloss must be given to the conceptual point about natural duties. Now, Rawls' argument about the principle of fairness is a general one, but he also argues that institutions, such as political institutions, 'which must inevitably apply to us since we are born into them', must be distinguished from 'those that apply to us because we have freely done certain things as a rational way of advancing our ends' (p. 344). Political institutions seem, therefore, to involve duties; I will return to the question of why, and how, some citizens have political obligations in a moment.

The only example of 'obligation' that Rawls discusses in any detail is promising. His discussion is very confusing and difficult to follow because he has to refer to 'choice' of the principle of fairness to explain why promises oblige. Rawls frequently refers to the social practice of promising, but his contradictory theoretical apparatus prevents him from following out the logic of the concept of a 'social practice'. The conceptual solution to the 'problem' of promising appears to Rawls as an erroneous 'conflation' of two different rules—the rule of fairness and the rule of fidelity—which 'at first sight ... may seem to be the same thing' (p. 349). They are, of course, the same. And they are the same as the natural duty of justice or obedience, which, in the case of the institution of promising, reads: you ought to keep your promises. Rawls, as noted in Chapter 2, tries to separate the non-moral 'constitutive convention' of the social practice of promising, or the rule of promising, from the moral principle of fairness (or fidelity in the case of promising). Rawls has to do this to maintain the ideological role of the original position in underwriting the general 'choice' of the principles of justice. He argues that, in saying 'I promise', I am performing a voluntary act in accepting the benefits of the practice of promising, so the principle of fairness is relevant. The 'problem' then arises of why I should recognize this principle.

The answer is the hypothetically voluntarist one: the parties choose it in the original position. This answer, however, merely pushes the 'problem' back a stage further: why should the parties be supposed to 'choose' this principle? Rawls has already answered this question in his discussion of the natural duty of justice, so it is not surprising that we learn that it is because of the need for stability. 'Choice' of the rule of fidelity enables individuals 'to set up and to stabilize small-scale schemes of cooperation, or a particular pattern of transactions. The role of promises is analogous to that which Hobbes attributed to the sovereign' (p. 346). But this is not an answer, or at least, not the one Rawls believes it to be. He is merely restating the point that one ought to (or ought to choose to) 'support' just institutions; in this case, by keeping promises. 'Cooperation', or as it might be put 'mutual aid', is necessary for 'social life', and 'cooperation' entails 'fidelity'. Rawls notes that he is relying on Hart's point that cooperation requires a 'mutuality of restrictions'.[33] Yet these 'restrictions', in turn, require 'fidelity', as the social contract theorists' laws of nature tell us. All Rawls is saying is that one should not act like a Hobbesian natural individual or a perpetual free-rider—in other words, that within a just institution we shall have good reason to, or ought to (or have a natural duty to), assume an obligation to do what is necessary to keep it in being.

Underlying Rawls' convoluted discussion of promising is the assumption that all social rules are of the same status. Having abstracted individuals from the social practice of promising, so that they can 'choose' the principle of justice, Rawls then has to bring them back again. All he can do is to reify the rule of promising so that they can 'take advantage of it' (and then a principle has to be invoked to explain the consequences of this voluntary act ...), but he also conflates the rules of other social institutions. Having gone to such unnecessary lengths to generate and solve the 'problem' of promising, Rawls is then able to assume that there is no problem about the obligation to obey any other rules, including the laws of the liberal state. I discussed the failure to differentiate between the rules that order the various dimensions of social life in Chapter 2. I shall not repeat my argument here, but it should be pointed out that the conflation of these different rules enables Rawls to assume that it is as meaningful to talk about the 'justice' of promising as it is about the justice of the institutions of the liberal democratic state. All institutions appear to be of the same status. Thus by 'choosing' the principle of justice (fairness, fidelity, obedience—the *same* principle), all the problems of obligation are solved for the rules of all institutions. On the other hand, by referring to 'fidelity', not 'justice' or 'fairness' in the case of promising, Rawls implicitly acknowledges that 'obeying' the 'rule of promising' is not quite the same thing as 'obeying' the laws of the liberal state.

The Benefits and Participation Arguments

There is a major problem in Rawls' argument concerning the relationship of *political* obligation to the natural duty of obedience and the obligations that arise from the principle of fairness. 'The natural duty of justice is the primary basis of our political ties to a constitutional regime' (p. 376): the most obvious interpretation of Rawls' argument is that, because all adult individuals occupy the formally equal status of citizen, or, as it might be expressed, the station of citizenship, then all, necessarily, have certain political duties, including the duty to vote. This argument does not, however, explain why, or how, it is that a few, socially advantaged citizens also owe (or owe instead) a political obligation, not merely a natural political duty. Nor is it any help to turn to the voluntarist reinterpretation of natural duties in terms of the principle of fairness, for this, too, is a completely general argument. It does nothing to explain the differentiation between the involuntary and voluntary relationship.

Another difficulty also exists about the formulation of Rawls' hypothetically voluntarist version of his argument about supporting just institutions. On the one hand, it appears as a version of Pitkin's hypothetical consent; the parties ought to, and would, choose or consent to, the principle of justice in the original position. On the other hand, Rawls also makes a great deal of individuals 'benefiting' from, or 'voluntarily taking advantage of', liberal democratic practices and institutions. This approach too can be formulated as an argument about tacit consent; consent can be inferred from these voluntary actions of individuals. But it is unclear whether the benefits formulation is anything more than restatement of the conceptual point about cooperation and the principle of fairness. If the 'benefits' cannot be independently specified apart from fair cooperation or participation within institutions, then all that is being said is that the 'benefit' *is* the existence of fair play, or mutual acknowledgement of the principle of fairness. However, arguments that infer obligation from acceptance of benefits, or participation within institutions, are also offered independently of each other, and independently of a conceptual approach to political obligation. I drew attention in the previous chapter to the way in which consent theorists tend to fall back on the benefits argument to avoid the embarrassment of having citizens who are unaccounted for. The benefits argument is also sometimes linked to obligations as a form of gratitude, and, before turning to the question of how some of Rawls' citizens come to have a political obligation, I want to examine the claim about acceptance of benefits.

The benefits argument is usually stated so briefly as to suggest that it is self-evidently valid. Any attempt to fill it out leads to a very different conclusion than is suggested by the abstract, general account of *A Theory of Justice*. The most obvious objection to the assertion about benefits is that,

> as a practical matter 'receiving benefits' and 'living in a political society' (especially one with a just constitution) are one and the same thing. ... No one who lived in a society would be exempted from political obligations by the benefits-received doctrine.[34]

This is, of course, exactly its advantage for most writers on political obligation! However, it either establishes too much or too little; either it applies to all political societies that ever existed, or will exist, or it applies only to 'just' political societies, and the criteria of justice then have to be established. Furthermore, to make the claim about benefits in the liberal democratic state is merely to restate a central tenet of liberal theory. The justification for the liberal state is that it provides certain benefits, notably protection of property. No one will enter the social contract if it is not to their advantage or benefit, so the claim is tautologous. The provision of protection by the state authorities 'is by no means a piece of benevolence or a gratuitous act. They are authorities only because they provide protection, and it is hard to see that any gratitude is due them'.[35] Or that anything substantive follows from this about political obligation.

If the claim about benefits is to be anything more than the assertion of the liberal contract theorists that all, by definition, benefit from the existence of the liberal state, then the benefits have to be specified and the question of their distribution considered. I have come across no attempts to specify what counts as a 'benefit', or what constitutes a proper distribution. Unless the 'benefits' are identified with the formal equality of citizenship then the distribution cannot be an equal one. The justification of the social inequalities of the capitalist market economy is a central part of liberal social contract theory, and Rawls' and Hegel's theories. Most writers on political obligation, unlike Rawls, nevertheless usually assume that all citizens have an equal political obligation. Significantly enough, if the most fundamental 'benefit' emphasized by liberal theorists, protection of the person, is considered, it is clear that it is not equally distributed in the liberal democratic state. Consider: Hobbes was concerned with protection in the basic sense of the physical security that would enable each individual to live his or her life to its natural span. The reality underlying the formal liberal democratic equality of citizenship is that, if you are born into the lower classes, you are likely to live less long than if you are socially advantaged. One survey of the relative class differentials in mortality rates concludes that, 'despite the multiplicity of methods and indexes used ... and despite the varigated populations surveyed, the inescapable conclusion is that class influences one's chance of staying alive'. Furthermore, it also seems that 'the differential between the lower class and other classes ... has not diminished over recent decades'.[36] One contributing factor to this difference in mortality rates is that one of the hazards of a worker 'voluntarily taking advantage' of the social institution of the capitalist organization of production, is dying from an industrial accident or disease. In Britain, for example, a realistic estimate is that some 3000 workers die from these causes each year.[37]

Consider again: the reason that individuals exchange their natural freedom and equality of the state of nature for the equal protection of the civil law, is to eliminate the insecurity and arbitrariness of individual punishment. All individuals who breach the civil law are, in principle, equally subject to the sanctions imposed on offenders, no matter what their substantive social position. Yet a recent study in the sociology of the legal process concludes that 'the poor do not receive the same treatment at the hands of the agents of law-enforcement as the well-to-do or middle class. This differential treatment is systematic and complete'. Not only are the poor more likely to be prosecuted and punished, but 'professional thieves and organized criminals enjoy an immunity from criminal prosecution second only to the immunity enjoyed by the very wealthy'.[38]

Consider once more: the liberal conception of equality of protection, so central to contract theory, implies also that all sections of the population are equally protected from each other. This has never been so in the relationship between the sexes. Men are conventionally held to be the protectors of women, who are seen to be 'naturally' incapable of protecting themselves and their interests. Yet the consent of the wife in the marriage contract has been held to constitute a continuing 'consent' to all sexual demands of the husband; rape is seen as impossible between husband and wife.[39] More generally, women are not afforded the same legal protection as men from physical assaults by men. Attention has only recently begun to be directed to brutality by husbands against wives and to the facts about rape.[40] Rape is formally regarded as a most serious offence. In practice, perhaps as many as two-thirds of rapes are not reported to the police, because women know that protection is lacking and dread the social stigma that attaches to the rape victim. It is the victim, not the assailant, who is subject to humiliating public examination and who, unless a child, is frequently held to have brought it upon herself. And it is difficult to secure conviction when men's careers are deemed more important than violent attacks on women.[41]

If actual examples of possible 'benefits', and their distribution, are considered, then it is no longer possible to draw the comforting conclusions about political obligation favoured by most political theorists. When the claim is made in general and abstract terms—we voluntarily take advantage of an institution and thus benefit from its existence—and examples such as promising are used, then it is easy to suggest that everyone is benefiting and is obligated (we all make promises and we all understand the connection between promising and obligation). Such formulations also very neatly avoid the question of—benefit compared to what? The contract theorists could at least answer this question; everyone benefits in civil society *compared to* their position in the state of nature. Rawls, and other advocates of the claim about benefits, can offer no such comparison. They are merely asserting that all benefit from the existence of liberal democracy. Yet if the comparison with the state of nature is not relevant, then the obvious comparison is between groups and classes within civil society. Rawls does not make any comparisons because the hypothetical choice of the principles of justice, and the abstract argument about benefits, *presuppose* the justice of the existing inequalities. The way in which the rules of justice are arrived at means that Rawls can set 'no moral restriction on the absolute size of "fair" inequalities',[42] and so it is pointless to make the brief investigation of the actual distribution of benefits I have just offered. But it is not so intuitively obvious as Rawls would have us believe that large inequalities in such a basic 'benefit' as protection of the person are compatible with justice, and hence with an inference that all are politically obliged or naturally bound. Rawls is faced with exactly the same problem of incorporating the working class and women into his system as other liberal theorists.

A major objection has already been noted to interpreting the claim about benefits in terms of gratitude, but it is worth looking in a little more detail at arguments about gratitude for they can play an important ideological role. It will be recalled that Hobbes talks about benefits and gratitude and, very significantly, he refers in this context to what is owed to superiors. Claims about gratitude, and what the grateful should, properly, feel and do, are frequently claims about the relationship that, it is argued, should exist between 'superiors' and 'inferiors'. For example, it is often said that the poor should be grateful for charity bestowed by their betters (if they are not, then this reveals that they are 'undeserving' poor; a good critique of this argument can be found in the films of Buñuel). Or, again, it is argued that wives should be grateful if they have been lucky enough to find a decent man who treats them in a reasonable fashion, and so should accept the generally disadvantaged and unequal situation of wives compared to husbands. Similarly, those who have to sell their labour should be grateful if they find an employer who pays good wages and provides decent working conditions. In all these cases it is claimed that the poor, wives, and workers should show their gratitude, and recognize the obligation it implies, by acting in the proper manner; a manner which maintains their unequal position.

As these examples illustrate, there is a close connection between the giving of charity and arguments about gratitude. The claim about benefits and political obligation can be seen as a contemporary version of the old argument about what is owed by the poor in respect of the benefit of the charity bestowed by the rich. This argument is now set in the context of an impersonal liberal society, with its welfare state and the benefits it has brought to the working class, but it performs the same ideological function as its age-old predecessor.[43] I am not arguing that gratitude never is appropriate or that there are no occasions when one should do something in return for a benefit. Rather, I am questioning the *political* uses and conclusions of the arguments. In any case, even if the benefits argument has more to recommend it, it does not follow from the fact that we 'ought' to do something in return for a benefit that we have an 'obligation' to do so, unless that obligation has been assumed by those concerned. I hope that my discussion has shown that the benefits 'argument' for political obligation is best decently buried.

An interesting question remains, however, about the frequency with which the benefits argument appears in discussions of political obligation. To be sure, its ideological usefulness, the fact that the inference from the acceptance of benefits leaves no one outside the net of political obligation, and that it can give a voluntarist appearance to arguments about involuntary or natural duties, goes a long way in explaining its popularity. But the popularity of the benefits argument derives also from the persistence of the abstractly individualist theoretical perspective. The idea that an individual benefits from participating in social life as such lies at the heart of the benefits argument. The argument implies that there is an alternative—without the benefits. Rawls states that he wants 'to account for the ... intrinsic good of institutional, community, and associative activities, by a conception of justice that in its theoretical basis is individualistic' (p. 264). In the original position, 'the combination of mutual disinterest and the veil of ignorance achieves the same purpose as benevolence' (p. 148). On the contrary, as Hobbes' theory shows so well, this combination works in exactly the *opposite* direction to 'benevolence', or the idea that there are certain actions that a moral person knows generally ought to be performed. The view of social life to which this combination gives rise is of a series of discrete benefits or mutually self-interested exchanges. The mutuality and reciprocity of social life, the mutual interest of social beings in one another's well-being that is presupposed in a coherent conception of 'social life', completely disappears from view. The claim that acceptance of benefits gives rise to obligations is thus an attempt to retrieve this lost mutuality and 'benevolence' of social life. Ironically, the theoretical perspective inherent in Rawls' frequent references to social practices, and the conception of the political association as a social union of social unions, shows that there is no need 'to account for' community and associative activities; these *are* social life.

Even if there were more to be said in support of the claim about benefits, it would not solve the problem of the origin of political obligation in Rawls' theory since it is a completely general argument. It is possible to find an answer to this problem by reformulating it in terms of participation within liberal democratic institutions, and concentrating on one form of participation, namely voting, although this causes difficulties for Rawls' arguments. He argues that everyone has a natural duty to 'support' just, or nearly just, institutions, but he gives no indication of what kinds of actions constitute such support; it would seem reasonable, however, that in the case of political institutions the support is given by citizens fulfilling their duty to vote.

The difficulty with this interpretation of Rawls' argument is that it does not account for the political obligation of the few—unless voting has a different, or additional, meaning for some citizens. In fact, this could be the conclusion that Rawls wishes his readers to draw, and it would explain why the first principle does not offer an 'ideal' of citizenship. Running for and taking political office is one way in which socially advantaged citizens assume their political obligation, and this may also be the meaning of their votes; we know that it is the middle classes who tend to be the most politically active (p. 344; also p. 113; 376).

Rawls has remarkably little to say about voting and its relationship to the liberty and equality of democratic citizenship on which he places so much emphasis. Nor does he appear to connect the liberal view of voting as an instrumentally functional activity with the social contract tradition. Rawls' view of voting is much more like Hegel's. He rejects the liberal analogy between the market and the political process, between voting and spending money. For Rawls, the voter, or the 'rational legislator', does not vote to protect his interests but to give his opinion about 'which laws and policies best conform to principles of justice' (p. 361). Rawls says that 'the fair value for all of the equal political liberties' must be preserved, but he also toys with the idea of plural voting (p. 225). The aim of government is to pursue policies that are to everyone's advantage and, to the extent that 'some men can be identified as having superior wisdom and judgement, others are willing to trust them and to concede to their opinion a greater weight' (p. 233). Thus the middle classes (whom liberal theorists have traditionally identified as the men in question) might be politically obligated and 'bound even more tightly' to the liberal state because they have extra votes (p. 344).

If this seems an odd way to secure 'fair value' for everyone, Rawls' distinction between liberty and the worth of liberty sweeps 'fair value' away. Immediately after introducing the possibility of plural voting, Rawls goes on to argue that the value of voting is that it strengthens self-worth and individuals' sense of each other as 'associates with whom one can cooperate' (p. 234). Rawls assumes that social and economic inequalities are irrelevant to this relationship:

> liberty is represented by the complete system of the liberties of equal citizenship, while the worth of liberty to persons and groups is proportional to their capacity to advance their ends within the framework the system defines.

The worth of liberty is not the same for all because 'some have greater authority and wealth, and therefore greater means to achieve their aims' (p. 204). Rawls takes it for granted that those whose liberty is worth very little nevertheless gain a sense of their worth by exercising the franchise; presumably because they understand the role of the second principle of justice and this reconciles them to their particular 'cross of the present'.[44] All this is extremely implausible. The least advantaged will surely find that the everyday impact of their unequal social position detracts more from their self-worth than the periodic exercise of a vote does to restore it. On the other hand, the socially advantaged would find that voting helped maintain their privileged social position and, hence, their self-esteem. This can be acknowledged by characterizing their relationship to the state as one of political 'obligation', and interpreting their votes differently from those of the moral proletariat whose citizenship is merely a formal status, and who have a natural duty to obey.

To refer to a 'moral proletariat' might seem too extreme because Rawls does argue that civil disobedience is a legitimate form of political action in a liberal democracy; indeed, 'a conception of civil disobedience is part of the theory of free government' (p. 385). Rawls' discussion of civil disobedience does not, however, affect my argument. Like Locke's right of resistance, civil disobedience is justified only when 'substantial or clear injustice' of a particular kind exists, or when the arguments for the natural duty of obedience or political obligation no longer apply. Furthermore, Rawls' conception of civil disobedience is, as I have noted in previous chapters, an exceedingly narrow one. It can make no impact on the position of the moral proletariat because he specifically excludes it as a means of remedying breaches of the difference principle; civil disobedience is relevant only to the formal equality of citizenship and the principle of equality of opportunity. Rawls comments that if formal equality is maintained (by civil disobedience if necessary) then 'the presumption is that other injustices, while possibly persistent and significant, will not get out of hand' (p. 373); in other words, they are not really 'injustices'.

Rawls attempts to provide a differential account of political obedience and political obligation, so that all individuals are held to be bound, yet their different social positions are recognized. However, he can include everyone only at the cost of reducing his argument to a completely abstract series of conceptual points, which fail to make the necessary differentiation between social classes. If the arguments are made more specific, and actual substantive inequalities are taken into account, then Rawls' arguments, like Hegel's, cannot successfully incorporate the working class or women.

The participation argument can also be used, as it is by Singer, to support the general identification of liberal democratic voting and political obligation. Singer's argument is interesting because it shows in a more concrete way why liberal democratic voting is different from promising and from other social practices of private life. If an individual joins a group in which each member in turn is buying, or shouting, a round of drinks, then, Singer argues, having voluntarily participated, the individual has assumed an obligation to buy the drinks when his or her turn comes. This is a version of the conceptual argument. The 'meaning' of the social practice of shouting drinks is, like the 'meaning' of promising, mutually understood, so that an individual who joins a group and accepts drinks knows that an obligation has been incurred. Singer presents the argument in terms of 'quasi-consent'. He argues that the consequences of participation are as if the individual had consented; actual consent is not involved so, Singer claims, the argument is different from tacit consent arguments.[45]

In fact, the argument is the same as the tacit consent argument; 'quasi-consent' is another version of hypothetical voluntarism. It is to argue that in performing certain actions the individual has acted as if he or she were consenting, so obligation can be inferred. The practice of shouting drinks is not, however, a good example with which to illustrate hypothetical voluntarism. Shouting drinks, like promising, is an example of the free creation of obligations, not an example of consent, hypothetical or otherwise. To participate in the practice of shouting drinks, like making a promise, is to assume an obligation. The consequences of so committing oneself are also similar to the consequences of promising, in that the individual knows what the consequences are, and they are limited. The content of the obligation is the same for each member of the drinking group (providing, that is, that when your turn comes the rest do not switch from glasses of beer to treble gins). In short, the political analogue of shouting drinks is the same as that of promising; it is participatory not liberal democratic voting.

Without making the distinction between the two forms of self-assumed obligation, it is all the easier to jump to the conclusion that 'participation' must be liberal democratic voting. However, there is less reason for Singer to draw this conclusion than many theorists. He begins his discussion using a model of a direct democracy, and he is more willing than most writers on political obligation to admit that citizens might refuse or withdraw consent. Public refusal to vote, for example, shows that citizens are not willing to assume an obligation.[46] And, as I mentioned above, Singer argues that liberal democracies are not, in practice, fair compromises. Nevertheless, he still argues that participation in liberal democratic elections gives rise to political obligation, even though a citizen may have voted 'because there was nothing better to do'.[47] But why should a citizen act in this way? In order to attempt to explain this action, it must be kept in mind that individuals are taught that liberal democratic voting is *the* method of democratic political action. A citizen may have thought seriously about political matters and reached the same conclusion as Singer, that liberal democracies are not fair compromises. Both voting and electoral abstention may appear equally pointless since both help maintain an unfair compromise in being—but what else can a citizen do who wishes to act democratically? Voting seems the only course open.[48] This can help explain why, despite the evidence cited in Chapter 5 about the way in which working-class voters perceive the electoral system, many continue to vote; there seems nothing better to do. The identification of consent (or quasi-consent) and voting is thus weakened further. Indeed, Singer refers to the 'weakness of the arguments for obedience' in liberal democracies, and he also comments that we might have to 'consider seriously the possibility that the basis of political obligation in Western democracies is in need of reconstruction ...'.[49]

Rawls, not surprisingly in view of the aim of *A Theory of Justice*, does not consider this possibility. But his arguments, perhaps to a greater extent than those of other liberal theorists, show why such a reconstruction is required, a reconstruction that goes much further than the reforms to the electoral and party system mentioned by Singer. The weakness of the liberal arguments for obedience extend far beyond political institutions as these are conventionally conceived. The problem of the locus and character of 'political' obligation, hinted at in Locke's theory, emerges clearly in Walzer's attempt to reconcile participatory pluralism with a justification of political obligation in the liberal democratic state. Because of the extremely abstract character of so much of Rawls' argument, it is not immediately apparent that exactly the same problems are inherent in his theory also. At one point, Rawls refers to Walzer's *Obligations*, and he remarks that the few citizens who are politically obliged owe this obligation 'to citizens generally' (p. 376). This raises the wider question of to whom it is that the natural duty and the obligation are owed; they prescribe the support of just institutions, so it would seem that they embody relationships that extend horizontally between the members of these institutions. However, if this is so, the question is then posed of how *political* institutions, and *political* duties and obligation, are to be distinguished from other institutions and non-political duties and obligations.

Here again, the conflict between the abstractly individualist parts of Rawls' theory and the conceptual and Hegelian parts is apparent. How exactly does Rawls intend us to see the relationship between individuals and the liberal state in his theory? Despite the close connection between his two principles and the view of liberal democracy as a political method, his is not a conventional liberal view; rather, Rawls implicitly relies on an Hegelian ambiguity about the 'state'. In his discussion of 'The Idea of Social Union' (pp. 520–9), Rawls argues that contract theory does not imply that 'private society is the ideal'. But, if this is so, then nor can the external 'umpire' state, or political sphere, be the ideal; as Hegel recognized, these two conceptions are inseparable. In contrasting the idea of a social union with that of private society, Rawls refers to the 'just constitutional order', and the 'public institutions of society', rather than to the 'state', but his discussion bears a striking resemblance to Hegel's discussion of the 'state' as an ethical order. The participants or partners in a social union, unlike individuals in private society, have 'shared final ends', in particular the end of 'the successful carrying out of just institutions'. They value the institutions as good in themselves, for within them they realize their 'natures as moral persons'. The constitutional order provides a 'framework' for the other social unions in the society, and thus, the 'state' can be seen as a social union of social unions. Moreover, it can be argued that through participation in (or by benefiting from) these institutions the partners acquire a political obligation, or have a natural duty, owed to each other, to uphold the rules that make the social union possible. Hence, the separation between private and political, on which Rawls' two principles depend and which is central to liberal contract theory, is systematically undermined by the conception of a social union.

Voluntarism and the Private Sphere

I now want to make some comments about obligation and the 'private' sphere of social life. In discussions of political obligation it is usually assumed that, whatever difficulties there may be about voluntarism in political life, the private sphere is a true example of a voluntary scheme. If, in arguments about political obligation, little account is taken of the realities of the liberal democratic electoral mechanism, or of other aspects of political participation, even less attention is paid to the realities of private, especially economic, life. Rawls, for example, refers to the 'democratic conception of society as a system of cooperation among equal persons', and to the social union as 'a cooperative venture for mutual advantage' (p. 383; 520). It is assumed that these general and abstract conceptions are actually realized within liberal democratic institutions, that they can accurately be characterized in these terms. In addition, the failure to distinguish between the kinds of rules that order practices and institutions in different dimensions of social life means that the institutions of the private sphere are treated as if they were all of a piece. 'Society' is viewed as if it is no more than the social practice of promising, or the social practice of shouting drinks, writ large. Conceptual points about 'membership', 'cooperation' and 'participation' can appear compelling, and seem part of a substantive argument, only because actual forms of membership, specific types of participation, and the manner in which 'cooperation' is achieved are totally ignored.

The voluntarist conception of political life is usually illustrated by reference to the 'voluntary associations' of liberal democratic life. However, the term 'voluntary association' itself is very misleading as a general description of all the institutions and organizations of the private sphere. Very few voluntary associations are like the social practice of shouting drinks. Some associations resemble it, because individuals are completely free to join or leave, and because it is of no particular importance whether one is a member or not. Associations and clubs concerned with leisure activities fall into this category. On the other hand, most associations will also differ from shouting drinks because they usually have an authority structure of a liberal democratic kind, with an elected body of officials to run the affairs of the club for its members. (These are the associations referred to in the conceptual argument about freely becoming a 'member', 'rules', and 'obligations'.) But not all institutions and organizations in the private sphere are of this kind; economic organizations provide a sharp contrast to such 'voluntary associations'.

'We are born into an economic system just as we are born citizens, and ... so must we work in order to live.'[50] (Although some women are able to obtain their subsistence indirectly from the market for paid labour by providing services for a husband in the home.) If, as is frequently argued, the fact that we are 'born citizens' renders voluntarism meaningless, then the same argument should be, but rarely is, applied to economic life. We are, involuntarily, participants within it. In principle, as Rawls' emphasis on equality of opportunity illustrates, individuals are free to train for and enter whatever occupation they choose, and are free to change their jobs; in practice the choice for most people, most of the time, is very limited. Working-class children, especially girls, are not trained for professional careers in the numbers one would expect; if one's trade declines it is hard, especially the older one gets, to retrain; prolonged periods of unemployment may well be the lot of the unskilled. There are, moreover, other basic features of the organization of economic production that show that references to 'voluntary schemes' are very misleading, and that reveal the ideological role of references to 'cooperative practices among equals'.

One of Rawls' numerous commentators has written that,

> the veil of ignorance has the effect of making all considerations on the production side so thoroughly hypothetical, so *abstract* ... that inevitably the difference principle comes to be construed as a pure distribution principle, ...[51]

Rawls takes no account of the organization of production. Indeed, this is precluded because the first principle, which is concerned with equality and authority, governs citizenship and political life; the second principle is concerned with non-political inequalities, and is designed to show why it is rational to accept or choose them. These inequalities are not, as Rawls suggests, merely inequalities of income or goods. They include inequalities of authority, of power and influence; the actual structure of authority in the workplace, that determines the mode of cooperation, what is produced and how it is produced, is ignored in Rawls' account of 'cooperation among equals'. Yet if it is hard to justify the assumption that political 'obligation' exists within the liberal democratic state, it is even harder to support the claim that 'participation' or 'cooperation' in the institution of capitalist economic production gives rise to an 'obligation' to support the rules that govern it. Rawls' discussion proceeds as if the rules governing the workplace were just like the rules constituting the practice of promising or the civil laws of the state. But the rules of the economic enterprise, unlike the laws of the state, do not rest on the formal equality of status of its members, nor are they made by elected representatives. Rawls' 'democratic conception' of social life stops at the gate of the workplace.

Locke's conjectural history of the state of nature and Rawls' second principle are designed to justify the division of the inhabitants of liberal democracies into two broad classes; those who own property in the form of material goods and the means of production, and those whose property is mainly in their persons, labour and skills. It is the former who have the right to make and enforce the rules that govern economic production. Their formal equality of citizenship is worth more, not only because they are more likely to use the opportunities offered by the electoral mechanism or attain political office, but because they make the rules governing economic production. This is an important reason why they have 'greater authority' than the citizens who sell their labour and obey in the workplace. Even the most casual examination of the realities of working life shows the hollowness of Rawls' assertion that liberal democratic voting compensates for the lesser worth of formally equal liberty to less advantaged citizens, and can mend the ravages to self-esteem and self-respect arising from the inequalities of economic life.[52] Not all workplaces reveal the basis of the 'cooperation of equals' in such stark fashion as those discussed in, for example, *Detroit: I do Mind Dying* or *Working for Ford*,[53] but all economic enterprises are organized in

A hierarchy where income differences are paralleled by other dimensions of economic inequality which may extend to differences in the regularity and dependability of income, and in the nature and extent of fringe benefits. There are also less tangible inequalities which relate to the content of work, to the kind of social relationships which people are involved in at work, and to the exercise of power.[54]

Once actual relationships in the workplace are considered, the abstractions of 'fair play', 'cooperation', 'accepting benefits' and 'obligation' are put into perspective. A more accurate characterization of the social relationships in economic production is—'workers are paid to obey'.[55]

In Rawls' brief discussion of forms of economic systems, he makes one reference to firms managed by 'worker's (*sic*) councils' (p. 266). He does not, however, appreciate the significance of workers' councils for his separation of the political and private spheres of social life, nor see that it poses a direct challenge to his assumption that the institutions of economic production are (nearly) just and a natural duty of obedience holds within them. Like the social contract theorists, Rawls bases his theory on the ideal of individual freedom and equality, and he must therefore answer the question why any free and equal individual would be willing, even hypothetically, to choose the existing structure of authority in the workplace. It is no answer to say that the hypothetical choices of the original position 'are ones that we do in fact accept' (p. 21). There is no good reason for free and equal individuals to make such a choice; they would not choose a system in which they are placed in a position of permanent subordination and inequality, and in which obedience is the price of the means of subsistence.

The election of a council to make decisions within the economic enterprise introduces liberal democracy into economic production.[56] Yet this is precisely what liberal theory, including Rawls' argument, rules out; 'democracy', whether liberal or self-managing democracy, is held to be a purely political concept and practice and can, therefore, have no place in the private sphere of social life. The separation of the 'political', and political concepts and practices, from everyday life enables theorists to identify liberal democratic voting and consent, and, at the same time (and with no sense of incongruity), allows them to regard as illegitimate the question whether obligation in other social institutions should not also be constituted through voting. As I have shown, the crucial separation of the 'political' and the 'private' is often undermined in discussions of political obligation, particularly by theorists attracted by pluralism and the conceptual argument; and it is also brought into question by arguments for workers' councils. However, it is not possible for the implications of these arguments to be explored without casting doubt on central and fundamental assumptions of liberal theory. If the logic of a genuinely pluralist conception of political life, the conception of the 'state' as a social union of social unions, or the extension of democracy into the workplace, is followed through, it becomes impossible to maintain the vertical conception of 'political' obligation that has been bequeathed by liberal contract theory. 'Political' obligation must be conceived as a horizontal relationship between citizens, that is assumed in a multiplicity of associations. But this conception cuts the ground from under the feet of the liberal 'umpire' state, and its claim to authority. I shall return to the problem of the character and locus of 'political' obligation in the final chapter.

The conceptual argument offers valuable insights for criticisms of abstract individualism, but its contribution to the argument about political obligation is considerably more limited than its proponents believe. Indeed, the elaborated conceptual argument, forming part of theories designed to show that the liberal state should be accepted as a necessary and rational form of political organization, is an argument about political obedience or duty, not political obligation. Moreover, the logical conclusion of the conceptual argument is that political obedience must be given unconditionally. If formally equal citizens have doubts about their station and their obedience, this merely shows that they failed to understand the rationality of the hypothetical choices in the original position. Yet neither Hegel nor Rawls presents a straightforward theory of political obedience or duty. Both give the conceptual argument a gloss of hypothetical voluntarism, a gloss that is necessary if the state is to be 'willed', or the ideal of social life as a voluntary scheme is not to be completely cast aside. But the introduction of political obligation, no matter how hypothetically, means that the intricate web of the conceptual argument begins to unravel to reveal the problematic character of the relationship between the citizen and the liberal state. Voluntarist arguments, however weak and implausible, expose the gap between the realities of liberal democratic institutions and the liberal political ideal, a gap that cannot be bridged by a resort to a series of abstract, conceptual points. The cost of trying to do so is that nothing substantive can be said about political obligation in the liberal democractic state.

Chapter 7

The Democratic Social Contract

Criticism has plucked the imaginary flowers from the chain, not so
that man shall bear the chain without fantasy or consolation, but so
that he shall cast off the chain and gather the living flower.

K. Marx, *A Contribution to the Critique of Hegel's 'Philosophy of
Right': Introduction.*

The philosophical anarchists and Rousseau argue very differently about political
obligation from the theorists I have discussed so far. They, also, begin their
arguments from the postulate of individual freedom and equality, but they reach
very different conclusions from the theorists of the liberal democratic state. The
philosophical anarchists conclude that all claims about political authority and
political obligation are illegitimate; Rousseau argues that the problem of political
obligation is soluble only in a participatory political association, which is, of course,
also my conclusion. Rousseau's social contract theory contains many valuable
insights for the development of a contemporary theory and practice of self-assumed
political obligation, but, before turning to his critique of liberal contract theory, it is
necessary to distinguish my argument from the claims of the philosophical
anarchists. The argument that the problem of political obligation is inherently
insoluble is often presented as a criticism of liberal theories of political obligation,
but it is, in fact, an argument located at one extreme of liberal theory itself.
Philosophical anarchism is one conclusion to be drawn from radically abstract
individualism.

Abstract individualism, as I have shown, gives rise to a general problem about all
social relationships; any constraint or limitation upon the private judgement of the
individual appears to compromise individual freedom and equality. The Hobbesian
solution to this problem relies upon the strength of the sword and reduces consent to
enforced obedience. Philosophical anarchists not only reject the sword but deny that
consent provides a solution. They argue that voluntarism is no solution to the
conflict between the right of individual judgement and the constraints imposed by
relationships of obligation and authority; 'the exercise of political authority', it is
stated in one of the most recent formulations of this argument, 'is simply
incompatible with the exercise of conscience. The exercise of moral judgement is
quite different from the acceptance of political authority'.[1] More generally, the logical
conclusion of philosophical anarchism, a conclusion which William Godwin, the
major theorist in this tradition, was quite willing to draw, is that all social
relationships involve the surrender of individual freedom and autonomy, or the right
of individual private judgement. Even promising, to Godwin, is an evil practice that
should be abolished.

The philosophical anarchist argument is usually conducted in terms of 'authority' rather than 'obligation', although contemporary philosophical anarchists are not usually as logically consistent as Godwin about promising. One reason for their concentration on 'authority' is that they are largely concerned with political laws and political rulers. Philosophical anarchists also, like all consistently radical individualists, fail to deal coherently with the mutuality and reciprocity of social relationships. 'Authority', for example, is treated not as a relationship but as a property of individuals (although it should be added that this view of authority is not confined to philosophical anarchists). It is more difficult to talk of 'obligation' in this way, unless it is assumed that individuals can owe obligations to themselves, or unless 'obligation' is reduced to a psychological sense or feeling. I have said very little about 'authority' except to indicate that voluntarist justifications of political obligation are also justifications of political authority; 'obligation' and 'authority' are both necessary corollaries of the liberal ideal of individual freedom and authority. This is precisely what philosophical anarchism denies and, in order to appreciate the nature and status of that denial, it is necessary to consider the concept of 'authority' in more detail. This is also necessary for a more important reason. A presently implicit, but nonetheless crucial, implication of my argument is that the democratic theory and practice of self-assumed political obligation is based upon authority, not power.

Philosophical Anarchism and Political Authority

Philosophical anarchist arguments were recently revived by Wolff, in *In Defence of Anarchism*. Wolff argues that 'authority resides in persons; they possess it ... by virtue of who they are and not by virtue of what they command'.[2] One result of treating authority as a property of individuals is to obscure the distinctively political character of 'authority'. In this respect 'authority' differs from 'obligation'. The practice of self-assumed obligation can exist both in everyday life and in political life; I have emphasized that the obligation constituted by a promise and political obligation are indeed both 'obligation'. However, 'authority' is a specifically political concept and is a correlative of political obligation, not the obligation arising from a promise. We do not usually say that the person to whom the obligation arising from a promise is owed has 'authority' to demand that it is fulfilled. On the other hand, conceptual considerations may suggest that 'authority' is as broad a concept as 'obligation'. Pitkin, for example, argues that although 'it is not at all obvious that government and law are indispensable to human social life. ... can we conceive society without any such thing as authority?'.[3] The conceptual argument reminds us that 'social life' requires certain 'rules' that we 'ought' to adhere to; so perhaps it also involves 'authority'. It might thus appear that the 'rule of promising' and 'authority' are connected at this basic level. But nothing is to be gained from using 'authority' in this way and detaching it from its relationship to 'law' and 'government'. Indeed, such a usage merely encourages the tendency to fail to differentiate between rules governing various dimensions of social life, a tendency common both to abstract individualism and the conceptual argument. 'Authority' is bound up with specific kinds of rules, namely those governing political institutions.

A further consequence of seeing 'authority' as a property of individuals is that it is impossible to distinguish political authority from the 'authority' of a person who has some special knowledge or skills. In other words, the notion of a person being 'an authority' on a given subject is confused with the idea of 'authority'. Wolff, for example, argues that a course of treatment from a doctor involves a patient in exactly the same loss of individual autonomy, or alienation of individual judgement, as submission to the demands of the state. Doctors have successfully contrived to surround themselves with a great deal of mystique and ritual, but this is a perverse way of describing the relationship with patients. Indeed, most liberal theorists would be unhappy with the comparison, because patients can throw away their pills, ignore the doctor's advice, or treat themselves, whereas their relationship to the liberal state is held to be one of an obligation to let the state decide for them; they do not have the choice of writing their own political prescription. However, the fact that patients are free to accept their doctors' advice or not illustrates an important similarity between the conceptions of 'an authority' and 'authority'; both are based on critical reflection and deliberate choice. In the social practice of promising, individuals judge whether they ought to commit themselves in any given instance; the political practice of participatory voting allows citizens collectively to engage in the same process of judgement and decision. If they decide to commit themselves, then they are, at the same time, creating or reaffirming a relationship of political authority. Political authority is constituted by the same political practice as political obligation.

This is not always apparent in discussions of 'authority' because it is frequently regarded as merely one form of power. 'The idea of authority embodies a presumption of legitimacy';[4] but the crucial question concerns the criteria by which legitimacy is to be judged. When authority is treated as legitimate power the criterion is often taken to be psychological states of individuals (do they feel obligated, or feel that the power is exercised legitimately) or to be hypothetical consent to its exercise. Rational commitment or reasoned persuasion is precluded. One reason is that 'authority' is usually seen in terms of the relationship between citizens and the liberal state. Theorists rarely consider another form of authority relationship; one in which citizens freely create relationships of authority for themselves. Thus definitions of 'authority' usually cannot encompass a democratic form of political organization in which members of a political association, in their capacity as citizens, exercise political authority over themselves as individuals. Or, to make this point slightly differently, authority is usually regarded as one way in which individuals can exercise power *over* others; it is not seen as a way of giving citizens collective power *to*, or the ability to, act for themselves.[5] It is seen as a form of control rather than as a means of citizens enlarging their collective capacity to create and take responsibility for their own political lives.

Bachrach and Baratz offer a definition of 'authority' that is compatible with a critical, democratic conception of political life. They argue that a relationship of 'authority' exists if persons freely choose to comply with directives and communications because they regard these as 'reasonable in terms of [their] own values'.[6] If this is amended to read that they 'create or comply with directives' it provides a foundation for a democratic conception of authority. Citizens take decisions (or create directives for themselves) compatible with their own political values or principles. If unanimous agreement cannot be reached about the decision, then the minority can decide, on the basis of the same principles, whether or not they ought to consent to, or comply with, these directives. (I shall return to the question of the minority at the end of this chapter.)

To a philosophical anarchist, however, 'all authority is equally illegitimate'.[7] Wolff reaches this conclusion only because he so defines 'authority' and individual 'autonomy' that it is necessarily true. Individuals, according to Wolff, obey authority whenever they act in a certain way simply *because* they have been told to. They exercise their autonomy or freedom of judgement, when they decide for themselves how to act. They can voluntarily forfeit their autonomy, or put themselves into a position of voluntary heteronomy, by, for instance, consenting to the authority of the state. It is not clear whether Wolff regards promises as examples of voluntary heteronomy, although logically he ought to. He refers to the 'obligation' that individuals have to take responsibility for their own actions, but the only example that he discusses is a promise to obey, or the liberal social contract. However, a promise to obey is a very special kind of promise. The liberal social contract, as my argument as a whole is designed to show, is a denial of, not an expression of, the practice of self-assumed obligation. Wolff, though, is not concerned with actual practices and institutions that can enable or prevent individuals from exercising autonomy. He reduces the problem of political obligation and authority to the 'problem' of a series of discrete encounters between two abstractly conceived individuals, one of whom possesses authority and the other autonomy. He concentrates on the latter's subjective 'final decision' about what to do. If the individual decides for himself to obey authority, then this is not really 'obedience' but, rather, 'acknowledging the force of an argument or the rightness of a prescription'. Providing that the individual makes the final decision whether or not to cooperate, he retains his autonomy and 'he thereby denies the authority of the state'.[8]

Such a 'denial' leaves everything as it is. Wolff offers an abstract 'solution' to a 'problem' generated by his own conceptual apparatus. No political ruler need quake at the implications of Wolff's 'anarchism'. Indeed, his argument forms no part of a political theory of anarchism; it is an extension of a purely philosophical scepticism, a scepticism which is inherent in abstractly individualist liberalism. Wolff's 'denial' of the authority of the state is of exactly the same character and status as the philosopher's 'denial' that there are other minds, or material objects—or that promises oblige. A proper understanding of the social practice of promising shows that the latter 'denial' is conceptually incoherent and, similarly, as I have already indicated, a proper understanding of the political practice of authority involves not the 'denial' but the presupposition of individual autonomy, or free, critical judgement and choice. Significantly enough, Wolff implicitly admits this. Although he claims that 'the just state must be consigned to the category of the round square, the married bachelor, and the unsensed sense-datum', he also allows that a coherent example of the 'just state' can be found. A direct democracy based on unanimity '*is a* genuine solution' since it combines both autonomy and authority; the difficulty is that it is empirically unrealistic.[9] I shall return to Wolff's reasons for hesitating to accept his own philosophical anarchist conclusions in a moment. Godwin, in his *Enquiry Concerning Political Justice*, was not so timid. Godwin's theory is extremely interesting for any discussion of political obligation because, like Hobbes' theory, it shows the full implications of one form of adherence to radical, abstract individualism.

Godwin's theory is a mirror image of Hobbes'. He ends where Hobbes begins, with a collection of individuals who each view the world through their own, subjective viewpoint. For Hobbes, the absolute freedom of individual private judgement leads to complete insecurity and arbitrariness; for Godwin, the 'unspeakably beautiful' practice of absolutely free exercise of individual private judgement is the only way to peace (p. 208).[10] Hobbes creates an artificial social union held together by the Sword and reduces 'obligation' to enforced submission and obedience. Godwin relies on reified Reason that speaks identically to each individual and he completely eliminates 'obligation' along with all other social relationships. Social institutions and social relationships, Godwin argues, merely stand in the way of individual judgement by preventing individuals seeing things as they really are.[11] Unhindered by governments, and other social institutions such as promising, each individual will be able to decide for herself what ought to be done and individuals' judgements will coincide. Reason will speak to all in a single voice because, in the absence of social institutions, reality will stand revealed in all its transparency.

Godwin's objections to the practice of promising are similar to his objections to political institutions. Promising is 'absolutely considered, an evil' (p. 218). It may occasionally be necessary to make a promise in order not to mislead other people about one's intentions, but a defence of necessity in specific cases does not detract from the essential evil of the practice itself. The evils of promising are twofold: first, promising binds future conduct and thus rules out further individual judgement as information and circumstances change. Secondly, promising encourages individuals to act from 'a precarious and temporary motive' (p. 219). It distracts attention from the consequences of particular actions, and hence obscures their intrinsic merits. If the individual judges that an action ought to be performed (and Godwin saw this judgement as a utilitarian calculation) then a promise adds nothing; it merely clouds the moral worth, or otherwise, of the judgement itself. Political institutions function in the same way to prevent individuals seeing things as they really are. For example, they give an appearance of permanence to opinions that prevail at their inception and thus cause the stagnation of judgement. Laws, like obligations, bind future conduct and, being general in form, can take no account of the fact that each case is unique and should be judged, according to Reason, on its own merits. Moreover, political assemblies impose a 'factitious unanimity' on their members. Decisions have to be reached in which all the members must acquiesce, thus pretending that they are something more than a collection of individuals, each with their own opinions. Deliberation has to be cut short by a vote and everyone, if their efforts are not to be for nothing, has to see themselves as 'obliged' to carry out the decision: 'Nothing can more directly contribute to the depravation of the human understanding and character' (p. 547).

Properly, according to Godwin, there are no obligations, only actions that ought to be performed, or refrained from; nor is there any political authority, only a coincidence of individual judgements that certain things ought to be done. Godwin's individuals, unlike those who enter a social contract, are 'bound to nothing'. If an individual joins in a 'common deliberation', he is, 'when the deliberation is over, ... as much disengaged as ever' (p. 234). This is not to say that he will never act with his fellows; they may independently have arrived at the same judgement as to the right course of action. Godwin also allows that individuals may sometimes defer to the judgements of an authority on a particular matter; this he calls 'authority' that depends 'upon the confidence of him with whom it prevails' (p. 242). This deference should, however, be rarely given, or it may tip over into a misplaced 'confidence' in alleged superiors who make judgements for others, and so inculcate those 'slavish feelings that shrink up the soul' (p. 232). This form of obedience is a greater source 'of degradation and depravity' than if the individual bows to political authority out of fear of the sanctions for disobedience. Here Godwin anticipates Wolff's 'denial' of the authority of the state. Wolff recognizes that there are many reasons for compliance, but these are irrelevant providing that the claims of the state are subjectively denied a 'binding moral force'.[12] Similarly, Godwin argued almost two hundred years ago that the individual who obeys solely to avoid punishment, 'may reserve, in its most essential sense, his independence. He may be informed in judgement, ... and suffer his understanding neither to be seduced nor confounded' (p. 141).

Godwin was confident that the philosophical anarchist 'denial' of authority and obligation could be put into practice. Through discussion and education, and the example of sincerity and frankness, individuals will become enlightened and develop an appreciation of the evils of social institutions and social cooperation. Godwin ruled out a sudden revolutionary change as this would not be based on the necessary development of individual understanding. As a transitional measure he advocated a system of 'juries', within small political communities or 'parishes', the juries dealing with individual offenders and disputes over property. He expected that disputes between parishes would be rare and that 'the obvious principles of convenience' would soon suggest a settlement (p. 546). A 'national assembly' might occasionally be necessary to adjudicate in such matters, but it would not be a permanent body. At first, all these institutions would exercise political 'authority' but, in time, Godwin expected that they would merely issue 'invitations' to individuals to cooperate in executing their verdicts, and, eventually, all political institutions and cooperation would wither away.

Abstract individualism rests on heroic assumptions. In Godwin's case he assumes that individual moral judgement can be exercised in complete absence of inter-subjective theoretical categories and communal relationships. The argument of the *Enquiry* implies that that which can be thought can be put into practice. Because it is possible to imagine an individual abstracted from social life, yet endowed with Reason and a capacity for moral judgement, Godwin also assumes that, given a sufficient period of education and social and political change, those individuals could actually exist, with their social past 'stored', as it were, within the consciousness of each one. They would exist largely in isolation and yet, on occasions, emerge, inspect reality and make an individual judgement that would coincide with judgements and Reason of others.

Godwin's theory has some extremely charming aspects, but they cannot hide the philosophically and sociologically bizarre consequences of radical individualism taken to one of its extremes. Everything, except their own judgements, and actions that flow immediately and unhindered from them, is foreign to one of Godwin's individuals. Even the individual's own physical needs or freely created relationships appear as impediments. A solitary individual, Godwin writes, is prevented from executing his judgements 'in compliance with his necessities, or his frailties' (p. 758). The evils of social cooperation are much worse, but technological progress will enable individuals to do many things for themselves in the future that now require the help of others. Godwin expects that concerts and plays will cease to be performed; what enlightened individual would want to mouth the words or play the compositions of another? Eventually, the individual will come to see society as 'not a necessary of life, but a luxury, innocent and enviable, in which he joyfully indulges' (p. 761). At this point, however, there is no 'society' for them to indulge in. Godwin relies on a reified Reason to link his individuals together but this cannot take the place of the social relationships he has wished away.

Once again, the impossibility of distinguishing between institutions in various dimensions of social life from within an abstractly individualist perspective is demonstrated. Godwin treats promising as just as much a constraint and impediment, and just as mystifying, as the laws of the state. It is worth emphasizing that Godwin ends by depriving his individuals of the means of transcending their own subjectivity. They have no social means of acting on their judgements and thus must remain totally immersed in their own assessments of what 'ought' to be done. The creative moral and social capacities of individuals are meaningless treated in the abstract; they presuppose, and, in practice, can only be exercised and developed as a part of social relationships including relationships of obligation.

A tacit realization of the peculiar conclusion of philosophical anarchism seems to underlie Wolff's equivocations about the 'just state'. In the last part of *In Defence of Anarchism*, Wolff offers some 'deeper philosophical reasons' why he is unwilling to accept the 'negative results' of his argument; the social world, unlike the natural world, is not 'irreducibly *other*'. Wolff is thus implicitly arguing against Godwin when he says that the state is 'no more than the totality of the beliefs, expectations, habits, and interacting roles of its members and subjects. ... The state, ... cannot be ineradicably *other*'.[13] In other words, instead of arguing that all authority is illegitimate, Wolff is now moving to the opposite theoretical extreme and putting forward a version of the conceptual argument; the state is no more than the association of its members and so necessary to them, so there is no problem about its authority. Wolff also suggests that there might be a practical solution to the problem of authority; political institutions must be decentralized and based on 'voluntary compliance' (although he may be arguing that a system based on 'voluntary compliance' does not involve authority at all). Curiously, Wolff does not appear to see anything odd in an 'anarchism' that proclaims the necessity of the state. The central argument of anarchism is precisely that the state, including the liberal democratic state, is inherently 'other', and so its claim to authority can never be justified.

Anarchists, philosophical or otherwise, it will be objected at this point, make a much larger claim than this. Like Wolff, they argue that all political authority, not just that of the state, is illegitimate. It is true that anarchist writings are full of statements to this effect. Kropotkin, for example, writes that 'anarchism ... works to destroy authority in all its aspects'.[14] Such statements are usually taken at face value. Flathman, for instance, criticizing Pitkin's comments on 'authority', argues that the state of nature in Hobbes' and Locke's theories provides an example of individuals living together without authority, and he asks 'what else have anarchists been putting forward as an ideal?'.[15] But, as I have shown, any social relationships existing in Hobbes' radically individualist natural condition are likely to be based on force and power, not authority, and Locke's state of nature, with its father-rulers and capitalist economy, would certainly not find favour with anarchists. Nor is it self-evident that the anarchist ideal does involve an absence of authority; not, that is, if anarchism is seen as a political theory and not merely as a variety of philosophical scepticism.

The political theory of anarchism is not a theory of the chaos with which 'anarchy' is popularly equated, but a theory of a specific form of socio-political organization that is, as it must be, ordered and rule-governed. Anarchists have usually been political activists and popular pamphleteers and not concerned with precise conceptual distinctions. They have tended to treat 'authority' as a synonym for 'authoritarian', and so have identified 'authority' with hierarchical power structures, especially those of the state. Nevertheless, their practical proposals and some of their theoretical discussions present a different picture. Kropotkin calls anarchism the 'no-government system of socialism',[16] but on one occasion he also distinguishes 'government' and the 'state'. He writes that 'it seems to me that in State and government we have two concepts of a different order'.[17] Unfortunately, Kropotkin does not pursue this distinction, but it suggests that one anarchist, at least, did not totally reject political authority. This conclusion is also suggested by the social and political changes advocated by Kropotkin. He argued that abolition of the political institutions of the state would allow 'mutual aid' to become the ordering principle of socio-political life. His discussion of this principle presents similar difficulties to the recent philosophically sophisticated discussions of cooperation, reciprocity and obligation. In part, Kropotkin's claim can be seen as a version of the conceptual argument: 'the practice of mutual aid ... [has] created the very conditions of society ...'.[18] He also used 'mutual aid' to refer to actual historical examples of cooperative institutions based on the voluntary agreement of the members, and it is the principle of free agreement that will govern an anarchist socio-political order. However, as I have argued, in political life self-assumed obligation and authority presuppose such 'free agreement'. Kropotkin's sketch of the internal organization of the communes that will replace the state is significant here. Kropotkin envisages

142

'committees' that will look after such matters as housing or trade, and he writes that,

> it is apparent that all these committees will perform some of the actual or possible functions of the present-day government, but it is no less apparent that they will not at all resemble the present-day government.[19]

There is no need, however, to move outside the social contract tradition to find a political theorist who argues that the political institutions that give expression to the liberal ideal of individual freedom and equality 'will not at all resemble the present-day government'. The social contract tradition of argument is not merely the *liberal* contract tradition, although most discussions about political obligation are conducted as if it were. Contract theory also includes Rousseau's *democratic* social contract, which, in both form and consequences, stands opposed to the liberal version of the contract story. Rousseau's theory does not 'deny' political authority, but it does deny that the authority of the liberal state can be justified by voluntarist arguments. Rousseau asks a dramatically different question from his liberal counterparts. He does not inquire how the ideal of self-assumed obligation can be made to appear compatible with the institutions of the liberal state. Instead he poses a radical question that has all but disappeared from contemporary discussions of political obligation: what kind of political system gives expression to the political practice of self-assumed obligation; or, how can citizens actually assume their political obligations for themselves?

Rousseau's True State of Nature

The contract theories of Hobbes, Locke and Rousseau are frequently 'compared and contrasted' by political theorists, but Rousseau's arguments are all too often seen through liberal democratic spectacles. They are treated as if he were discussing the same contract as his liberal predecessors, and as if his picture of the state of nature, and his concept of 'consent', differed from their's only in detail. It would be very odd if this were so, for Rousseau denounces the liberal social contract as an illegitimate fraud, and argues that the characteristics of the possessive individuals of the liberal state of nature are corrupt, vicious, and appropriate only to individuals who believe that they are free but who, in reality, are in 'chains'. In one sense, it is suprising that more attention has not been paid to Rousseau's arguments about obligation, because his contract sets up precisely the horizontal relationship between citizens implied by the argument that political obligation is owed primarily to fellow citizens. The difficulty for contemporary theorists, however, is that Rousseau also shows that such a conception of political obligation cannot be reconciled with the institutions of the liberal democratic state.

Nor are Rousseau's arguments compatible with the attempt to abstract individuals from the market economy and the liberal state, and to present them in a 'natural' condition. The characteristics and social relationships must therefore be seen as ahistorical, timeless, or as unchanging. The need for the liberal social contract is explained by reference to human 'nature', and 'natural' possessive relationships, which remain constant after the contract is concluded, although now regulated and constrained. In contrast, Rousseau discusses individuals in the context of actual social relationships. He argues that individual characteristics and social relations are interrelated and mutually reinforcing, and that both develop together through the same historical process. Allegedly 'natural' attributes are nothing of the sort. Rousseau's account of the state of nature includes a conjectural history of its development that forms a striking alternative to Locke's history. With great 'dialectical ingenuity' Rousseau traces the stages of the mutual interaction of human consciousness and the social institutions of civil society.[20] Rousseau postulates two great transformations of human consciousness or human nature. The course of the first transformation is charted from the emergence of consciousness itself, from the latent potentialities of the animals that inhabit the true state of nature, to its development into the corrupt, competitive and possessive conciousness that helps create the conditions for the liberal social contract. The second transformation is a possibility for the future; it will begin when free and equal individuals create a democratic political order based on self-assumed political obligation.

Rousseau's conjectural history of the state of nature in the *Discourse on the Origin and Foundations of Inequality* is divided into two parts. In the 'First Part' Rousseau is concerned with the conception of an 'individual' and what this implies. In the 'Second Part' he traces the social development of individuals. Rousseau's history contains many references to empirical matters, both about animals and great historical advances such as the invention of agriculture and metallurgy, but this does not mean that he should be read as attempting to write an actual history of human development. Rather his account forms a logical or rhetorical sequence, the aim of which is to enable us 'to judge our present state correctly' (p. 93).[21] We can, in Rousseau's famous phrase, 'begin by setting all the facts aside' (especially the 'facts' as presented in religious accounts of human origin), for the task is 'to clarify the nature of things [not] to show their true origin' (p. 103). Such an investigation will show just how much of bourgeois civil society is due to social development, not nature, and so cannot be justified by liberal appeals to natural law and natural rights. Once this clarification has been completed it is possible to understand the character of our 'present state' of liberal society, and why its inhabitants are in 'chains'; enchained by bonds 'justified' by the liberal social contract. The conjectural history also provides the necessary basis for understanding the character of a new socio-political order in which actual, substantive freedom and equality is maintained through the free creation of political authority and political obligation by individuals themselves.

Rousseau 'it must be emphasised ... was *not* a liberal and individualistic thinker'.[22] For Rousseau, the state of nature, in the true sense, does not contain 'individuals' at all, but animals of different kinds, some of which are potentially human individuals. In the first part of the *Discourse*, Rousseau criticizes the attempt to abstract individuals from their social relationships and portray them in a social or 'natural' condition. Theorists, he argues, in

speaking continually of need, avarice, oppression, desires, and pride, have carried over to the state of nature ideas they had acquired in society: they spoke about savage man and they described civil man (p. 102).

Rousseau's reference to 'savages' here is misleading since the theorists he is criticizing intended the inhabitants of the state of nature to be perfectly familiar to their readers, not foreign savages (they were not 'natural' because they were 'primitive'). However, Rousseau is correct to emphasize that the alledgedly 'natural' characteristics are those of individuals in civil society. In a true 'state of nature', Rousseau argues, individuals could not exist, nor could all the concepts and relationships, summed up under the heading the 'laws of nature', be present. He criticizes natural law theorists both for contradicting each other and for assuming, in their accounts of the laws and the social contract, powers of reasoning on the part of 'natural' individuals which depend upon 'enlightenment which only develops with great difficulty and in very few people in the midst of society itself' (p. 94). Genuinely 'natural' human creatures would lack all the capacities required to understand such concepts as 'law'—or 'obligation'. Rousseau's true state of nature, like Hobbes' natural condition, contains no obligations, but the reason for this emptiness is very different. In Hobbes' state of nature relationships of obligation always remain a possibility, even though it is very unlikely that completely possessive individuals will ever enter into them. In Rousseau's true state of nature obligations are absent because none of the species of animals can understand the idea of an 'obligation'.

Human animals are distinguished from other animals because they have the potential to develop into 'individuals'. Before that potential is realized, members of the human species differ among themselves in exactly the same way as other animals, because of natural differences in physical strength, agility, health, and so forth. Again, like the other animals, their life is based solely on their physical needs and sensations, and their desires will never go beyond their physical requirements. Rousseau argues that the needs of the human animals will be satisfied by each one largely in isolation from its fellows. The sexes will have fleeting encounters, and infants will leave their mothers as soon as they are capable of shifting for themselves (it should be noted that males and females are implied to be equal in strength and ability to protect themselves). The inhabitants of the true state of nature will also probably lack the ability to recognize each other and, both as a consequence of, and a condition of, their isolated existence, they will have no language. They live entirely within a world of their own sensations and lack the capacities for thought, judgement and knowledge.[23] Thus the intentions, selfconsciousness and relationships imputed to individuals in the natural condition by the liberal theorists are literally inconceivable to the human animals in Rousseau's true state of nature.

There are, however, two 'principles' to be found in the state of nature that are 'anterior to reason' and to sociability (p. 95). The first principle is that of self-preservation, and the second the sentiment of pity or compassion for members of one's own species. Both are entirely natural and common to all the species of animals in the state of nature. Neither of these 'principles' has anything in common with the 'natural rights' of the liberal contract theorists. Nothing could be further from Rousseau's 'principle' of self-preservation than the urge which drives Hobbes' individuals. Rousseau's human animals have no consciousness of 'self' to move them ceaselessly to strive for self-esteem and mastery over others. Moreover, 'an animal will never know what it is to die', so that even Hobbes' most basic passion of fear of death is absent (p. 116). Although it might metaphorically be said that the animals have the 'right' to all that they need to keep themselves alive, this does not lead to war, nor to accumulation of property. The true state of nature is basically peaceful because the animals rarely come into contact with each other. Occasionally, a stronger animal may seize food from a weaker one, but this is seen not 'as an insult which must be punished', rather as a 'natural event' (p. 134; 222). Food or shelter will not be viewed as 'property' since they will not have 'the slightest notion of thine and mine' (p. 133). These languageless animals will have no moral or social notions at all; neither 'rights' nor 'wrongs' mean anything to them. If they are naturally 'good' this is only because morality has yet to develop, together with the 'vicious' characteristics of individuals who can also be immoral.

There is no conception of 'obligation' in Rousseau's true state of nature and similarly, there is no idea of 'authority' or 'power'. None of the animals tries to govern another or to force another into servitude; such relationships of inequality and obedience develop only when social life itself has developed and taken a certain form. Rousseau asks:

> What is the use of wit for people who do not speak, and ruse for those who have no dealings? I hear it always repeated that the stronger will oppress the weak. But let someone explain to me what is meant by this word oppression. ... A man might well seize the fruits another has gathered, ... but how will he ever succeed in making himself obeyed? And what can be the chains of dependence among men who possess nothing? (p. 139).

In the true state of nature 'to be obeyed' is meaningless. The oppression of, or the exercise of authority over, one individual or group by another can take place only when the human potentialities of the animals of the state of nature have developed and they are living sociably together. Social life, selfconsciousness, language and morality all develop together and are all necessary to each other; when they have emerged it is possible for inequality and relationships of authority and obligation to be established. Unlike the other animals, humans have the potential to act not merely on the basis of instinct or sensation but from rational deliberation and choice, and on the basis of moral principles; that is, they have the potential for what Rousseau calls 'perfectability'. They can create a collective life together, but in so doing, they can also undermine their freedom and equality and wrap the chains of inequality and forced dependence or servitude round each other. The conjectural history shows how these chains are forged and how the liberal social contract, made between rich and poor, enables these relationships to be presented as legitimate.

The Fraudulent Liberal Social Contract

A major distinction between Rousseau's social contract theory and the theories of liberal writers is that Rousseau, in his conjectural history of the state of nature, is able to explain how the liberal social contract comes about, and how it is presented as something other than it really is: namely, a device of the rich to secure and strengthen their dominant social position. Liberal theorists, in contrast, cannot recognize that there might be an alternative to their version of the social contract story. Because the liberal contract is an hypothetical abstraction, entered irto by 'naturally' free and equal individuals separated from their actual social relationships, it can only be presented by liberal theorists as *the* contract, derived from reason and nature and to the advantage of all. Liberal theorists cannot admit that their contract is a hypothetical justification of the development of a specific form of consciousness and a specific form of social relationships. Rousseau's conjectural history charts the development of these social relationships and the emergence of the liberal state. He argues that the claim of the liberal theorists that the liberal state is based on political obligation is totally fraudulent.

In liberal theories the passage from the state of nature to civil society is clearly marked: marked by the social contract. In Rousseau's theory matters are not so clear cut. When the liberal social contract is instituted the true state of nature has long since vanished. Human social life has passed through a period that resembles the liberal theorists' state of nature, and that is crucial to Rousseau's argument. In the 'First Part' of the *Discourse*, Rousseau dwells on the difficulties of explaining how the transition from the true state of nature to social life could have come about. He notes, for example, that 'if men needed speech in order to learn to think, they had even greater need of knowing how to think in order to discover the art of speech' (pp. 121–2). How could the animals in the true state of nature ever have made this momentous step and developed human speech and thought? However, Rousseau says that he will leave to others the problem of 'which was most necessary, previously formed society for the institution of languages; or previously invented languages for the establishment of society?' (p. 126). The requirements of human social life all develop together, mutually reinforcing each other. In the 'Second Part' of the *Discourse* Rousseau assumes that this process is underway, and he is able to give an account of the 'different accidents' that have brought individuals to 'the point where we see them'. Although the history is conjectural, Rousseau states that his conclusions 'will not thereby be conjectural', because they follow from the understanding that has been gained of the present condition of social relationships (pp. 140–1).

The 'Second Part' of the *Discourse* opens with the famous proclamation that the 'true founder' of civil society was the man who first fenced in a piece of land and said, '*this is mine* and found people simple enough to believe him' (p. 141). Civil society and private property thus develop together, but there is a long process of development between the action of this founder and the emergence of 'civil society', in the sense in which the term is used in liberal theory. 'Civil', or bourgeois society, with its liberal state, requires the development of the division of labour and exchange necessary for the capitalist market economy and a specific consciousness or sense of self and others. When this stage of development is reached the 'epoch of the first revolution', the happiest time of human history, has come and gone (p. 146). This revolution, which marks the disappearance of the true state of nature, occurs as a result of the evolution of hunting and fishing and population increase. Consciousness evolves too, and human 'individuals' begin to appear and then settle down in family groupings.

The dialectic of social development is then properly underway. These 'little societies' are united by bonds of 'reciprocal affection and freedom', that is, moral notions are developed. As the families begin to associate together, new needs come into existence and a new sense of 'self' appears. Individuals begin to want to be valued by others for their abilities, which is 'the first step toward inequality and, at the same time, toward vice'. The seeds of *amour propre*, of self-interest, vanity and competition, are sown, replacing the unselfconscious *amour de soi*, or instinct for self-preservation, of the true state of nature (p. 147; 149). Nevertheless, this stage of history is the 'happiest and most durable epoch. ... the best for man, ... he must have come out of it only by some fatal accident, ...' (p. 151). This time was the best because individuals still retained, though already in a socially transformed fashion, much of their natural independence and equality. (Or, at least, this is so for males; I shall return to the position of women later on.) At this period families are virtually self-sufficient and individuals are content with very little. The 'fatal accident' that irrevocably disturbs this balance between nature and society is the invention of metallurgy and agriculture, which leads to transformations in social relationships and human 'nature' that culminate in civil society and the liberal social contract.

Rousseau's conjectural history follows Locke's quite closely from this point, but his conclusions are very different. Once agriculture is established, inequalities arising from natural differences in strength and ability are accentuated and, eventually, displaced by *social* inequalities, especially inequalities of property. Rousseau writes that:

> from the moment one man needed the help of another, as soon as they observed that it was useful for a single person to have provisions for two, equality disappeared, property was introduced, labor became necessary; ... slavery and misery were soon to germinate and grow with the crops (pp. 151–2).

Rousseau agrees with Locke that labour is the only basis for property. Originally, natural inequalities led some individuals to accumulate more than others, but the size of the disparities was naturally limited. Once agriculture is established, and all the land is appropriated, social inequalities continue to grow until Locke's two classes, or in Rousseau's terminology, the rich and the poor, are established and mutually at war.[24] As property is accumulated so consciousness and a possessive morality are further developed, and desires continually expand. Locke does not explain in his conjectural history why 'consent' to money leads to an expansion of desires, but Rousseau links increasing inequality of property to an increase in interdependence and the development of *amour propre* and competition, which stifle the natural sentiment of compassion. Individuals' social position no longer depends on their natural abilities but on how they can present themselves to others. In turn, their social appearance depends on how much property they can accumulate: 'it was necessary to appear to be other than what one in fact was. To be and to seem to be became two altogether different things' (p. 155). Property is crucial because 'my possession of material goods can overcome my lack of natural gifts'.[25] As social relationships change so 'the soul and human passions, ... change their nature'; society becomes 'an assemblage of artificial men and factitious passions which are the work of all these new relations and have no true foundation in nature' (p. 178).

As the two classes of the rich and the poor are consolidated, so independence is completely swept away. The division of labour, the expansion of needs and exchange, ensure that everyone is dependent on everyone else, and in the worst possible sense; everyone tries to enhance their own self-interest and self-esteem at the expense of others. The rich depend upon the services of the poor; the poor cannot manage without the charity of the rich. Once all the land has been appropriated the property owners can increase their holdings only at the expense of someone else, and those without property must either work for, or steal from, the rich: 'Between the right of the stronger and the right of the first occupant there arose a perpetual conflict ... the most horrible state of war' (p. 157). It is at this stage of social development, when the 'vices' of civil society are fully revealed, that the liberal social contract is instituted. Rousseau agrees completely with Hobbes and Locke that the contract is required because of the state of war, but he disagrees about its foundation and its consequences. Both Hobbes and Locke, in different ways, argued that the state of war was a 'natural' outcome of conditions in the state of nature, and that all individuals, no matter what their social position, could independently use their reason and appreciate its advantage to everyone. The argument of Rousseau's conjectural history is that the liberal contract has no basis in 'nature'; it is a result of a particular form of social development, and far from securing all individuals' 'natural rights' merely stabilizes inequality and gives an appearance of legitimacy to the dominance of some over others.

The liberal social contract is in fact a deliberate political contrivance. It is a stratagem of the rich to secure and maintain their own position of socio-economic dominance through political means. The rich use the argument about security and protection as a superb piece of political mystification to procure the agreement of the poor to an arrangement that will ensure that they remain subordinate. The rich say to the poor:

> Let us institute regulations of justice and peace to which all are obliged to conform, which make an exception of no one, and which compensate in some way for the caprices of fortune by equally subjecting the powerful and the weak to mutual duties.

The poor are easily seduced by this plan. They have too much 'avarice and ambition to be able to do without masters for long'. Therefore, the liberal social contract is concluded: 'All ran to meet their chains thinking they secured their freedom; ...' (p. 159).

Rousseau defends the idea of a social contract as the legitimate foundation, or 'origin', of government, against arguments in favour of conquest or patriarchy. However, this does not mean that he is, after all, agreeing that the liberal contract establishes justified political authority and political obligation. It follows from the ideal of individual freedom and equality that a social contract, or, more broadly, voluntary agreement, is the *only* possible basis on which political authority can rest.

The agreement, however, has to be of a certain kind if it is to establish genuine political obligation. The liberal contract 'changed a clever usurpation into an irrevocable right', but this is a 'right' of the same spurious status as the 'right' of the strongest (p. 160). The liberal contract covers the inequalities and servitude of civil society in a facade of formal equality and freedom. Natural independence is exchanged for formally equal subjection to the civil laws of the state. Rich and poor alike are formally equal before the liberal state, which creates an *appearance* of political right and obligation, but it makes the contract no less a deception and no less illegitimate.

It is true that the poor agree to the contract, but Rousseau argues that agreement or consent, taken in isolation, does not in itself create proper obligation. If it did, an individual foolish enough to consent to a contract which placed herself or himself in slavery would be validly bound, purely by virtue of consent. For Rousseau, the form, content and conditions of the contract, not merely agreement in the abstract, are crucial. This constitutes another important difference between Rousseau and liberal contract theorists. In a valid contract, Rousseau argues, the freedom and equality of both of its participants must be recognized, or, to put this another way, the contract must be reciprocal. Rousseau writes that, 'it would be difficult to show the validity of a contract that would obligate only one of the parties, where all would be given to one side and nothing to the other' (p. 166). In the *Social Contract* he says that the action of anyone who made such an 'agreement' is illegitimate and void (indeed such a person must be mad).

Similarly, the social contract cannot be abstracted from the conditions in which it is made and its real aim ignored. Liberal theorists of political obligation insist that formal equality under the law is what counts; once the contract is instituted then social inequality can be disregarded. Rousseau argues that the private and political spheres of social life cannot be separated in this fashion. The liberal contract is made precisely to stabilize and reinforce socio-economic inequality—that is, the market economy and the liberal state must be seen as part of a single social order. Merely because the rich called this regulation 'just', and the poor were simple enough to agree, does not justify these relationships. Indeed, inequality now appears to be rightful and the laws which maintain it are seen as imposing obligations, so that the deleterious social and individual effects of civil society will be promoted and enhanced. Rousseau concludes that the liberal contract 'gave new fetters to the weak and new forces to the rich' (p. 160). The contract is fraudulent because it is presented as being to the benefit of everyone but the poor actually lose from it. They can no longer exercise the natural 'right' of the strongest by seizing the property of the rich which is now secured by the laws of the liberal state; their propertylessness is institutionalized. Moreover, the reason for inequality has been obscured. The rich have persuaded the poor that formal civil equality will compensate them for 'caprices of fortune'. The dominance of the rich is thus doubly secured. The liberal social contract is accepted at face value as establishing rules of political right, and the poor now also believe that social inequality results from 'fortune', not the logic of the development of civil society.

The liberal contract is freely entered into, but the agreement is procured by deception. It is a contract that gives 'all to one side' and is based on inequality; its function is to maintain and foster that inequality by legitimizing political regulation by the liberal state. No such contract can establish justice or political right; it cannot give rise to political obligation or justify the authority of the liberal state. Rousseau, it must be admitted, does not explicitly spell out this conclusion, but

> to do so would have been extremely dangerous at a time when writers to whom the authorities took exception could be imprisoned without trial. However, the material by which the reader could draw his own conclusion was all to hand.[26]

Rousseau's Participatory Social Contract

It has sometimes been suggested that Rousseau advocated a 'return to nature'. The absurdity of this suggestion is revealed by Rousseau's account of the true state of nature, and he expressly rejected such an idea:

> What! must we destroy societies, annihilate thine and mine, and go back to live in forests with bears? A conclusion in the manner of my adversaries, which I prefer to anticipate rather than leave them the shame of drawing it (p. 201).

The *Discourse* looks backward and traces the social process through which individuals voluntarily enchain themselves. Having gained this understanding it is then possible to look forward to a new political order and another transformation of human nature or consciousness. In the *Social Contract* Rousseau shows 'men models of what they could be, if only they were to abandon their chains'.[27] The necessary conditions for casting off the chains and reconstituting political life have been established in the conjectural history. Individuals cannot return to the first 'happy epoch' of independence and equality, but they now know why it was 'happy' and that it is necessary to reinstate these two conditions, though in a new socially transformed fashion: 'man's innocent ignorance, ... cannot be regained. The most modern man could conceive of, ... is a new set of circumstances for a new independence'.[28]

The argument of the *Social Contract* shows that 'the most' that can be conceived is, in fact, a very great deal. Rousseau wrote 'what more certain foundation can obligation among men have, than the free agreement of him who obliges himself'.[29] If there is to be genuine free agreement, a valid social contract, and justified political obligation, then the material conditions of social life have to be transformed, as well as political institutions and the consciousness of individuals. Rousseau's democratic social contract, like the liberal contract, is hypothetical, but it is an hypothesis of a very different kind. The liberal contract serves to justify social relationships and political institutions that already exist; Rousseau's contract is to provide an actual foundation for a participatory political order of the future. Liberal theorists provide a continued justification for the authority of the liberal state through hypothetical voluntarist arguments; Rousseau's political order is kept in being through the free creation of political obligations by its members. I have noted that Rousseau asks the radical question: what is necessary to establish a political association based on self-assumed obligation? He also asks another crucially important question, namely how can citizens decide for themselves that they are assuming genuine 'obligations'? In other words, Rousseau's theory offers an answer to the repeated charge that consent theory, or self-assumed obligation, is entirely arbitrary and so can provide no secure foundation for political life.

The liberal social contract, as I have shown, is a two-stage contract. One way of reading the *Social Contract* is as a rejection of the liberal claim that the second stage of the agreement is necessary. Rousseau's social contract, like the first part of the liberal contract, is an agreement between individuals to establish a political association or community. For Rousseau, as the argument of the *Discourse* establishes, the second stage of the liberal contract is no different from a 'contract' to sell oneself into slavery; to agree to obey a few representatives who decide upon the individual's political obligation is to deny that individuals are free and equal. A promise to obey is a very special kind of commitment which puts the individual into a position of voluntary heteronomy, and thus contradicts the liberal ideal of individual freedom and equality. This is why Rousseau thinks that no one making such an agreement 'could be in his right mind' (p. 54).[30] (Recall Hobbes and an agreement that placed life in danger.) Rousseau argues that 'if a people promises simply and solely to obey, it dissolves itself by that very pledge' (p. 70). The comparison with the first stage of the liberal contract can be misleading because, as I argued in some detail in my discussion of Locke's theory, the first stage, for liberal theorists, is purely formal. It is formally required because individuals must 'leave' the state of nature and form a new political association, but it is the second stage that is vital. Rousseau's contract, in contrast, forms the actual basis for the new political order and has substantive content and consequences. It is more than a formal pact of association; it constitutes the members of the association as a sovereign body or as their own participatory legislative assembly: 'A people, since it is subject to laws, ought to be the author of them' (p. 83).

Rousseau's contracting individuals enter into a reciprocal commitment with each other not just as individuals, but also to constitute their new status as legislators. Each individual is bound 'first, as a member of the sovereign body in relation to individuals, and secondly as a member of the state [political association] in relation to the sovereign' (p. 62). They enter into a double-sided agreement, collectively to make laws for themselves as citizens, and to obey those laws as individuals. Thus Rousseau is able to claim that the 'essence of the political body lies in the union of freedom and obedience', and that 'each individual, while uniting himself with the others, obeys no one but himself, and remains as free as before' (p. 138; 60). Strictly speaking, this last statement is not quite accurate, since each individual obeys not merely himself but himself as part of a politically authoritative body. Each citizen forms part of the political authority which governs the political association. He also assumes the political obligation that he has helped create with his fellow citizens. Political obligation, in Rousseau's political association, is thus owed by citizens to each other (they *are* the association) and it binds them in a horizontal relationship together.

The consequence of Rousseau's contract is not the formal equality of political subjects of liberal theory, but a substantive equality of active citizens who are political decision-makers, or the sovereign, in a participatory political association. The distinction between 'sovereignty' and 'government' is central to Rousseau's argument, but it has not always been taken into account by his commentators, who have thus further blurred the distinction between Rousseau's democratic contract and its liberal counterpart. Rousseau's 'government' is a purely administrative body. He argues that it will be impossible for all citizens to execute political decisions (a system Rousseau calls 'democracy'); they need a smaller body to perform that task. It has been argued that the 'existence of a government is in ... sharp contradiction with Rousseau's general principles of social philosophy', but this is to assume that 'government' is a liberal democratic form of government.[31] Rousseau rejects the alienation to representatives of the right of political decision-making that is the essence of liberal government. There can be no contract between the people and the government: 'a contract which stipulates between the two parties the conditions under which the one undertakes to command and the other to obey. ... is a strange way of contracting' (p. 144). Rather, the sovereign assembly elects representatives to carry out certain tasks on its behalf.[32]

Rousseau's elected representatives, or government, are not 'representatives' in the liberal sense; they have no independent political authority. Rousseau defines 'government' as

> an intermediary body established between the subjects and the sovereign for their mutual communication ... whose power the sovereign can limit, modify and resume at pleasure, since the alienation of such a right would be incompatible with the nature of the social body and contrary to the purpose of the social union (p. 102).

Rousseau's representatives are thus agents or delegates of the political association. They can act on behalf of citizens but they cannot decide for them: political authority remains in the hands of the assembled citizens. They do not consent to the decisions of their representatives, rather the acts of representatives must be subject to the authority of citizens. 'Representatives' in this sense are compatible with self-assumed political obligation: 'the holders of the executive power are not the people's masters but its officers; ... the people can appoint them and dismiss them as it pleases' (p. 146).

Rousseau's social contract is not a hypothetical agreement which is assumed to be ratified subsequently by hypothetical or inferred consent. It is kept in being, and regularly renewed, through the decisions of the citizens in the participatory political community. Despite the fact that Rousseau's conception of the relationship of citizens to the social contract, to each other and to their decisions or laws presents such a striking contrast to the familiar liberal conception of political life, it is often claimed by his commentators that Rousseau's aim was to make law, not men, supreme. Certainly, Rousseau wished to eliminate 'masters', and the relationships of dependence that the term implies, but this is not to say that he was endorsing the liberal idea of the 'rule of law'. Nor is it the case that Rousseau wished his form of law to 'eliminate, not merely limit, political authority'; if he is not an advocate of liberal constitutional government, neither is he a philosophical anarchist.[33] Rousseau's political theory has a place both for law and political authority, but in a democratic, not a liberal sense. He does not abstract 'law' from the wider social relationships of which it is a part, and then claim that the mere existence of civil law (or the liberal state) is sufficient to show that political obligation exists. In Rousseau's theory it is 'legislative will, and not law itself, [that] is supreme'.[34] Or, to make this point in another way, it is not the rule of law *per se* that orders socio-political life, but the critical judgements and decisions of citizens.

It is this feature of Rousseau's theory that immediately provokes the charge of arbitrariness. If legislative will, or the judgement of citizens themselves, is supreme in political life, then, it will be argued, there is nothing to prevent citizens acting in a completely arbitrary manner. Individual whim and caprice are, as Hegel claimed, enthroned at the heart of Rousseau's theory. It is true that Rousseau places no external limits on the scope of citizens' decision-making. They can, for example, even revoke the social contract itself if they deem it necessary to do so, but this is not to say that there are no constraints at all upon legislative will. Rousseau's famous conception of the 'general will' serves exactly this purpose. It provides Rousseau's citizens with 'a political morality of common good', or a principle of political right by which they can evaluate their own judgements.[35] Rousseau states that 'every authentic act of the general will, binds or favours all the citizens equally' and that the general will 'is an institution in which each necessarily submits himself to the same conditions which he imposes on others' (p. 76). Citizens can thus ascertain whether their own decisions do constitute 'laws', or are in conformity with the general will. It is necessarily true that 'the general will is always rightful and always tends to the public good'; it could not function as a principle of political morality if it were not the case (p. 72). If a decision is a 'law', and thus benefits or burdens all citizens equally, then citizens know that they ought to assume the obligations consequent upon that decision.

I have noted at various points of my argument that a democratic theory of political obligation must include some principle of political right to enable citizens to make such a judgement, just as they are able to decide whether they have good reason to make a promise, and are able to assess whether a promise should be broken. But does Rousseau's general will offer an example of the kind of principle required? Riley has argued that Rousseau took his conception of the general will and political morality from the polities of the ancient world, and these polities were not voluntary associations. Rousseau's theory is therefore based on 'a philosophical paradox of willed non-voluntarism'.[36] Before looking at this specific argument about Rousseau's theory I want to look more closely at the paradox of willed non-voluntarism itself. From certain theoretical perspectives it can appear that the paradox is inevitable if any limitations are placed on the individual's judgement.

For example, for a philosophical anarchist, if the individual really decides freely then no constraints can be admitted; individuals are always superior to their judgements and obligations. Alternatively, a proponent of the conceptual argument will also run up against the paradox, for it will appear that the most the individual can do is to recognize or assent to rules and 'oughts' that seem to exist independently of her judgements. In a recent discussion of consent it is argued that either consent is completely arbitrary or reasons must be offered to justify consenting. If reasons can be offered, then consent ought to be given, it cannot rightfully be refused: 'my obligation is not really voluntary ... I have no justifiable choice but to consent'.[37] The paradox of willed non-voluntarism will appear unavoidable if individuals are separated from their social relationships, for it is then impossible to give due weight to the fact that individuals are, at one and the same time, both superior to and bound by their rules, oughts and obligations. As I have shown in my discussion of the social practice of promising, the practice presupposes constraints on what counts as a 'promise', and criteria that enable individuals to evaluate their commitments at a later date. Similarly, such criteria are implied in the practice of free agreement (or the social contract) and the ideal of social life as a voluntary scheme; the idea of a voluntary association 'always implies placing certain prior limitations in principle, however vague they may be, on what may legitimately be willed'.[38]

Riley does not argue that willed non-voluntarism is inevitable, but that Rousseau's particular conception of the general will provides an example of the paradox. The importance of the ancient world as an inspiration for Rousseau's political theory cannot be denied and, like the ancients, he was concerned with the political virtue of citizens as well as political obligation, a concern to which I shall return shortly. But this is not to say that his conception of political morality is no different from pre-modern ideas. Rousseau, and the other contract theorists, had to answer a problem that is specifically modern: the problem of justifying any claim to political authority when individuals are 'naturally' free and equal. Hence Rousseau, unlike the ancients, had to find a conception of political morality or right that is compatible with political 'obligation', or with voluntarism. Riley argues that Locke's natural law provides such a conception but, as I argued in Chapter 4, for Locke, God's law exists externally to and independently of individuals. It is therefore 'voluntarist' only in the sense that they can 'accept' it, rather as Hegel's citizens can 'accept' the rationality and necessity of the liberal state.

If principles of political right are to be compatible with the ideal of social life as a voluntary scheme, they must be created and agreed to by citizens themselves, and be internally, not externally, related to their political judgements and actions. This is one of the major insights of Rousseau's theory, and it provides an important part of the foundation for any contemporary democratic theory of political obligation. His conception of the general will provides an example of 'willed voluntarism', notwithstanding the importance he attached to the example of the ancient world. The social contract, or the agreement upon a principle of political morality, is made only once. However, because the association is a participatory one, citizens always have the opportunity to reassess their 'beginning'. They do not have to decide anew upon the general will each time they meet, but it is always open to them to amend or change the rules that govern their political association, or to revoke the social contract itself. Citizens are bound by the political obligation and political authority they have created for themselves, but they also remain superior to them; they have created their own rules and they can change them. They are members of a political association who decide themselves on the terms and conditions of membership. It is because principles of political right, and the rules and laws that govern social and political institutions, can provide an internal and voluntarily assumed constraint that (unlike the 'rule of promising') can be amended and revoked, that it makes sense to speak of social life as a voluntary scheme. The realization of this ideal, as Rousseau is well aware, requires radical social and political change. A truly voluntary association is an association of individuals who are substantive, not merely formal, equals. Rousseau's conception of the general will both presupposes the existence of the material conditions necessary for equality and operates to sustain it.

The radical distinction between Rousseau's general will and the purely procedural and external regulation provided by the liberal democratic political method is not always appreciated, and theorists attempt to assimilate the general will to the liberal democratic political method. For example, it is suggested that Rawls' two principles of justice have 'shown how Rousseau's theory of the general will ... can be given a new lease of life'—a lease of life that presents as rational the social inequalities of the capitalist economy and the liberal democratic state, and that offers a doctrine of non-voluntarist political duties![39] Moreover, Rawls' argument that his two principles would be chosen in an hypothetical original position by parties who know nothing of themselves is completely opposed to Rousseau's argument that the general will, in specific socio-economic conditions, would actually be decided upon by people who know all about themselves. In a similar fashion it is claimed that the general will should be discussed 'without reference to any particular political condition, in reference rather to politics in general'.[40] But 'politics in general' assumes that political life can be discussed in the abstract, separated from specific social conditions. This is exactly what Rousseau's critique of liberal theory denies, and it is impossible to understand what he has to say about the general will if it is torn from the context of the material conditions specified in the *Social Contract*.

If Rousseau 'is always able to say what a general will must *exclude*', rather than 'what it *is*', he is nonetheless saying something extremely important.[41] The general will excludes the social and political inequality of civil society, and thus constitutes a rejection of the central liberal claim that these inequalities are compatible with political obligation. Economic equality is central to Rousseau's argument because it provides the necessary material basis for individuals to become and remain free and equal, in the sense of being independent. No independent individual has any reason to call another 'master', and no reason to allow 'obligations' to be imposed upon him. This is not the unselfconscious 'independence of the happy epoch', but a specifically *social* independence that is maintained in the context of a wider interdependence in social and political life. Rousseau does not argue for absolute equality, but a substantive economic equality that is sufficient to maintain the independence of each citizen. He writes that

> laws are always useful to those with possessions and harmful to those who have nothing; from which it follows that the social state is advantageous to men only when all possess something and none has too much (p. 68).

This means that 'no citizen shall be rich enough to buy another and none so poor as to be forced to sell himself' (p. 96). I have looked at the question of what this might mean in contemporary economic terms in my *Participation and Democratic Theory*.

By definition, the 'general will' entails that the benefits and burdens of membership of the political association are shared equally by all citizens. The problem, of course, is why citizens' decisions should conform to the general will; why should they judge according to this standard of political morality? Rousseau's answer is that with independence established, the logic of the participatory process itself has an educative effect, or brings about the second great transformation in human nature. Possessive individualism is transformed into civic virtue, and citizens come to judge according to what Rousseau calls their 'constant wills', rather than from self-interest or *amour propre*. Rousseau states that during participatory democratic voting 'there is no one who does not take that word "each" to pertain to himself' (p. 75). This helps explain how individuals learn to distinguish between their 'private wills' or judgements of self-interest, and their 'constant wills' or judgements about their 'interest' or good as part of the political association as a whole. Because all citizens are independent (or free and equal) there is no reason for anyone to vote for a proposal that puts him at a disadvantage. This is true for every citizen. Thus the only acceptable proposals are those in conformity with the general will. In a situation of independence, each citizen has to think of his own advantage *as a member of the political association*, not as a single individual; he has to think of himself along with everyone else, or in terms of the good of 'each' member of the community. For 'each' member, the maintenance of equality is the only acceptable policy. Thus individuals are gradually educated to think in terms of the general will; they become conscious of themselves, and act politically, as citizens, not only as private individuals.

The participatory formulation of the general will is thus a process that 'forces' constant wills to the fore. Rousseau does not actually use his notorious phrase 'forced to be free' in this context, but he speaks of individuals being 'compelled to act on other principles' than self-interest (p. 64). It has recently been suggested that *forcer d'être libre* should be translated as 'to strengthen to be free', and this does capture the educative effect of political participation.[42] It helps to emphasize that, if citizens are not to fall back into the 'chains' of inequality and servitude, they must judge and act according to their principle of political morality, and that, because this is a large departure from possessive individualist ways of thought and action, they need 'strengthening' to do this. The 'strength' is provided by the transformation of their consciousness that is gradually brought about through the participatory process. The constant will eventually becomes integral to citizens' judgements and actions. This is why Rousseau claims that the citizen is compelled 'to consult his reason rather than study his inclinations' (p. 64).

The reference to benefits and burdens in connection with the general will should not be taken to imply that, despite my criticisms in the previous chapter, there is something to be said for the benefits 'argument' about political obligation. Rousseau's conception of self-assumed political obligation has nothing to do with accepting benefits. If a proposal is judged to be in accordance with the general will, this gives citizens a good reason for voting for it; it gives them a good reason to assume the obligation to do what is required to implement it. It is not the fact that the proposal has been judged rightful, or that it ought to be put into effect, that creates political obligation, but 'an act of the citizens' own'. They create and assume their political obligations through participatory democratic voting. Rousseau's theory allows the conceptual argument about 'membership' and 'fair play' to be put into perspective. The making of the social contract would be meaningless unless those involved understood that they were constituting themselves as members of a political association, and that 'association' necessarily implies a mutuality of restrictions upon its members. The contractors, in other words, understand the meaning of 'membership', 'fair play', and so forth. But they also know that the purpose of the democratic social contract is to give practical expression to their ideal of social life as a voluntary scheme. The conceptual argument is presupposed; the real problem is whether their membership actually enables them to assume their political obligations for themselves and to continue to do so. It is an empirical problem of social and political organization.

The empirical problem includes the question of the conditions which will make it possible for *all* individuals to assume their own obligations. I have deliberately referred to the citizen as 'he' in discussing Rousseau's theory, for his arguments, both in the *Social Contract* and the conjectural history, refer to males only. The transformations of 'human' nature are actually transformations of the attributes of *male* individuals. Rousseau is one of the most male chauvinist political theorists, and his assertions about the respective characters and social roles of men and women provide a stark reminder that radical theorists may confine their argument to one half of humankind. For all the brilliance of Rousseau's critique of liberal theory he therefore shares in the liberal failure to include everyone in the argument for political obligation. For Rousseau, of course, there is no problem about the position of the poor, because he has postulated an economic transformation to eliminate poverty, but all he has to say about female individuals stands in blatant contradiction to the fundamental tenets of his political theory.

Rousseau does not, like Hegel, assume that the physical differences between the sexes can be incorporated into the structure of the political association; nor does his theory imply, like Locke's, that women can be concluded by their fathers or husbands. Rousseau simply excludes women from political life by virtue of their 'natures'. Women can never be educated to become independent citizens of a participatory community; they are, Rousseau asserts, 'naturally' fit only for dependence and servitude. The contrast between Rousseau's treatment of males and females—and his prejudices—are most clearly displayed in Book V of *Emile*, which discusses the education appropriate for Emile's future wife. Emile is educated to take his place as a citizen of the community depicted in the *Social Contract*; he is educated for independence and taught to judge for himself. Sophie is educated to serve and obey Emile. Her education is designed to foster all the 'vices' that Rousseau condemns—in males—in his conjectural history. Women must be educated to please others (i.e. men), and look always to the effect that they have on others; their reputation is all. They must also be educated for obedience: 'woman is made to please and to be in subjection to man', therefore 'they must be trained to bear the yoke from the first, ... and to submit themselves to the will of others'.[43] Emile's tutor tells Sophie that when she married Emile, 'he became your head, it is yours to obey; this is the will of nature'.[44] (Although male commentators can still refer to the

158

'unusual equality of Emile and Sophie in their marriage'—unusual indeed!)[45]

Now, as I noted above, in Rousseau's true state of nature both sexes are held to be equal in their ability to protect themselves; both sexes are naturally independent. Rousseau gives no reason at all why female human animals should not transcend nature and undergo the same social transformations of character, capacities and consciousness as male animals. But they do not. At the stage of the 'happy epoch' Rousseau has already relegated women to a dependent and unequal position in the family.[46] He suddenly, and quite arbitrarily, announces that 'the first difference was established in the way of life of the two sexes, ... Women became more sedentary and grew accustomed to tend the hut and the children, while the man went out to seek their common subsistence'.[47] Women are thus thrust into dependence upon men for their subsistence; their independence disappears and their servitude is then alleged to be a 'natural' fact—by the very same theorist who makes so much of the *social* character of the relationships of civil society, which include those between the sexes. Women are asserted by Rousseau to be such that they cannot gain the self-mastery necessary to develop a 'constant will'; political obligation is irrelevant to them. Moreover, their education emphasizes appearances and purely personal relationships, and women are recommended by Rousseau to use deceit and cunning to gain their desires within the family. The characteristics that are developed mean that women are not merely outside of political life but a permanent threat to it.[48]

In addition, because the life of women is wholly bound up in the family, their influence is a standing temptation to their husbands to falter in their citizenship. The family could become one of the 'sectional associations' which attempt to subvert the formulation of the general will. Rousseau does not consider the family in this light and this is perhaps because he, in effect, separates the family, symbolized by Woman, from political life, notwithstanding his criticisms of liberal theorists for their separation of the private and public spheres. However, there is no good reason for excluding the family from among the groups which can develop their own 'private will' in opposition to the general will. Rousseau states that 'it is imperative that there should be no sectional associations in the state' (p. 73). This is sometimes taken to imply that his political society consists merely of a collection of individuals, yet Rousseau allows for the existence of both families and a government. It is not groups as such to which he objects, but groups which obtain a particular advantage for themselves at the expense of the community.[49] In fact, the government always poses such a threat; if it is to perform its task it must develop a 'consciousness common to its members, ... a will of its own', so the people must always be alert to prevent attempts by the government to usurp their authority. They must assemble more frequently if the government becomes stronger and 'be ready to sacrifice the government to the people and not the people to the government' (p. 106). In order to prevent the development of sectional private wills Rousseau recommends that groups should be as numerous and as equal in power as possible. Rousseau's political association can thus be seen as comprising a plurality of groups, which, like their individual members, are equal and independent: 'These are the only precautions which can ensure that the general will is always enlightened and the people protected from error' (p. 74).

These precautions may not always be effective. There can be no certainty or guarantee that a specific group will not try to gain special advantages or privileges, nor that the citizens will always judge rightfully. Neither will voting always be unanimous. Rousseau argues that once the social contract is entered into 'the votes of the greatest number always bind the rest' (p. 153). But do they *always* do so? The problem of political obligation and the minority cannot be solved quite so simply as that.

Majorities and Minorities

Rousseau's participatory political association is grounded in the free creation of political obligation by its citizens. However, self-assumed obligation as consent will also be important, since the minority will always have to decide whether they ought to consent to the judgement of the majority. Rousseau assumes that the minority ought always to consent. He implies that because the conception of the general will as a principle of political morality entails its rightfulness, then a majority vote will always actually be in conformity to it. So there is no problem for the minority; their judgement was mistaken and they must consent. There is to be no right of political dissent or resistance in Rousseau's political association. Just as he refuses to extend his arguments to women, so he fails to pursue the logic of the participatory social contract to its conclusion: that the right of dissent and disobedience is implied by the practice of self-assumed political obligation.

Rousseau's arguments, like those of the liberal contract theorists, allow for only two alternatives: either everyone agrees that political obligation ought to be assumed, or the very foundations of the political association have crumbled. Moreover, Rousseau follows Hobbes in his view of dissent and lawbreaking. Although Rousseau's theory is based on a critique of abstract individualism, he shares Hobbes' view of the fragility of the political association. Hobbes' artificial social union is indeed fragile, but Rousseau completely overlooks the fact that the transformation in consciousness and capacities brought about through political participation is itself a source of strength. The members of a participatory association are continuously educating themselves in a fashion that serves to maintain their political system in being. Rousseau, therefore, falls back on external means of fostering citizens' commitment to their principle of political morality, or strengthening their civic virtue. The civil religion, which is not a religion in the usual sense, but a profession of 'sentiments of sociability', fulfills this function. Rousseau argues for tolerance of private religious beliefs, but any action which may appear to pose a threat to social bonds meets with the strictest intolerance; the severest penalties are required to aid virtue. Anyone who has acknowledged the dogmas of the civil religion and then 'behaves as if he did not believe in them' may be executed (p. 186). Similarly, the bonds of the family must also be protected; adultery by a wife is 'not infidelity but treason'.[50]

Rousseau makes no distinction between different kinds of offence. All lawbreaking is of the same status and, for Rousseau, all offenders are traitors. If the social contract is to have any meaning, anyone who 'refuses to obey the general will shall ... be forced to be free' (p. 64). It is possible to interpret this statement purely as a reference to 'moral liberty', and I followed this interpretation in my earlier comments on being forced to be free.[51] However, Rousseau is concerned with more than the transformation of consciousness, or development of a sense of moral liberty, which enables individuals to see collectively created and imposed laws as extensions of, not merely constraints upon, their freedom. He also means his graphic phrase to apply to those who are 'forced to be free' by being punished for lawbreaking, and to the necessity for the minority to consent to the decision of the majority. If one takes an Hegelian view of punishment it is possible to see the punishment of criminals, or those who have broken the law purely for personal gain, in this light; they are being forced to recall their own judgement of the law.

But not all lawbreakers act from criminal intent. The law can also be broken for political reasons, to further or maintain equality, freedom and justice. In this context it is less easy to give a benign interpretation to 'forcing to be free', as relevant only to moral liberty, or to citizens' psychological sense of freedom. If the law is broken for political reasons the disobedients are denying the claim implicit in this reading of Rousseau. They are denying that the content of a particular decision is such that they ought to consent to it; they are denying that it is a 'law'. To consent would be to limit or undermine, rather than to enhance their freedom and equality. Rousseau is concerned not only that citizens *feel* free, but that they *are* actually free and equal. This is exactly why he criticized liberal contract theory, and why his political association is participatory, and based on substantive economic equality and authority, or 'power to', not 'power over'. Power cannot completely be eliminated, since it is legitimately exercised over criminals when they are punished, but Rousseau is also arguing that power may be exercised over the minority; they must be forced to 'consent' or be 'free'. This argument contradicts the basic principles of his theory. By being forced to 'consent', the independence of a section of the citizenry is denied. Far from safeguarding the political association, compelling the minority to 'consent' can only lead to its 'degeneration' by reintroducing inequality and forced dependence.

Rousseau states that 'we always want what is advantageous but we do not always discern it' (p. 72). Nevertheless, he refuses to admit that the majority's decision may sometimes be incompatible with the general will. In Hobbesian fashion, Rousseau argues that, after the social contract, a citizen can 'no longer ask if the law can be unjust, because no one is unjust to himself' (p. 82). Here, he is completely ignoring his own distinction between 'myself' and 'each' citizen. Even if it is impossible to be unjust to myself, I do not vote for myself alone, but for myself along with everyone else. Questions about injustice are always appropriate in political life, for there is no guarantee that participatory voting will actually result in decisions in accord with the principles of political morality. Rousseau, however, merely asserts that a citizen 'consents to all the laws, even to those that are passed against his will, ...' (p. 153). Like recent advocates of the conceptual argument, Rousseau also implies that voluntary participation is in itself sufficient to preclude any further problems about political obligation. He argues that if I am in a minority in any vote then 'this proves only that I have made a mistake and that what I believed the general will was not so'.

He qualifies this by noting that 'this presupposes, ... that all the characteristics of the general will are still to be found in the majority', but this is merely to assert that either everyone ought to consent, or the political association has already 'degenerated' (pp. 153–4).

If these two all-or-nothing alternatives, characteristic of liberal rather than democratic theory, are to be avoided, the right of free judgement and choice must be extended to the minority. Political obligation is both like and unlike promising and other social obligations. Everyone understands that the meaning of 'I promise', or the meaning of joining in the social practice of shouting drinks, is that an obligation has been assumed. Similarly, the political practice of participatory voting rests on a collective selfconsciousness about the meaning and implications of citizenship. The members of the political association understand that to vote is simultaneously to commit oneself, to commit one's fellow citizens, and also to commit oneself to them in a mutual undertaking. Political obligation is a collective obligation that binds the whole community. But what is the position of those who do not vote, or those who vote against a given proposal?

If an individual refuses to make a promise, or refrains from joining with a group of drinkers, then she remains uncommitted. The meaning of inaction or abstention is also mutually understood. In the political practice of democratic voting a refusal to vote on a particular occasion indicates that the refusers believe they have good reason for abstention; the proposal on which the vote is taken infringes the principles of political morality on which the political association is based. A refusal to participate can thus be seen in a similar fashion to Rawls' conception of civil disobedience. Rousseau's individuals have been politically educating themselves in political morality or developing a 'sense of justice'. A refusal to vote could be seen as an appeal to the 'sense of justice' of their fellow citizens, or as a way of drawing their attention to the fact that, on a particular occasion, the general will, or principle of political right, is not being followed.

There are two reasons for participating in a democratic political association that do not apply to liberal democratic voting: first, all citizens take part in creating their own political obligations; and, secondly, any decision can be reassessed by them at a later date, and, if necessary, changed or revoked. The principles of political morality provide the criteria by which all citizens can evaluate their own actions, and also allow the minority to judge whether the decision of the majority is indeed a 'law'. If the minority decide that they ought to consent to the majority vote a kind of unanimity results, but they may decide to abstain from voting, or that they cannot consent. Rousseau's statement, that the majority retain all the characteristics of the general will, implies that they have been trying in their deliberations not to infringe the principle of political morality. The good faith of the majority is important for the minority's decision, for there is evidence to show that the majority are more likely to be right than any single voter if 'everyone is co-operating to find a mutually beneficial answer ...'.[52] Nevertheless, this fact is not necessarily sufficient for them to agree that they are mistaken. Rousseau assumes that it will be fairly easy to decide upon the consequences of a particular decision, but there may be genuine disagreement whether it really will preserve independence and equality. A minority may decide that they are justified in consenting, at least provisionally, to see how things actually turn out, but there is no reason why they should *always* do this. Nor will the majority necessarily act in good faith; if they have looked only to their own advantage and interest then the minority ought not to consent. If they do, they are contributing to a slide back into inequality and 'chains', and undermining the basis of the political association.

The action that follows from a refusal to consent, or a refusal to vote, depends whether the political consciousness of the community is sufficiently well developed that such an 'appeal' to them is all that is needed for the matter to be reconsidered. If the majority have acted in bad faith this is unlikely to be all that is necessary. The minority will have to take political action, including politically disobedient action if appropriate, to defend their citizenship and independence, and the political association itself. In a self-managing democracy, political action is not a symbolic act of authorization by individuals who have donned a political 'lion skin', but is the means through which the political association and its goals are maintained. Political disobedience by citizens, far from being 'treason', may be the only way in which freedom and equality can be preserved.

This is a very different view of political disobedience from that presented in the orthodox account of civil disobedience. From a democratic perspective the formal characteristics of the disobedient action are not all-important, nor is disobedience uniquely in need of justification, setting it apart from other forms of political activity. All political actions of citizens must be evaluated to see whether they are compatible with the principles of political morality ordering the association, and whether they contribute to the democratic ideals and goals of the community. Political disobedience is merely one possible expression of the active citizenship on which a self-managing democracy is based. Within a self-managing democracy, political obligation is explicitly recognized to be a permanent problem; citizens have continually to create political obligation, and sometimes it may be constituted only after politically disobedient, or other action, by a section of the citizenry. The social practice of promising involves the right to refuse or change commitments; similarly, the practice of self-assumed political obligation is meaningless without the practical recognition of the right of minorities to refuse or withdraw consent, or where necessary, to disobey.

Chapter 8

Political Obedience or Political Obligation?

Either the State for ever, ... *Or* the destruction of the States, and new life starting again in thousands of centres on the principle of the lively initiative of the individual and groups and that of free agreement.

P. Kropotkin, *The State: Its Historic Role.*

Despite recent attempts to deny that political obligation in the liberal democratic state constitutes a genuine problem, the 'old-fashioned' view of political obligation as the fundamental problem of liberal democratic theory is still valid. The problem is fundamental because it challenges basic beliefs about the character and necessity of the liberal democratic state. Liberal political theory has been very successful as ideology and has obscured the subversive character of its own political ideals of individual freedom and equality and self-assumed political obligation. For three centuries liberal theorists have claimed that the relationship between citizens and the liberal state rests upon the voluntary creation of, or agreement to, political obligation. It is now so widely accepted that the liberal democratic state is based on consent, on 'will not force', that this has come to be treated as a fact about the state. A critical analysis of the liberal theory of political obligation, and an examination of some aspects of the realities of the liberal democratic state, shows that this claim, like the social contract, is a political fiction. Liberal voluntarism is hypothetical voluntarism—and the hypothesis is unfounded.

In the preceding chapters a very large number of questions have been touched upon that are related to central, and very difficult, complex matters in social and political theory. It is not possible in the space of this final chapter to discuss them all; however, this is rather less important for my argument than the fact that the questions have been brought to the surface. In recent discussions of political obligation so many questions are avoided or suppressed that a major part of any critique must consist in making these explicit. In this chapter I shall confine my discussion to two areas. First I want to say something about the significance of my argument for liberal democratic theory. Despite all the criticisms that can be made of the liberal theory of political obligation, and the more positive points that emerge from an analysis of the conception of self-assumed obligation, it could be argued that my conclusion—that a relationship of political obligation is possible only in the context of a participatory or self-managing democracy—does not obviously follow. It might be pointed out that not all liberal theory is social contract theory, and my discussion has been concerned only with the latter. If the main alternative to contract theory, utilitarianism, is considered, then the problems surrounding political obligation may prove less intractable. Discussion of this objection will allow the

164

ideological nature of liberal theory to be spelt out more fully. Second, I shall examine some selected aspects of the democratic theory and practice of self-assumed political obligation.

Liberal Theory and Political Obedience

The more abstract and implausible that hypothetical voluntarism becomes, the more it invites the question whether political obligation must always contrast so strikingly with promising. Liberal theorists reply that this must be the case, and the basis of their response is an implicit appeal to empirical necessity, an appeal that reflects the shift that has taken place in liberal theory over the centuries. The liberal contract theorists provided a justification for a new form of political organization, and they had to argue in terms of obligation. The liberal state is now successfully established, and such a familiar part of our lives, that it can be treated as if it were a natural feature of the world. That is to say, it is assumed that 'democracy' has been achieved and that further democratic development is not empirically feasible. However, given this perception of the state, utilitarianism, not voluntarism, is the most obvious and economical argument about the relationship between citizens and the liberal state. If the liberal democratic state is empirically necessary, and actually operates as liberal theorists claim, then there are good utilitarian reasons for obedience; it is in citizens' interest to obey. The force of this argument is one reason why, looking back from our present vantage point, the social contract and consent can be treated as largely irrelevant to Hobbes' and Locke's arguments.

It is not difficult to provide a utilitarian reading of the liberal contract theorists. The state of nature can be interpreted as revealing the awful, or at least, unacceptable, consequences of an absence of civil government and so showing why it is in the individual's interest to obey the liberal state. The social contract, or a promise to obey, can therefore appear completely irrelevant, or even as an evil which stands in the way of individuals perceiving that social utility or self-interest provides a sufficient reason for obedience to the state. Bentham, in his usual forthright fashion, would have no truck with stories of social contracts:

> But the season of *Fiction* is now over: ... I bid adieu to the original contract: and I left it to those to amuse themselves with this rattle, who could think they needed it.[1]

It is possible to move directly from the liberal conception of free and equal individuals, competing with each other in the market to protect and further their interests, to the argument that there are good prudential or instrumental reasons for obedience to the state that protects them in this enterprise. This argument presupposes that the state takes a form which ensures that obedience is reasonable; that it is a liberal state exercising an external constraint on individuals' actions, or operating as an impartial procedure or political method to regulate their possessive interactions. Schumpeter was quite clear about the relationships between the development of the capitalist market and the liberal state:

> democracy in the sense of our theory of competitive leadership presided over the process

of political and institutional change by which the bourgeoisie reshaped and from its own point of view rationalized, the social and political structure that preceded its ascendancy: the democratic method was the political tool of that reconstruction. ... modern democracy is a product of the capitalist process.[2]

There are, therefore, good instrumental reasons for political obedience to the liberal state. This is especially so when universal suffrage is introduced and all citizens have the means to protect their interests and authorize an orderly succession of governments.

A utilitarian approach has obvious attractions but it also has one crucial drawback. As I have indicated, the utilitarian argument is an argument for political *obedience*, not political *obligation*. If voluntarism is abandoned, it cannot be held that the relationship of citizen to state is one of political obligation. This is important, for an instrumental relationship is a very much more fragile bond between citizen and state than a voluntary assumed commitment of political obligation. Considerations of self-interest may not always dictate obedience: 'it is [men's] duty to obey, just as long as it is their *interest*, and no longer'.[3] Few contemporary writers on political obligation are willing to leave the argument at that point. They wish to place the authority of the liberal democratic state on an unassailable basis. The surest way to do this is to give arguments about political obedience a voluntarist gloss; the liberal democratic state is such that individuals ought to consent, and can be said to do so. Political obedience is thus turned into political obligation—and political obligation is claimed to be unproblematic. Voluntarist arguments cannot be set aside without removing one of the major ideological planks of liberal democratic theory and practice. Utilitarianism provides no mechanisms of mediation between the demands of self-interest and the claim of the state.

I have shown it is impossible to give a coherent account of the social bonds that underlie individuality, communality, and social and political creativity, from a radical, abstractly individualist perspective. At one level this is a purely conceptual or theoretical problem; such a radical individualism can 'be thought but not lived'.[4] At another level, however, it is a practical problem, and a problem for a utilitarian account of political obedience, because the social and political consciousness of the inhabitants of the liberal democracies is, in part, shaped by the ideas and practices of possessive individualism. It is no accident that political theorists are now preoccupied by problems of free-riding and the rationality of voluntary cooperation, exemplified in the prisoners' dilemmas of game theory.[5] The totally isolated, possessive individual is a figment of the political theorists' imagination, but self-interested activity is not. Concepts and forms of social life are not independent; the theoretical imagination reflects the fact that in liberal democracies individuals are encouraged to act, and to believe that in major areas of their lives they ought to act, in a self-interested or possessive manner. Or, more accurately, some individuals are encouraged to act in this way. Women are held 'naturally' to be differently motivated, and the organization of capitalist economic production has restricted the extent to which working-class males can act possessively. In addition, completely self-interested action has been constrained by love, friendship, solidarity, altruism, and remnants of religious and other traditional world views.

However, many of these contraints are being steadily eroded by social developments in the liberal democracies. For example, Gauthier has noted that one effect of recent liberation movements has been to extend a possessive consciousness more widely throughout the population; the 'natural morality' of the self-interested individual is becoming more widely diffused and 'awareness of oneself as an appropriator undercuts one's willingness to accept the constraints of the political order'.[6] If citizens come to accept, and to act as if, political obedience was a matter of self-interest alone, and if theorists, politicians and the mass media spoke only in terms of prudential reasons for obedience, the political authority of the liberal state would begin to crumble against the rocks of possessive individualism. The 'triumph of radical contractarianism', or the triumph of possessive individualism,

> leads to the destruction, rather than the rationalization, of our society, for what real men and women who believe the ideology need to keep them from the war of all against all is ... the Hobbist sovereign, and he is not available.

Or, at least, he is not available at present. A contemporary version of Hobbes' absolute sovereign is not inconceivable. The liberal democratic state could turn into an authoritarian state, based visibly on the sword, and administered by technical (and military) experts. Political obligation would then be irrelevant, and liberalism and the potential it contains for democratic development would be no more, but I shall not pursue this pessimistic possibility.[8]

Rather oddly, Marxist writers on questions related to the problem of political obligation usually interpret liberal theory as a purely utilitarian theory. In the 'Introduction' I referred to the current revival in political theory, and part of this revival has been in Marxist and neo-Marxist theory, including the discussion, notably by Habermas, of the legitimation crisis in the liberal democratic state. This discussion is very relevant to arguments about political obligation, but it is usually ignored by liberal democratic theorists. They also fail to take account of Macpherson's arguments, which bridge the gap between liberal and Marxist theory and are, in part, specifically concerned with political obligation. From the other side, Marxist and neo-Marxist theorists, including Habermas who is an eclectic writer and widely read in anglo-american theory, usually neglect liberal discussions of political obligation. This is a curious failing for Marxists, since they are ignoring a crucially important aspect of the ideology of the liberal democratic state, but it is not surprising in the light of their failure to take account of the social contract tradition.[9] I criticized Macpherson's discussion of Hobbes and Locke for this reason in Chapter 3, and, similarly, Habermas argues that the classic liberal justification for the liberal state was derived directly from the market: 'the bourgeois constitutional state finds its justification in the legitimate relations of production'.[10]

Macpherson argues that the seventeenth-century justification for political obligation is now irrelevant because the laws of the market have ceased to be perceived as an inevitable or natural feature of the world. This change also reflects a change in the function of the state. The liberal state is no longer Locke's 'umpire' exercising a nightwatchman function over an autonomous market. Capitalist economic production is now largely state-managed; a development that forms the basis for Habermas' argument in *Legitimation Crisis*. Habermas argues that the crucial role of the liberal democratic state in economic management and planning means that economic crises can no longer be seen as 'a natural fate of society'.[11] They tend to become political crises which tend, in turn, to develop into crises of legitimation. Liberalism depends upon 'civic privatism', requiring the minimum of participation from citizens, although the latter are very interested in the outcome of the state's economic management. The other side of civic privatism is that individuals are largely concerned with consumption and occupational achievement. However, the 'motivations' of civic privatism and achievement are tending to break down. The former is undermined by the increasing involvement of the state in social life; for example, an unintended effect of social planning is that it provokes demands for citizen involvement. Consumption and achievement 'motivations' are under stress because schooling, for instance, no longer necessarily leads to a job commensurate with formal qualifications—or even to a job at all—and the professions are becoming increasingly routinized. Yet the legitimation of the state is increasingly dependent on the 'motivations' produced by bourgeois culture, because the state is no longer underpinned by traditional values, such as religion. However, since these 'motivations' are being eroded by the internal development of liberal democracy, crises orginating in the economic sphere can become political crises and then, perhaps, a crisis of legitimacy.

Habermas states that 'legitimation needs *do not have to* culminate in a crisis'.[12] But in ignoring the social contract, consent, and voluntarist liberal theory, Habermas is overlooking a specifically *political* justification of the authority of the liberal democratic state, and a 'traditional' source of legitimacy that helps prevent the culmination of the crisis. The authority of the liberal state is not based directly on the prudential 'motivations' of bourgeois culture, but, it is held, on political obligation, on the voluntary moral commitment of citizens. The bond of obligation is not so easily cast aside as is obedience based on prudential calculations, hence a legitimation crisis is less likely than a purely utilitarian view of liberal theory might lead one to suppose. Moreover, economic and social concerns, or considerations of self-interest, do not, in fact, have the direct impact on the authority of the state that discussions of the legitimation crisis suggest. Their impact on the state is mediated through *political* mechanisms, through the formal equality of citizenship and through claims and beliefs about consent which cast doubt on the relevance of economic and social factors for political obligation. Voluntarism is a practical source of cohesion in the liberal state. It is the ideological heart of liberalism, which is precisely why liberal democratic theorists cannot give up voluntarism, no matter how implausible their arguments may become or how many problems they engender.

Habermas, significantly, passes over the function of liberal democratic voting in the most cursory way. He comments that 'legitimation can be disassociated from the mechanism of elections only temporarily and under extraordinary conditions. This problem is resolved through a system of formal democracy'. In this system, citizens have 'only the right to withold acclamation'. Habermas also states that formal democracy is justified by technocratic systems theories and democratic elite theories that, he says, go back to Weber and Schumpeter.[13] But, as I have shown, liberal democratic elite theories go back much further than Schumpeter (or Weber). Classic liberal social contract theory provided a political justification for the liberal state, and anticipated Schumpeter's conception of the liberal democratic political method. Once universal suffrage is introduced, all individuals are incorporated into the state as formally equal citizens. They occupy the same political status, and enjoy a common interest as citizens, which appears to transcend and compensate for social and economic inequalities, and render them irrelevant to questions of political obligation or legitimacy. Voting is a political resource enjoyed equally by all, through which citizens can protect their interests. The operation of the liberal democratic political method, or the method of consent, therefore insulates the state from economic criticism and the erosion of social 'motivations', notwithstanding its function of managing the contemporary capitalist economy.

The realities of liberal democratic voting are very different from the account given in, or implied by, arguments about consent. But there is one other feature of the liberal democratic state that is important to an understanding of how the state can be presented as something it is not. The liberal democratic state is no longer Locke's 'umpire', but it can nevertheless be seen as an 'umpire' of a different kind. If the development of the labour movement undermined an earlier perception of the laws of the market, it also contributed to the achievement of universal suffrage, to the development of the economic functions of the state, and to the building of the welfare state. The existence of the welfare state makes it much more plausible for liberal theorists to present the liberal democratic state as an impartial 'umpire', that protects all interests, albeit that the 'umpire' has changed its character from the time the metaphor was first used. Working-class citizens are now tied to the state by a material bond, a bond which also helps prevent the culmination of a legitimation crisis. Moreover, this material bond, in the ideological 'argument' about benefits and gratitude, is also claimed to be something more, to be part of political obligation.

The inescapable and insoluble dilemma for liberal theory should now be clear. Liberal democratic theorists treat the state as if it were a natural feature of the world, and it is assumed that the liberal democratic political method does actually constitute an impartial procedure protecting all interests. *The basic liberal argument about the relationship of citizens to the state is that there are good reasons for obedience. Yet, the argument must be given a voluntarist appearance.* It follows from the postulate of 'naturally' free and equal individuals that political authority must be grounded in individual commitment (and it was a stroke of theoretical genius for the contract theorists to abstract individuals from the market to the state of nature and so provide an 'original' justification for the liberal state based on human nature and reason). The hypothesis must therefore be maintained that the liberal democratic state rests on a relationship of political obligation. Furthermore, a utilitarian account of political obedience cannot provide the secure grounding for the liberal state that is offered by a theory of political obligation; without hypothetical voluntarism the emperor is indeed naked. Recourse to claims about a natural duty of obedience treat obedience as unproblematic, but they contradict three centuries of liberal argument that political relationships are conventional. Political obedience must be presented as political obligation. At the same time, however, voluntarist arguments call attention to the existence of a problem about political obligation in the liberal democratic state.

If 'obligation' is taken seriously, and examined critically, it becomes clear that the practice of political obligation is not, and more importantly, cannot be, given expression in the liberal democratic state. The dilemma for liberal theory is that it cannot afford to abandon hypothetical voluntarism, and talk merely of political obedience, or the liberal state is deprived of a major ideological support. But nor can it really afford to retain voluntarism, because the concept of 'obligation' is a standing reminder that the liberal state is being presented as something other than it really is, and that there is a democratic alternative to liberal theory and practice.

The idea of the social contract is central to this dilemma. The origin of the fiction of political obligation is to be found, of course, in liberal social contract theory. Like the utilitarians, but for very different reasons, democratic theorists have no use for the idea of a social contract, or for contractual conceptions of 'obligation'. *A democratic theory of self-assumed political obligation is not a contract theory*. The idea of the social contract is central to an abstractly individualist theoretical perspective that attempts to reduce social life, and the practice of obligation, to a series of discrete contracts and exchanges. The exchange embodied in the liberal social contract is then treated as if it were equivalent to a promise.

During my argument I have used 'voluntarism' to cover all the ways in which individuals freely commit themselves. But although promises, contracts, covenants, agreements and votes have many aspects in common, there are fundamental differences between them. In particular, the examples of a contract and a promise are not merely different ways of characterizing the same act of commitment, but form part of contrasting theoretical perspectives which help constitute different forms of social and political life. The ambiguity about the relationship between promising and political obligation has its roots in the conception of political obligation as a contractual relationship, or as arising from the liberal social contract. Individuals in the state of nature have been abstracted from the social relationships of the capitalist market where they make contracts with each other embodying exchanges which each has independently judged to be in his interest. The liberal social contract is another such exchange. All participants in the contract are held to be able independently to see its advantages; they thus exchange their 'natural' freedom and equality for civil freedom and the formally equal political status of subject, or, they receive the protection of the liberal state in exchange for political obedience. A similar exchange of obedience for the protection of the two principles of justice takes place in Rawls' original position.

However, the social contract is held to give rise to political obligation, not merely to political obedience. The liberal social contract is treated as if it were a promise, or, at least, as if it were a certain kind of promise: namely, a promise to obey. By virtue of being a promise it transforms obedience into obligation. At the beginning of my argument I remarked upon the peculiar nature of this form of promising. It is a promise which, instead of exemplifying and enlarging the freedom and equality of those who enter into the social practice of promising, denies or limits that freedom and equality in certain, or all, areas of life. The effect of the 'promise' in the liberal social contract is that substantive political freedom and equality, necessary if citizens are to create their own political obligations, are given up or exchanged for the protection of the liberal state. The liberal social contract is, in this respect, exactly like other contracts in which obedience is exchanged for protection; it is like the traditional marriage contract, the employment contract, and even like a contract of slavery, for the master must protect his slaves if he is to obtain satisfactory service. The liberal social contract is precisely what the words imply—a contract, not a promise. It is a contract that embodies an exchange of security for obedience, but the contract is then presented as a promise, and the hypothesis of political obligation in the liberal democratic state begins its long history.

Hegel was correct to emphasize that neither the relationship between the sexes nor political life is contractual, but this is not to say, with Hegel, that the only alternative to contractual models and abstract individualism is the conceptual argument and acceptance of the 'rationality' of the liberal democratic state. The practice of self-assumed obligation, of promising, points the way to another alternative. A promise is not an exchange to the mutual advantage of possessive individuals but the creation of a relationship (a difference marked by Hobbes' distinction between a contract and a covenant). A promise is based on trust, keeping faith and responsibility, not the 'natural morality' of possessive individuals, which is why it is promising, not contract, that is fundamental to social life itself. The conceptual and empirical significance of the difference between contracts and promises is exemplified in the difference between liberal contract theory and Rousseau's democratic contract theory. In fact, it is extremely misleading to call Rousseau's theory contractual (but hard to avoid since he uses the term himself). Rousseau's 'contract' is *not* a contract, or an exchange of obedience for protection, but a voluntary agreement, or promise, between individuals to create a political association that will give expression to, and maintain, their substantive freedom and equality.[14] The association is sustained through time, not by renewals of a contract of obedience by voting for representatives, but by the free creation of political obligation through participatory democratic voting, the political counterpart of promising.

The distinction between contracts and promises also throws more light onto the doubtful political status of liberal democratic voting, about which I commented in Chapter 5. Liberal democratic voting is central to hypothetical voluntarism because it is a clear 'act of one's own' that can be presented as consent or a promise to obey. However, a liberal democratic vote is not a promise, or consent, but a continuation of the self- interested exchanges of the capitalist market. This is why economic models of the liberal democratic political method are so popular. In voting, individuals exchange obedience for the protection of the liberal democratic state, but, as in other exchanges, self-interest should be secured as cheaply as possible. If it is possible to obtain protection without voting, so much the better; thus political apathy is the 'natural' condition of the liberal democratic citizen. Voting appears to be different from other ways of pursuing self-interest, and to be more than a renewal of a contract, because it takes place beneath the 'lion skin' of liberal democratic citizenship; it appears to be a qualitatively different activity from those in the market, to be a 'political' activity, and like a promise, and so to give rise to political obligation.[15]

Liberal theorists cannot clarify the status of voting, or develop an explicitly political account of citizenship, without moving away from contractual conceptions, and so undermining the ideological function of liberal theory. Indeed, liberal theory is not able to take its own political ideals seriously. If an ideological rationalization of the authority of the liberal democratic state is to continue to be provided, the fiction of political obligation and hypothetical voluntarism must be maintained. The problem bequeathed by liberal contract theory must continue to be ignored or glossed over. This is illustrated by the problem of differential political obligation.

From the outset, liberal writers have had difficulties in incorporating all individuals into the liberal state. The difficulty in the case of women has gone largely unnoticed, since most theorists implicitly regard the 'individual' as a male. Women pose a particularly acute problem for liberal theory. The theory began life in conflict with the patriarchalists, but disagreement did not extend to beliefs about women. Liberal theorists were content to ignore their own arguments about the conventional character of authority relationships, and to fall back on arguments from 'nature' for female individuals. Once again, liberal democratic theorists now face an uncomfortable dilemma. Either their arguments for political obligation have to be explicitly developed as arguments about males only (and women will remain as a constant threat to the state), or the unfinished attack on patriarchal theory must be brought to a conclusion. The latter alternative, however, means that suppressed problems about self-assumed obligation will have to be confronted and radical questions about social and political change will have to be faced.

The problem about the inclusion of working-class males in arguments about political obligation is easier to gloss over than the problem about women, since all males appear 'naturally' to be free and equal individuals. They all exercise authority over women in the family, and, traditionally, it is fathers of families who have been seen as participants in the liberal social contract. But are all males included in the contract? Again, this may appear to be the case if the market is seen in abstract terms as a series of discrete economic contracts and exchanges between equal male individuals. But fathers of families occupy different and unequal social and economic positions, and most importantly, when working-class fathers enter into capitalist economic production they must *obey* in return for subsistence. Hence, there is a doubt that they have, or can develop, the civil personality (to use Kant's phrase) appropriate to participants in the liberal social contract. Rawls' theory illustrates this ambiguity very nicely. The parties in his original position can be seen as heads of families, yet the formally equal citizenship of the majority of these heads is actually worth very little. This difference is recognized in Rawls' distinction between political obligation and the natural duty to obey. When the reason for the difference in the worth of liberty is examined it becomes clear that this is not merely a matter of the inequalities of wealth, income, and material goods, on which Rawls concentrates, but reflects the fact that middle-class males are most likely to be politically active and to govern, and the same individuals make decisions about economic production.

The 'free and equal individual' is, in practice, a person found much more rarely than liberal theory suggests. An abstractly individualist perspective enables the position of the middle-class male to be generalized, while the actual social position of other individuals is never seriously considered within the limits imposed by basic assumptions of liberal theory. Liberal theorists cannot look too closely at ambiguities about the relationship of men and women, and the working and middle class, to the liberal state, nor at the problems and contradictions of their own arguments, if they are to continue to maintain the fiction of political obligation.

The necessity of such reticence can also be illustrated by an examination of the other problem with which I have been concerned, the problem of to whom it is that political obligation is owed. As I have shown, this problem gives rise to the crucial question of what counts as 'political' obligation, and I now want to take this up in order to provide an example of the way in which the transformation of liberal theory can proceed from the groundwork of an internal critique. Liberal theory contains the basic material for its own transformation or 'reconstruction'.[16] It must always be kept in mind that the conceptual revision required for the reconstruction is not an end in itself. It is part of democratic social and political change. I have presented empirical evidence to show the feasibility of one aspect of this change, the democratization of the workplace, in *Participation and Democratic Theory*, so I shall not canvass this here.[17] Nevertheless, democratic social and political change cannot take place unless we also begin to think differently:

> Conceptual revision is not, ... a sufficient condition of political change, but it is indispensable to significant political change. It is part of that process by which events once considered mere facts come to be seen as the outcomes of a political process. ... Conceptual revision is involved in any political strategy that aims at reconstituting social life in modest or in radical ways.[18]

To cease to see political obligation as a 'mere fact' about the liberal democratic state, to see it as a problem, as a relationship that has yet to be created, is to place in question the entire liberal democratic interpretation of political life and the concepts, including the 'political' itself, that help constitute it.

Democratic Theory and Political Obligation

Political theorists are beginning to look beyond the conventional liberal view that each citizen can be said to owe obligation to the state:

> we must understand that our primary obligation must be to those with whom we are engaged in a common undertaking. The government or the regime is an institution born of the necessity to administer and carry out the aims of the common life ... Our obligation to the regime—even to that savage and holistic abstraction known as the state—is at once secondary and prudential.[19]

It is not difficult to see why theorists are beginning to turn away from the vertical conception of political obligation. One reason is that the moral emptiness of this conception is a powerful incentive to look to the richness of everyday practices and institutions for an account of the voluntary acts of individuals which are held to constitute political obligation. But if 'private' associations are the locus of meaningful moral—and political—life, then it is hard to explain why the state has a claim at all, or what kind of bond remains between citizen and state. One response to these problems, which follows easily from the conceptual approach, is to argue that the obligation to the state is an obligation between citizens because the state is a special kind of association; it is an ethical order, the embodiment of the 'common life' of its members, or the social union of their social unions. Participation in the associations of the state can thus appear to give rise to political obligation. But Hegelian legerdemain with the term 'state', even if brilliantly executed, merely serves to obscure rather than solve the problems, and, by presenting political obligation as a horizontal bond between citizens, begins to point towards a different conception of the relationship.

Although an Hegelian ambiguity about the 'state' exists in many recent discussions of political obligation, the 'state' is usually treated uncritically by liberal democratic theorists, and taken for granted as a 'fact'. In liberal social contract theory the 'political' is identified with the 'state', and the latter is identified with a specific set of institutions that stand separate from, but regulate, as an impartial 'umpire', the private sphere of social life. The political sphere, or the state, is an arena for representatives, for experts or professionals, not, except on special ocassions when representatives are chosen, a sphere in which citizens are active. The vertical conception of political obligation is integral to this view of the state; indeed, it is no more than an interpretation of the periodic alienation of political authority to representatives as 'consent'. Now, I have argued that, today, the state as 'umpire' requires that the historical development of the functions of the liberal state be taken into account. But, at the same time, this development provides a second reason for dissatisfaction with the traditional liberal conception of the state. State-management of the capitalist economy, and the increasing involvement of the state in other areas of social life, makes it hard to maintain the separation of the state from the common life of its members. If the state is part of, rather than separate from, the associations and practices of everyday life, then it becomes more plausible to see it as a special kind of association in which political obligation is assumed.

However, to see the state in this fashion is to see it as much more than an external 'umpire', or as comprising a specific set of governmental institutions. The state is now being conceived as part and parcel of the mechanisms that maintain and reinforce the inequalities of everyday life:

that thing called the government can only do what it is supposed to do if behind it is an apparatus responsible for the reproduction of the social system within which the government operates. That other thing, which cannot in fact be directly touched or seen, is the state.[20]

Liberal democratic theorists cannot afford to 'see or touch' this wider conception of the state, however much their arguments may rely on it, because it undermines the presentation of the liberal state as an impartial 'umpire', and also introduces a wider conception of the 'political'. Both these factors pose a challenge to the success of liberal theory as ideology. If the 'political' ceases to be identified with the 'state' in the narrow sense, then the crucial separation between the 'private' and the 'political' breaks down. But the liberal hypothesis about political obligation depends on precisely this separation: political obligation is essentially different from promising. In view of the present character of the state, it is not surprising that definitions of the 'political' can be found in standard works of political science that refer broadly to the existence of structures of power or authority, and to the authoritative allocation of values. The organizations of economic life are certainly 'political' according to these definitions, but few political theorists explore their significance or implications for liberal democratic theory and practice.

Such definitions, like radically pluralist conceptions of consent, and the broad conception of the 'state', lead away from a liberal democratic and statist conception of political life. Any account of the liberal democratic state must give a central place to its essential feature: namely, to the alienation by citizens, through elections, of their right to make political decisions. An account of the liberal democratic state that recognizes its present wide-ranging functions is, therefore, more than an extension of the conception of the 'state' as an ethical order or social union of social unions. The idea of the 'state' as an association has no necessary connection with the authorization of representatives. The 'state', in this sense, comes into being at the first stage of the liberal social contract (although Locke's new political community is undifferentiated, or, at least, contains only families). Rousseau's theory shows that, if the new political association is to be grounded in self-assumed political obligation, there can be no second stage to the contract—that is to say, there can be no liberal state. Rather, citizens collectively must create their political obligation and political authority through participatory voting in a democratic community; there can be no alienation of political authority to representatives, which is then called 'political obligation'. Hegel was right to be suspicious of the implications of liberal voluntarism for the constitutional state. To take self- assumed obligation seriously as a political ideal is to deny that the authority of the liberal democratic state and the (hypothesized) political obligation of its citizens can be justified. It is to deny the central contention of liberal contract theory that the liberal state is necessary for an ordered democratic life.

The view of 'political' obligation as a horizontal relationship between citizens cannot be reconciled with a liberal conception of the 'political'. It is compatible only with a revised democratic conception, and it presupposes a non-statist political community as a political association of a multiplicity of political associations. The members of the community are citizens in many political associations, which are bound together through horizontal and multifaceted ties of self-assumed political obligation. The essential feature of a democratic revision of the 'political' is that it is no longer conceived as separate from everyday life. The political sphere is one dimension, the collective dimension, of social life as a whole. It is the area of social existence in which citizens voluntarily cooperate together and sustain their common life and common undertaking.

It is important to emphasize that although, in this revised conception of the 'political', the everyday dimension of social life is not independent of political life, it is still *distinct* from it. It is sometimes assumed that the only alternative to a liberal view of the political is the assimilation of the two dimensions of social life; witness the currently popular slogan, 'The personal is the political'. This is a useful slogan, provided that it is not taken too literally. To identify the personal and the political no more captures the mutuality or communality and individuality of social life than does the liberal reification of the political. A democratic conception of political life must show how it is constituted by rules that are grounded in, yet transcend, everyday life, just as the social practice of promising presupposes yet transcends the 'rule of promising'. The two dimensions of social life have their own character and are ordered by distinct, though related, rules. A great deal of theoretical work remains to be done in this area, in particular in exploring rules or principles of political right compatible with the practice of self-assumed obligation. A democratic theory of willed voluntarism has to 'combine the seemingly incombinable',[21] in that it has to encompass freedom and equality, and also reason and substantive principles of political morality. One implication of the practice of political obligation is that there will be occasions when citizens know that they ought to assume, or refuse to assume, an obligation, or when they ought to consent or refuse to do so. There is little need to stress the contrast between this conception of political action, and the organization of political life, and the liberal argument that political life should be governed by formal rules of procedure that constitute a neutral political method.

It is often assumed that the 'political' refers to power relationships (which, in view of the character of contemporary sexual and familial life, is one reason why it can be supposed that the personal is the political). A democratic transformation of the liberal democratic state can then appear to presage an end of the political itself.[22] However, philosophical anarchism notwithstanding, the collective dimension of social life cannot disappear; rather, the aim of democratic political change is, as far as possible, to transform power relationships into relationships of authority in which citizens collectively exercise political authority. Their decision-making will determine the content and boundaries of the 'political' dimension of their lives. This will sound imprecise and arbitrary to political theorists who take a 'realistic' view of the political. However, as shown in Chapter 2, once abstract individualism is left behind, there is no reason to suppose that this decision will be any more, or less, arbitrary than other aspects of participatory decision-making. Openness is part of the political creativity of citizens; 'once we have acknowledged the nonexistence of ... a boundary "in nature" ', between political and everyday life, it will be possible

> to conceive of a society ... that formed a single voluntary association for certain purposes and that consisted of a plurality of voluntary associations for other purposes; both the respective purposes (of the largest associations and the others) and the identities and the memberships of the subassociations could be conceived of as fluctuating in response to conditions.[23]

A reconceptualization of the 'political' in the manner outlined attempts to move into a non-abstractly individualist and non-contractual theoretical perspective (which implies that some concepts, inextricably tied to abstract individualism, must be discarded, not revised). To conclude my argument I want to comment on three aspects of this perspective, beginning by emphasizing one dimension of the contrast between liberal and democratic theory. A democratic theory, as my remarks on the 'political' suggest, is a theory of interrelationships; it is concerned with relationships between individuals, their characteristics and forms of social and political institutions, between concepts and social life, between concepts themselves, and between political theory and political practice.

Liberal theory tries to separate these things, seeing 'human nature', for example, as independent of specific social and political institutions. In Rousseau's critique of liberal contract theory, freedom and equality are treated as integrally related to each other. In liberal theory, the two concepts are seen as independent of each other, and so it can appear that 'contemporary demands for equality are made in the language of freedom, e.g. "women's liberation" '.[24] But women are not merely demanding equality (insofar as their demands go beyond the extension of formal equality of opportunity to women as well as men); nor are they demanding freedom as understood in liberal theory. Feminist demands are designed to remedy three centuries of liberal accommodation to patriarchy; they are designed to secure the practical recognition that women are 'individuals' like men or are autonomous persons, free and equal individuals, beings who can enter into the practice of self-assumed political obligation. Independence or autonomy is, as Rousseau saw, central to *both* freedom and equality. The freedom and equality demanded by women presuppose each other. Women are believed to be 'naturally' inferior to men in strength, character and abilities, and so they are unfree because treated as men's 'natural' dependants, and unequal because treated as men's 'natural' subordinates; or, alternatively, they are unequal because dependent, and unfree because subordinate.

If it is widely believed that women are 'naturally' excluded from the ideal of individual freedom and equality, it is also widely believed that men are 'naturally' possessive individuals. My earlier remarks about the diffusion of this 'natural morality' might suggest that to talk of self-managing democracy and social life as a voluntary scheme is indeed Utopian, and that the state is needed to enforce social cooperation. My second comment is concerned with the question, 'on what basis does the critical theorist found [her] hopes for the future?'.[25] This was a question that also concerned Rousseau. He wrote,

> the social spirit which must be the product of social institutions would have to preside over the setting up of those institutions; men would have to have already become before the advent of law [the general will] that which they become as a result of law.[26]

Every form of social life requires a specific form of consciousness or 'social spirit' in its members. The problem is that any form of radical social and political change seems to presuppose that Rousseau's second great transformation of human nature has already taken place; the form of consciousness needed for, and that will be further developed within, the new social order must, it seems, already be in existence or change will not be possible. How then can political theorists have hope for the future? Rousseau's answer to this problem, or rather, the way in which he avoided it, was to introduce the ancient and awesome figure of the Legislator or Lawgiver to institute the new political association. The Legislator is sometimes seen as central to Rousseau's argument, but he usurps none of the people's sovereign rights and takes no part in government, which indicates that he is precisely what Shklar argues that he is not: namely, a contrivance 'invented to give utopia a start'.[27]

To fall back on Lawgivers, or their modern equivalents, encourages the view that participatory democracy, and the practice of self-assumed political obligation, is indeed a Utopia, but, from the perspective of contract theory, there seems no alternative. Contract theory suggests that socio-political change emerges from a 'beginning' and is grounded in a timeless 'human nature'. From this abstractly individualist perspective the construction of a voluntarist political order, like the practice of promising, appears to pose insoluble problems. But the war, or inconveniences, of the state of nature is not the outcome of an ahistorical 'human nature'. Rather it results from the actions of social individuals, abstracted from the market, equipped with the consciousness of appropriators, which works against voluntary cooperation when the constraints of civil law (or all social relationships) are imaginatively removed.[28] The actual political consciousness of the inhabitants of liberal democracies is more complicated than contract theory suggests. It is shaped by friendship, love, solidarity and relationships such as obligations as well as by self-interest. Moreover, if the labour movement has assisted the development of the liberal democratic state, it has also fought against it and kept alive democratic concepts and forms of action and organization. Similarly, the diffusion of possessive individualism is only part of the legacy of liberation movements. The feminist movement, for example (which reemerged despite the much-emphasized effectiveness of the socialization process in fitting women for a subordinate, dependent and apolitical place), aims to transform liberal society in a fashion necessary for the construction of a self-managing democracy.

The patriarchalists and conservatives claim that everyone is involuntarily born into a specific social order; therefore, there can be no voluntarist social contract. A non-contractual political theory does not depend on a 'beginning' and can meet this objection to voluntarism. It is true that no one comes into the world fully mature, free, and equal and free from all social ties; but it is only abstract individualists who argue as if they do. The fact that humans are social creatures, born into a network of social relationships, is the foundation for, not a barrier against, the construction of a democratic political association. It is during their social life together that individuals learn how to cooperate, and in which they develop the capacities necessary for the creation and maintenance of a voluntarist social order. Hopes for the future depend upon the potentiality for social and political education, and upon social and political action and organization, not the magical beginnings of social contracts.

A great deal of thought needs to be given to the kinds of political action that will foster democratic political change. I have commented on the poverty of liberal theory which identifies 'democratic' activity with a narrow range of electoral and inter-electoral activities, to which civil disobedience is assimilated. No means are provided to discriminate between 'unorthodox' activities, so that completely different actions tend all to be lumped together and labelled as 'undemocratic' or 'violent'.[29] Unfortunately, the critics of liberal theory have not given much attention to this area: 'insights that illuminated the critiques of electoral-representative processes have been entirely overlooked in the few studies that have been done of the nature of protest itself'.[30] The development of democratic criteria to evaluate different forms of political activity is an important aspect of the restructuring of liberal theory.

One such criterion is the extent to which political activities contribute to the political education of the participants, and this brings me to my third, and last, point. Political education is central to a non-abstractly individualist theory. Not political socialization, but education. 'Socialization' is the process which encourages individuals to accept the liberal democratic state, and their place within it, as rational and necessary, as 'natural'.[31] I have offered some empirical evidence on the educative effect of participation in *Participation and Democratic Theory*, but a more basic political education is also required if individuals are to participate effectively. The social practice of promising presupposes certain critical abilities and moral self-consciousness. Similarly, the practice of political obligation requires that individuals develop the capacities that enable them critically and self-consciously to appreciate the foundation, and operation, of their political association. One reason why the identification of 'consent' and 'democracy' with liberal democracy is so rarely challenged is that 'many people are linguistically inhibited from thinking theoretically about politics'.[32] They are neither taught nor encouraged to think in a critical and systematic way about their relationship to the liberal democratic state, least of all encouraged by writers on political obligation. Habermas' discussion of the requirements for free, rational discourse is extremely valuable for the development of this area of democratic theory. However, Habermas draws a sharp distinction between 'communicative action', which is part of political life, and work, or technical or 'purposive-rational' action; a distinction between two dimensions of social life which is incompatible with the practice of political obligation.[33] 'Communicative action' is basic to political obligation over the whole of collective life, including economic production.

The linguistic and other capacities which underlie the individual's ability to perform and understand speech acts are continuous with those necessary for participation in the practice of political obligation. The rules of linguistic usage are very different from rules governing other social and political institutions, but the concept of self-assumed obligation provides a necessary continuity between language, everyday life and political life; it brings together in a coherent whole, and yet differentiates, the rules of language, the moral life of the individual, and the collective life of the community. The idea of the social contract has no place in democratic theory, but to ignore the social contract tradition is to fail to appreciate the value of the practice of self-assumed obligation, or to see that it can form the basis for a critical analysis of liberal theory. Self-assumed obligation, and the vision of social life as a voluntary scheme, are invaluable democratic kernels that deserve to be extracted from the shell of liberal hypothetical voluntarism.

Afterword (1985)

The questions and forms of argument that come to the attention of political theorists at a particular time always reflect the political circumstances in which they are writing. In view of the social and political developments of the past decade it is not surprising that other discussions of political obligation appeared at about the same time as my own, or that liberal arguments have begun to be treated more sceptically. The social realities in the liberal democracies now make it much less easy to take claims about consent at face value, to take it for granted that all citizens are equally obligated, or to assert that political obligation poses no general problems. Most of the contemporary literature that I examined was written during the post-war consensus on the aims and policies of the liberal democratic welfare state. The relationship of citizens to the state looks much less secure now that the consensus has broken down.

The comforting view of the world presupposed by hypothetically voluntarist claims was always based on slender empirical foundations, but circumstances are now very much bleaker. Large-scale (permanent?) unemployment has re-emerged—and soup kitchens have been established in the big cities of the richest and most powerful country in the world. Class and racial inequalities and divisions are increasingly visible. The organized feminist movement has demonstrated how enormous the gap is between claims made about citizenship and the actual social position of women—and the feminization of poverty is one consequence of the reductions in welfare benefits and social services. The traditional allegiances to the major political parties are splintering and many voters, particularly in the USA, seem reluctant to go to the polls at all. The allocation of public funds to building up nuclear and other means of warfare is increasing, and liberal democratic states are now much more heavily armed against their own citizens than was the case a decade ago. When I was writing this book in the late 1970s, I would not have expected to hear the British Prime Minister, Margaret Thatcher, use the language of 'the enemy within' when speaking in 1985 of the coal miners' strike; nor, in the same year, the President of the United States, Ronald Reagan, referring to the 'Contras' currently attacking Nicaragua—who specialize in destroying health clinics and murdering and torturing medical workers—as 'the moral equivalent of the Founding Fathers'.

Despite these developments, by no means all the new discussions are sceptical about finding a convincing justification of political obligation in the liberal democratic state. Attempts are still being made to shore up hypothetical voluntarism, and, in one central respect, arguments about political obligation are still exactly where they were when this book was first published. The reasons *why* political obligation is a problem in the liberal democratic state are still not addressed. My approach thus remains distinct from more recent contributions, but in the light of my more recent research, in which I have looked at some of the problems raised in this book from an explicitly feminist perspective, I now see that, in one respect, my argument did not go far enough, and I shall return to this later.

The most sceptical writers merely show that the conventional liberal arguments are unconvincing and therefore fall firmly within the tradition that is usually called philosophical anarchism. The conventional arguments cannot be accepted, but the problem goes much deeper than that. My aim was to show that the problem of political obligation is *insoluble* unless political theory and practice moves outside the confines of liberal categories and assumptions. The modern problem of political obligation arose with liberalism, but liberalism cannot provide a solution. The problem is generated by the liberal premise of 'natural' individual freedom and equality that entails a voluntarist account of the relation between citizen and state, i.e. an account in terms of 'obligation'. A corollary of the liberal view that social relations are conventional, which I did not perhaps sufficiently emphasize, is that social contract theory is central to liberalism. Paradigmatically, contract is the act through which two free and equal individuals create social bonds, or a collection of such individuals creates the state. Social life must be created *ab initio* because liberal theorists assume that argument must begin from a picture of the individual abstracted from his social context. Political obligation would not have become central to political theory without this assumption, but it also gives rise to the numerous, seemingly insoluble problems of fidelity and arbitrariness that surround contract. Voluntarism (contract) thus threatens the authority of the state and the stability of the relationships it is designed to secure.

One apparent solution is to transform liberal theory into an instrumental argument, or, more recently, into a series of conceptual points, and so eliminate reference to contract. Although there has been a revival of contract theory since the publication of Rawls' *A Theory of Justice*, liberalism is not usually seen, first and foremost, as social contract theory, and this more thoroughly obscures the basis of the problem of political obligation. Thus contemporary writers on political obligation see no need to explain why liberal social contract theory and arguments about consent are so persistently or so easily reinterpreted as arguments about benefits, or why there is so much uncertainty about whether political obligation is or is not self-assumed. In the absence of these explanations, recent discussions, like those earlier examples criticized in this book, suppress all the complicated theoretical and empirical questions about democracy. Moreover, it is still being claimed that the problem lies in the language of obligation and consent rather than the political realities of the liberal democratic state.

Jules Steinberg's *Locke, Rousseau, and the Idea of Consent* provides a more thoroughgoing example than many I discussed of how liberal theorists' uneasiness with the basic assumptions of their own arguments leads to completely hypothetical voluntarism. Steinberg acknowledges that the problems with consent are now so serious as to be beyond repair (and he devotes a chapter to the difficulties of identifying consent with voting). He concludes that all talk of consent should be abandoned. However, for Steinberg, this drastic reformulation of liberal theory does not suggest that there may be something amiss with liberal democratic institutions. Rather, the need to abandon consent shows that the concept was inappropriate all along, and has merely hindered theorists' attempts to display the moral legitimacy of the liberal state. Unlike many writers on the subject, Steinberg recognizes that the question of why 'obligation' is self-assumed is central to the understanding of liberal claims about political obligation, but he nevertheless insists that 'consent' is the problem. Locke's references to consent are reinterpreted as entirely metaphorical, used only to indicate that certain acts are rational. And this, Steinberg argues, is how all references to consent must be understood. No acts of commitment are required for political obligation. Rather, argument should begin from the fact that the liberal state promotes certain ends and purposes, and, therefore, since we already know that the state is morally legitimate, citizens ought to obey. They act rationally (metaphorically, 'consent') if they do.

This comforting conclusion looks a great deal less plausible as soon as questions are asked about the character of the ends and purposes and whether the liberal democratic state actually secures them. Steinberg says little about these matters. The most popular reinterpretation of arguments from contract and consent is not in terms of the ends and purposes of the state but the promotion, receipt or acceptance of benefits from schemes of social cooperation or from the state itself. My own efforts to present a decisive theoretical argument against this influential approach are now supported by John Simmons in *Moral Principles and Political Obligations*. Having examined the deficiencies of arguments about consent and tacit consent, which, like Steinberg, he sees as irreparable, Simmons turns his attention to what he calls the 'consent-implying' acts to which consent theorists have often resorted in their claims about political obligation; that is to say, acts from which, it is said, obligation could be inferred or hypothesized, notably the enjoyment of benefits.

Simmons scrutinizes various versions of the claim about benefits as they appear in the fair play, natural duty and gratitude arguments. He finds these arguments as implausible as I do. He concludes that it is hard to account for any political obligations from the principle of fair play, which 'has very little to recommend it, either as a supplement to or a replacement for principles of fidelity and consent' (p. 141). Simmons further concludes that the duty to support just institutions cannot account for political obligation in a particular state, and that gratitude arguments are completely unsatisfactory. Having demolished the central arguments about political obligation, he is 'forced by this examination' to acknowledge that liberal theory 'cannot offer a convincing general account of our political bonds' (p. 192). This is, of course, exactly my own conclusion, but the way in which we each arrive at this point and what we see as following from it, are very different.

In Chapter 7, I distinguished my argument from that of philosophical anarchists or radical, liberal sceptics. From William Godwin onward, there have always been a few liberal thinkers willing to push abstract individualism to one of its logical conclusions (the other is Hobbes' conclusion) and deny that the state has a legitimate claim to authority. My argument is not merely sceptical about political obligation. In order to sort out and discuss some basic problems (including establishing why political obligation *is* a problem) this book is written using a certain mode of (modern) political argument. Perhaps that form of argument now seems so 'natural' that it can be read in only one fashion, as my reviewers appear to have read it. But the book can also be read in the light of another political argument; not philosophical anarchism, but the social and political theory of anarchism. The latter is less concerned with denying the claims of the state as showing why a socio-political transformation to a non-statist order is required. These are two very different projects; the political theory of anarchism is fundamentally concerned with empirical questions about the structure and operation of social and political institutions, whereas the narrowly philosophical inquiry of the doubting liberal all too easily embraces what Unger (1984, p. 88) has called 'the ancient alliance of skepticism and surrender'.

Simmons does not ask any empirical questions, but the manner in which they enter into his argument illustrates how philosophical anarchism can lead to support for, rather than a challenge to, the liberal democratic state. He rightly points out that the argument that political obligation cannot be justified, or that the liberal state has no legitimate claim to authority, does not entail that no distinction can be drawn between good or bad, better or worse forms of government. Philosophical anarchism does not mean that liberal government is no different from any other. He then goes on to argue that the real place of arguments about benefits is not in bolstering claims about political obligation (which are spurious) but in evaluating governments. After all, then, it may well turn out that although citizens are not bound to the liberal state by ties of obligation, they are bound because of empirical facts about the benefits provided by liberal democracies. Simmons does not draw this conclusion, but, from the philosophical anarchist perspective, the fact that the empirical basis for the benefits argument looks even more shaky than it did when I was writing this book, is less relevant in assessing the worth of governments than the still relatively favourable comparison of liberal democracies with other forms of state.

Radically sceptical arguments are a welcome antidote to most treatments of political obligation, but they cannot go beyond a denial of legitimacy and provide the theoretical perspective necessary to think about the democratic transformation of the liberal state. The philosophical anarchist conclusion does not disturb the liberal assumption that political obligation is a vertical relationship that exists only between the citizen and the state. The benefits argument is about the advantage of social co-operation, fair play and following rules, and it thus implicitly appeals to horizontal relations between participants. Simmons is doubtful whether 'modern political communities' can plausibly be seen as large-scale co-operative schemes, but he does not pursue the question of what relationship, if any, there is between the vertical and horizonal conceptions of political obligation in liberal theory, or whether the concept of obligation as a bond between citizens may not suggest that criticism can be taken further than a mere denial of the validity of arguments about political obligation. Nor does he ask whether the consent, fair play, natural duties and gratitude arguments— which are entirely general in their scope—are not just as implausible when applied to other major institutions such as the workplace.

If the benefits, or conceptual, argument will not work, rational and social choice theory shows why a return to radically individualist theory is no solution. The social and political developments to which I referred earlier have been accompanied by, and are in part reflected in, an increasingly individualist mode of discourse and activity. One of the most striking features of the past two decades is the extent to which the assumptions of liberal individualism have permeated the whole of social life. The assumptions are exhibited in the new right-wing political movements; in the economic and social doctrines of the Reagan government in the USA, of the Thatcher government in the UK and of an influential faction of the Liberal party in Australia; in arguments and policies about equal opportunity in the so-called sexual revolution; and, in academia, particularly clearly in work in social choice and rational choice theory.

These fields are highly technical, but they hark back to classical liberal contract doctrines and claims that social order is founded on the interactions of self-interested, utility-maximizing individuals, protecting and enlarging their property in the capitalist market. Ironically—although not altogether unexpectedly in the light of Hobbes' arguments of three centuries ago—both rational choice and social choice theory have served to show how very difficult, if not impossible, it is to generate orderly social interaction and contract from abstractly individualist premises. Rational choice theory is preoccupied with problems of co-ordination, co-operation and free riding. Social choice theorists are concerned with the problems of aggregating individual preferences, and the work of the latter is directly related to arguments about political obligation and consent since it further undermines the claims made about liberal democratic voting.

In *Liberalism Against Populism*, William Riker takes voting to be 'at the heart of both the method and ideal of democracy' (p. 8). He argues that social choice theory shows that only 'liberalism', in a very minimal form, is feasible. The problem revealed by social choice theorists (a problem first noticed by Condorcet in the eighteenth century) is that there is no way, using different procedures of liberal democratic voting, in which preferences can be aggregated to give a determinate outcome independent of the procedure used. There is also no way of knowing, in any particular case, whether the aggregations have been subject to manipulation. Riker's conclusion is that social choice theory has shown that 'populism'—in which the outcome of a voting procedure is held to embody the will of the people that is then implemented by governmental officials—is untenable; there can be no popular will.

However, the liberal state (or 'democracy') is feasible because liberalism requires only that a liberal democratic voting procedure provides a decision on the election of candidates. Liberal democratic voting offers the possibility that representatives could be turned out of office, and this is compatible with all the aggregation problems uncovered in social choice theory. Riker does not discuss consent, but his argument suggests that the only way in which consent could be linked to voting is through voting as authorization. However, it is far from clear that social choice theory leaves even that comfort to the liberal claims about political obligation. Criticizing Riker's conclusion, Coleman (1985) has shown that if social choice theorists are right, then liberalism is no more defensible than Riker's populism. If the outcomes of voting procedures differ according to the procedure used, then the removal (or not) of representatives from office is an entirely arbitrary process, since the result could well have been different if another procedure was used. In which case, consent is rendered meaningless, and the connection between liberal democratic voting and political obligation is severed once again.

Social choice theory is also significant in another respect. One of my reviewers objected that I was mistaken in arguing that the liberal democratic state entailed the alienation of the citizen's right to make political decisions. Contemporary technology means that it is now possible to install voting devices in the homes of all citizens and policies could be determined directly by their votes (Dagger, 1980). The argument that participatory democracy could be implemented by technological means is often put forward, but such a system resembles Riker's 'populism' rather than participatory democracy. The proposal also founders upon the problems of aggregating individual preferences and upon the equally severe problems of finding a way of reducing alternatives in a non-arbitrary fashion so that they could be presented to the voters to record their preferences in a suitably simplified form. The host of other practical problems surrounding this seemingly straightforward technological solution—for instance, by whom, and how, are the policy questions to be formulated, and how are the voters to learn of the arguments for and against the various proposals and what their implications are?—make it extremely implausible. Moreover, even if it were possible to overcome the technical problems of aggregation of votes and the practical difficulties, the technological solution is an embellishment to, rather than a real change in, the political lion-skin of liberal citizenship.

Technology of this kind extends liberalism instead of moving toward democracy; the representative structure of the liberal democratic state is augmented by numerous and regular referenda on policy questions. Such proposals take for granted the liberal conception of the citizen and of the political, so that obligation is seen as a vertical bond between each individual and the state. Voting would become more frequent, instead of being confined to special occasions, and would authorize policies as well as the choice of candidates, but it would still be an isolated, privatized act, unrelated to daily life or other aspects of political activity. Indeed, to have voting devices in the home would reinforce the view that citizens vote in pursuit of their private interests, and would do little to restore the right of political decision making, in the wider, democratic sense of 'political', alienated through exercise of the franchise in the privacy of the voting booth. Nor would it develop the capacities required collectively to create and maintain political life. Recording an individual preference (based on what criteria?) at a computer in the home is unlikely to develop an understanding of the significance of a relationship of *obligation*. Political obligation is a much more complex matter than determining the outcome of the aggregation of subjective calculations or preferences.

Liberal abstract individualism requires that mechanisms must be found to bring individuals together with institutions. The structure of liberal theory suggests that the liberal state is created (through the social contract) after the individual has been constituted, but the individual and the state (institutions) are two poles of one theoretical construct (the individual must be abstracted *from* something). However, since liberal theory cannot admit that individuals and institutions are integrally related without acknowledging the incoherence of abstract individualism, it is committed to a continuous search for ways in which individuals can be connected to institutions in a manner binding them to uphold the rules. The search gives rise to two characteristic features of discussions of political obligation.

First, at one level, citizenship becomes subsumed under voting (legal electoral activity). Voting comes to occupy its peculiar place as *the* political act, as the individual act that is *sui generis* because it is the one political activity equally open to each individual (as a right), which, when performed, creates a vertical, unmediated bond between each individual citizen singularly and the institution of the state. At the same time, voting is also seen as nothing more than the extension of the private activities of individuals as they protect their property. This paradoxical act, carried out in isolation from the rest of the individual's social and political life, then has to bear the weight of three-hundred years of hypothetical voluntarist arguments to secure the citizen firmly to and under the authority of the state. Second, at another level, citizenship becomes subsumed under the law of the state, or, more broadly, under the rules and procedures which regulate associations and organizations. Citizens are obligated because of the advantages they derive from voluntarily participating in rule-governed associations, including the liberal state. The major task of citizenship is then to ensure that the rules are impartial in form and are fairly applied. Liberal argument thus continually bounces to and fro from concentration on the individual act (a vote, an agreement, a choice or a preference), which takes the institution for granted, to concentration on general rules (the law, the rules of a club, the rule of promising), which retains the individual act only as a ghostly hypothesis.

Neither pole of the liberal theoretical oscillation can encompass the richness, complexities and tensions of our moral, social and political life, because each pole has to exclude the perspective gained from the other. Individuals and institutions can never be considered or given due weight together; the focus is always on one at the expense of the other (Fishkin, 1982, provides another recent example). Democratic theoretical inquiry has to make the break with abstract individualism and its other side, the fixation on rules. My argument that (a participatory form of) voting is the political analogue to promising does not, I now think, provide a sufficiently clear break; voting still has too privileged a place. A major deficiency in contemporary political theory is that the relationship between voting and other forms of political participation is so little discussed. A comprehensive theory of political obligation would have to remedy this neglect. In a democratic political order, voting would be one form of participation through which citizens could create political obligation, but various other political activities would also be explicitly understood as constituting commitment (or refusal of commitment).

Before the theoretical turn from abstract individualism can be made it is necessary to have grasped the significance of the liberal achievement in imagining that individuals could be entirely independent of their social relations and thus have to make them for themselves. Without this theoretical feat the non-liberal understanding of the individual and individuality could not have been developed in criticism of the liberal abstraction. The legacy of a concept of individuality that is, at one and the same time, embedded in and constituted by social relations, and yet able critically to judge, to change and recreate them, allows the development of a theory of a democratic socio-political practice of political obligation in which individuals can educate, enlarge and use their capacities to transform their social contexts.

In many respects the theoretical break has been made again and again. There is a long and varied philosophical tradition that emphasizes what Durkheim called the non-contractual basis of contract, that stresses intersubjectivity, common meanings, the social character of individuality and the dialectic between individuals and social relations. Hegel is one of the greatest figures in this tradition, and a pale reflection of his profound insights can be seen in the proponents of the conceptual argument and Rawls' idea of social union. In my attempt to go beyond, rather than to criticize liberalism, I drew on Rousseau, one of the earliest critics of abstract individualism. All the furiously contested questions of the interpretation of Rousseau were thus opened up. But there was one very good reason for using Rousseau as a starting point—his arguments are couched in terms of the social contract tradition and leave no doubt that the problems are about political *obligation*.

Using Rousseau complicates matters, because most other writers critical of abstract individualism are either also critics of contract theory, (rightly) seeing it as part of the theoretical perspective they are attacking, or—in the case of marxist and neo-marxists—interpreting it as a utilitarian justification of the state. So one difficulty with using existing criticism of abstract individualism is that, if one turns to Rousseau, the non-contractual basis of his critique of liberalism is obscured by his use of social contract language; if one turns elsewhere, it is usually to find that the relevant issues are discussed as questions of legitimation rather than obligation. The problems of legitimation and obligation are not the same, since legitimation centres on questions of belief and meaning: do citizens believe in the claims of the state, or in their own obligation?; do they accept the meanings with which the state surrounds its claims? Legitimation problems, that is, overlap with the problems of hypothetical voluntarism, and do not address the questions central to the problem of obligation; such questions as why the meanings and beliefs are discussed in terms of individual freedom, equality and consent, or whether—and if—beliefs about the claims of the state have any empirical basis. Recent social, economic and political developments have increased the legitimation crisis, but it is not presently clear how far the specifically political mechanisms on which arguments about consent depend, and to which social contract arguments direct our attention, have been shaken, or to what extent the crisis provides avenues for democratic transformation.

There are some recent contributions to this critical theoretical tradition that bear directly on my argument. In particular, there has been a revival of interest in political judgement. Political judgement is central to a theory of democratic political life. Judgement will always be necessary in deciding when to assume obligations, what kind of obligations they should be or when it is necessary to refuse to commit oneself in certain ways. Ronald Beiner (1983, p. 8) offers an account of judgement as a capacity that can 'potentially, be shared by all. It enables us to appraise particulars without depending upon rules or rule-governed technique, and it involves release from the confines of private subjectivity since we can support our judgements with publicly adducible reasons or grounds.' But, Beiner argues, if valid judgements are to be made, 'there must exist a way of breaking the twin stranglehold of methodical rules and arbitrary subjectivism' (p. 2). Contemporary liberal arguments about political obligation are caught in this stranglehold as they oscillate from arguments about subjective reason, preferences and self-interest, to arguments about the fairness of rules and decision procedures. Beiner links his analysis to the claim that political judgement is connected to a renewal and revival of citizenship, but he says nothing about the form of education through which the capacities necessary for judgement might be developed, or the social conditions and forms of political organization necessary if we are self-consciously to understand ourselves as certain kinds of political beings.

In a participatory democracy citizens would exercise their judgement about all aspects of their lives, so that their political judgements would be part of this wider exercise of capacities. But their collective, political judgement is of particular importance. When judgement (or legislative will) is primary, and not rules or law, it is necessary to have socially understood and communally agreed upon principles of political morality. Here, my borrowings from Rousseau have worried reviewers who have objected that the criterion of judgement which I cited from Rousseau—that decisions should benefit and burden all citizens equally—is inappropriate because any decision will benefit some more than others, and treat some differently from others (Markus, 1982: Mansbridge, 1980). However, from a democratic rather than a liberal perspective, this is exactly the point: to maintain the autonomy that enables individuals to judge politically and play a full, active role as citizens who must create and uphold their own political obligations, different treatment may be necessary. The important issue is not Rousseau-interpretation, but the contrasting place and meaning of equality in a liberal and a self-managing democratic system.

The claim that benefits and burdens will not be equally shared if there is differential treatment implies that 'equality' means 'the same'. The current political battles over equality of opportunity, affirmative action and other policies to assist the presently disadvantaged illustrate that this is the liberal notion of equality, and also how difficult it is to use the language of equality, except in a specific context, outside of the liberal framework. The liberal standpoint looks to the impartiality and fairness of rules that are independent of any substantive notions of political morality or the common good. Such rules regulate the interactions of individuals who are also conceptualized independently of common ends and morality, and who, therefore, can all be regarded as identical or interchangeable (Rawls' original position and notion of equality of opportunity are the logical conclusion of this standpoint). Fair treatment under the rules, or equal allocation of benefits and burdens, can thus only mean that all individuals who fall under the relevant rules must be treated in the same way. Equality, as can be seen from the liberal accounts of the state of nature, thus has a primary place in liberal theory, but it has a more limited role in a democratic theory.

Citizens in a democratic political order will have an equal, i.e., the same, standing as citizens (that is, in part, what citizenship means); they will have the same rights or liberties. The status of citizen is fundamental, but this does not mean that, in a substantive sense, it is completely encompassed in the language of equality. Equality is a primary category of liberalism because individuals, pictured abstractly, necessarily have no characteristics that ('naturally') distinguish one from the others— and so 'individual' becomes a universal category. Once liberalism turns into pluralist liberalism and tries to take account of variations among individuals and the variety of social associations within which they actually live their lives, the content of 'equality' becomes more and more uncertain and diffuse. Similarly, democratic citizenship can be said to require 'equality of social conditions', but the difficulty is in specifying what 'equality' involves here. It is plainly not identity or sameness in all respects, even if economic circumstances were transformed so that all citizens had a very similar income, or accumulation of wealth. The liberal categories of equality and freedom must be reconceptualized in a democratic theory of political obligation. Equality will be relevant primarily to the standing of citizens, and autonomy will be the fundamental category. Democratic theory begins from a social conception of individuality constituted within the diverse social contexts in which real, complexly differentiated human beings live. If the conditions for individual autonomy are to be created and enhanced, the requirements of individuals and groups may differ if some are not to bear lighter burdens or enjoy greater benefits. Moreover, it is citizens themselves who will have to develop the capacity to judge whether the social conditions for autonomous democratic citizenship (and hence political obligation) are being furthered or weakened.

A democratic theory of political obligation and political judgement will, therefore, involve a conception of practical reason. In another new, and rather opaque, contribution to the debate about political obligation, John Dunn (1980) claims that questions discussed under the heading of 'obligation' are really about what, politically, citizens have good reason to do. 'Obligation', he states, 'is an overbearing word' that is best dispensed with (p. 252). He argues that in the past (and, I assume, the recent past), theories couched in terms of obligation have been 'an exercise in superstition' (p. 297), and have given a misleading impression of the central problems. Dunn sees no hope that a theory of political obligation, as it has generally been conceived, can be developed because it has to deal with too much at once. Instead, a theory of political duties is required that is part of a more general account of reasons for acting politically. Leaving aside Dunn's failure to explain why 'obligation' has been so central to the problem of the relation between the citizen and the liberal state, and his attempt to dissolve the problem by merely asserting that we *do* have political duties in the liberal democratic state, there is no political theory that could provide what he demands.

No general theory of rational action or political reason can answer the question of how citizens in a specific historical time and place, confronting particular problems, should act politically. Political theory can give some guidance, in the sense that a theory of political obligation can, for example, help citizens understand how it is that citizenship is seen in a certain way, how the character of the liberal democratic state and their relationship to it is best interpreted, and how a democratic conception of social and political life differs from liberalism. But the question of what actions ought to be taken, here and now, that might be successful in furthering a democratic transformation of social life and creating relations of political obligation between citizens, can be answered only by the deliberation and judgement of the citizens involved. They have to make the decision, for good or ill, and no general political theory can provide the political knowledge and experience that is derived from actual political participation.

There is also another fundamental limitation to the help that can be gained from political theory about questions of political action. At various points in this book I commented on the problem of incorporating women into arguments about political obligation. I have now concluded from my more recent research that I greatly underestimated the depth and complexity of the problem.

When I wrote *The Problem of Political Obligation*, I had begun to appreciate the significance of the extraordinarily far-reaching questions that the feminist movement and feminist political theorists were raising, and I tried to provide some indication of how important the classic writers' arguments about the sexes were to their wider claims about political obligation. Nevertheless, the passages about women are largely an addition to my own use of more familiar, radical criticism of liberalism. I believed that the difficulty was not in the categories of argument, whether those of liberals or their critics, but in extending what were, in principle, universal arguments and concepts to women as well as men. I assumed that the classic writers had either contradicted their own arguments when they wrote about women (e.g., Rousseau) or that their views on the relation between the sexes were historical accidents (see also Brennan and Pateman, 1979). I now see that I was mistaken.

The claims about the sexes made by the classic writers are central to their theories; their arguments about political life are dependent upon what they have to say, or what they silently take for granted, about relationships between men and women. The modern, liberal conception of the individual is not a universal conception that, contingently, initially excluded women; rather, the manner in which the idea of the free and equal individual was constructed was sexually particular. The 'individual', and the public world for which his capacities naturally fit him, are not universal but sexually particular, or masculine. The classic texts (if read appropriately) make it clear why the masculine individual is treated as universal, as representative, as 'everyman'. However, in both liberal theory and that of its critics, the masculine character of the individual remains unacknowledged and, instead, the 'individual' is implicitly presented as sexless. Radical critics of liberalism have vigorously attacked the abstract character of liberal theory but have never extended their criticisms to the greatest abstraction of all—the assumption that it is possible to talk of 'the' individual and 'the' citizen. To talk of 'the' individual presupposes that only *one* of two real individuals, the feminine and the masculine, is taken as universal. Now that women have finally won a large measure of formal, civil equality with men, including the franchise, it appears as if there can be no question about the extension of liberal and democratic arguments to both sexes, the arguments seem to have been shown to be sexually neutral. On the contrary, when liberalism is formally universalized, the conception of what it is to be an individual and a citizen remains sexually particular. The present bitter controversy over the substantive social position of women is hardly surprising when liberalism has no place for women *as women*.

Another reason why there are difficulties in making use of the radical theoretical tradition opposed to liberalism (and in this area the difficulties are profound) is that, despite the long history of criticism, both traditions rest upon shared assumptions about the character of and relationship between women and men and the private and political worlds. This means that the social transformation required to create a genuinely democratic political order, and political obligation, is much greater than suggested in this book, for it involves not just the creation of a non-statist form of social life but a transformation of our conceptions of, and the way in which we live out, masculinity and femininity.

My claim that the category of the individual and his public world are sexually particular depends on an appreciation of the relationship between the three terms 'individual', 'private' and 'public', only one aspect of which is usually considered (see Pateman, 1983a). The familiar argument that promising is not like political obligation depends upon a separation of the political—the sphere where voluntarism can, at best, be only hypothetical—from the social, the private arena of voluntarism. Social contract theory is a great deal more complicated than is usually supposed. The social contract brings into being a new public world (civil or political society); the world of the individual, of universalism, of impartial rules and laws, of freedom, equality, rights, property, contract, self-interest, justice—and political obligation. However, this world gains its meaning and significance in relation to and in contrast with the sphere that is created simultaneously; the modern, private or personal and domestic sphere. The private sphere is the world of particularism, of subjection, inequality, nature, emotion, love and partiality. Neither the public nor the private world can be understood in isolation from each other, although this is taken to be possible in the conventional understanding of the 'political' and the subject matter of political theory.

The separation of the two spheres is the cornerstone of the development of modern liberalism—and it remains unexamined by the critics of liberalism. The separation is most economically exemplified in Locke's separation of paternal from political power, but that formulation, and the long history of political theory built upon it, systematically obscures the fact that the separation between the two spheres *is also a separation of the sexes*. Only men have the natural capacities to take part in public life; the universal sphere is a masculine arena. Women are natural subjects, who, as Rousseau and Freud spell out, are inherently subversive of the civil order (see Pateman, 1980a), and so have their proper place in the private, feminine sphere. Moreover, this means that political theory, including discussions of political obligation, is based on the implicit assumption that the sexes are divided and opposed. The ultimate irony is that feminists are now accused of setting women and men against each other, and of introducing irrelevant sexual divisions and differences into political theory.

However, this fundamental, *patriarchal* separation between private and public is *not* the relevant division for the comparision between promising and political obligation. The contrast between the voluntarist sphere of 'society', or private, everyday life, and the non-voluntarist sphere of the state, of public citizenship, is a division drawn *within* what I have been calling the public world. The latter division takes for granted that the public world, or political society, has already been constituted in opposition to the private, personal and familial sphere. The latter is then repressed and lies 'forgotten' as political theorists concentrate on their object of study, the universal, public realm which is then seen through the familiar liberal notions of the private (private enterprise, promising, 'society') and the public (citizenship, political obligation, the 'state'). The inquiries of political theorists presuppose the existence of a sphere that, when explicitly mentioned (a rare occurrence in most contemporary theory, unlike the classics), is treated as the natural foundation of civil life. Precisely because the private world is 'forgotten' in the familiar controversies over political obligation and democracy, the assumption that the individual and other associated categories are universal appears completely sound.

An instructive example of the lack of understanding of the patriarchal character of modern political theory occurs in another review of this book. Rogowski (1981) argues that I was mistaken in looking for a political equivalent to promising; rather, obligation arises from functioning membership in a community. He suggests that the family provides the model of such a community which can be 'applied' to political associations. To argue that the family provides the model for political life is to disregard, in a rather startling way, the foundation of modern political theory in the assumption that women and the private form of association—family life—stand in contrast to, opposed to, and even as a threat to, political life.

The family has its origin in the marriage contract and the consent of a women to become a wife (see Pateman, 1984)—but theorists do not ask what significance these examples of contract and consent may have for arguments about political obligation. For example, consider the crucial question of consent. The problems with the standard accounts of consent that I criticized actually form only part of the difficulties surrounding consent. If the question of women and consent is examined (see Pateman, 1980b) the full theoretical poverty of contemporary argument becomes tragically evident, and the extent of the wider problem about women and political obligation begins to be revealed.

One paradox is immediately evident. Women are held to lack the capacities required by individuals who can give consent, yet, in sexual relations, where consent is fundamental, women are held always to consent and their explicit refusals are reinterpreted as consent. Radical critics of liberalism have always paid a good deal of attention to the contradictions between formal equality and liberty and substantive social conditions. Their criticism has never, however, extended to the social conditions that undermine the claim that women are now 'individuals' like men. The contradiction between women's formal equality as citizens and their substantive position as individuals (or, more accurately, lack of recognition as individuals) is nowhere more starkly revealed than in the structure of the relationship between husband and wife within marriage (the family). The assumption that women are naturally subject to men is not an antiquarian relic of the classic texts that has now been firmly rejected, but an assumption still lived out today. Consent has had no place within marriage. When a woman marries, her husband gains the right of sexual access to her body even against her will. Marriage ceremonies now usually omit the promise to obey by the wife—but that so few legal jurisdictions have, even now, reformed marriage law to make rape within marriage a criminal offence clearly indicates the depth and tenacity of patriarchal perceptions of the characters of men and women and what it means to be masculine and feminine. Any argument that is going to cite participation in the family as a model for incurring political obligation thus has to explain how such a model can be derived from an institution which continues to deny women's status as free and equal individuals and presupposes that our consent is irrelevant.

In wider personal relationships the distinction between normal and coerced (hetero)sexual relations depends upon the presence or absence of consent. In working on my paper 'Women and Consent', I found that the empirical evidence revealed that the heart of the problem of rape is that it is 'the extreme expression of, or an extension of, the accepted and 'natural' relation between men and women' (p. 161). Public opinion and the courts are all too willing to treat enforced submission as consent, a willingness that reflects the widespread conviction that a woman who says 'no' never means what she says, but really means 'yes'. Women's words, that is, are not taken at face value but are persistently and systematically invalidated and reinterpreted. 'Consent' and the refusal of consent thus become completely emptied of meaning. In the debate about political obligation, theorists do not discuss consent in the context of personal relationships (although Rousseau, for example, was well aware of its relevance) so they can therefore ignore the enormous problem of how individuals whose words are invalidated in the central matter of consent in private life can give consent as citizens. Nor do the critics of liberal theory ask how women can take their place as full members of a community in which speech, argument and deliberation are essential to the creation of political obligation.

The development of a democratic theory has to take criticism of social life a good deal further than I pursue it in this book. Apart from my brief references to promising to obey and marriage, I concentrated on the private and public spheres as conventionally discussed. But argument has to be extended to the repressed private realm of personal, sexual and familial relations. Social conditions have to be created in which genuine free agreement and promises—on the part of both sexes—can replace the myth of consent and the domination currently presented as free contract.

Moreover, the task does not end there. The development of a genuinely democratic theory of political obligation (i.e., one that includes both sexes as full citizens) has also to consider the *connection* between the public and private spheres. Radical criticism has stopped short because political theorists ignore both the construction of the individual within the patriarchal separation between private and public, and the fact that, although the two spheres are separated, they are also the two, interrelated sides of the one coin of liberal democratic social and political life. When women gain access to civil life they do not magically become transformed into examples of 'the' individual or citizen. Public laws, policies and practices also work against the development of the social context necessary for democratic citizenship, although this aspect of the problem has been less discussed in recent feminist scholarship than the manner in which women's status as wives and mothers works against their involvement in public life. Social welfare policy, especially, frequently serves to reinforce women's position as economic subordinates to men. The arguments of the advocates of participatory democracy have been as blind to the significance of these features of the liberal democracies as have the liberals they criticize.

They—including myself in my earlier work—have also failed to examine the very different positions of women and men within the (public) workplace, despite the importance of the argument that active, participatory citizenship can be developed through the education provided by democratic participation in the workplace (see also Pateman, 1983b). The 'worker', too, is a sexually particular category that presupposes that the necessities of daily life are taken care of in the (private) domestic sphere so that the worker can sell his labour power in the public market and work, undistracted, for eight hours for his employer.

The empirical evidence shows that women typically work at the low-status, low-skilled jobs in which it is unlikely that any opportunities to participate will be taken up.

Furthermore, since married women workers have two jobs—one unpaid in the home, and one in paid employment—there is a very serious question about why they would or should be eager to take on the further responsibilities of democratized workplaces. Nor is it clear that women, as workers, are acknowledged to have the standing necessary to be active participants. Conceptions of femininity and masculinity, and the capacities they are held to embody, are maintained and reinforced in public as well as private life. Over the past few years a practice that has come to be known as sexual harrassment has received some publicity, but its implications for citizenship are rarely commented upon. For women, the discipline of the factory is also sexual discipline, and this underlines the continuity between assumptions about women's natural subordination in private life and their position as participants in public life. Some new discussions of participatory democracy no longer refer to 'men' and are instead self-consciously couched in terms of 'men and women'—but indicate no awareness of the profound difficulties in extending existing arguments to women.

My more recent research has led me to the conclusion that a distinctively feminist perspective in political theory provides as searching and as fundamental a critique of radical democratic theory as it does of liberalism, precisely because both theories are sexually particular, predicated upon the patriarchal separation of private and public, women and men. At first glance, liberal abstract individualism appears emancipatory since it denies that sexual difference is politically relevant and so appears to be sexually impartial. The impartiality is bought at the expense of a conception of feminine individuality. The great critics of liberal contract theory, Rousseau and Hegel, insisted that sexual difference was important for political life, but both argued in some detail that, because of women's passions, citizenship must be sexually particular. The enormous task facing anyone who wishes to develop a genuinely democratic theory of political obligation is to formulate a universal theory, including civil equality, that also embodies a social conception of individuality as feminine and masculine, that gives due weight to the unity and the differentiation of humankind.

My comments in the final chapter about a non-statist, horizontal view of the political fail to break through the confines of standard, radical arguments about citizenship. If the political is to become the dimension of social life in which citizens build and maintain their common undertakings, in any genuine sense of 'common', as much attention as is presently given to the workplace has to be paid to sexual relations and to activities dismissed as 'women's work'. A democratic recasting of the relationship and distinction between the personal and the political cannot be achieved when theoretical investigation denies any moral and political significance to areas of social life which encompass some of our deepest and most lasting attachments.

Arguments about citizenship and education have also completely ignored the long history of feminist argument and political activity that has been every bit as preoccupied with civic virtue and political education as the theorists and social experiments always cited by democratic theorists. Women's activities and political struggles, never drawn upon by the proponents in the controversy over democratic theory and political obligation, have frequently taken very different forms and had different aims than the men's activities which have been seen as definitive of political life. The long history of women's political activity has been dramatically brought to

194

attention since 1981 by the women's peace camp at Greenham Common nuclear missile base in England, where, in 1982, 30,000 women surrounded the perimeter fence and decorated it with symbols of life, including baby clothes. (It is now an offence to thread wool through the fence of a missile base.) No wonder the liberal conception of citizenship is so impoverished and its major alternative truncated, when neither side has accepted that women's tasks and political struggles could enrich our understanding of what it is to be an active citizen, or that conceptions of commitment, obligation and what we morally ought to do could be deepened and strengthened by looking beyond the abstract individual, the workplace or universal rules.

Reconstruction of democratic theory has to reach into the heart of the conventional understanding of sexual identity as well as into the structure of the state. Despite the magnitude of the theoretical task, there are some hopeful signs. Liberal justifications for political obligation in the liberal democratic state are now in tatters, and there are indications that political theory and philosophy are taking a turn away from long-established modes of liberal argument and criticism. Feminist theorists have begun to ask radical questions about sexual difference, and there are various examples of the contextual, relational, differentiated, theoretical approach that is needed in an account of political obligation, although it has to be said that such work is proceeding independently of feminist scholarship which points in the same general direction. On the other hand, whether the democratic, social basis required for long-term advance in theoretical inquiry can be developed is another matter. There are examples of imaginative communal action to be seen in a wide variety of settings from local government, land rights campaigns and the feminist movement, to the labour, peace and green movements, but the liberal democratic state is no longer Locke's umpire, nor armed only with Leviathan's sword. For citizens faced with increasing numbers of biological, chemical and nuclear weapons, cluster bombs and other anti-personnel and citizen-control devices, democratic political transformation was never more difficult, nor more urgently required.

Carole Pateman, Center for Advanced Study in the Behavioural Sciences*

* I am very grateful to the Center not only for material support but for providing such a marvellous environment for theoretical work. My thanks also to Graham Baugh and Nancy Fraser for their helpful comments.

Notes

Introduction

1. See for example McPherson, T. (1967), *Political Obligation*, Routledge, London; Pitkin, H. (1972), 'Obligation and consent', in P. Laslett, W. G Runciman and Q. Skinner (Eds), *Philosophy, Politics and Society*, Fourth Series, Blackwell, Oxford; and, for an earlier example of this argument, Macdonald, M. (1960), 'The language of political theory', in A. Flew (Ed.), *Logic and Language*, First Series, Blackwell, Oxford.
2. Riley, P. (1973), 'How coherent is the social contract tradition?', *Journal of the History of Ideas*, **XXXIV**, 543.
3. Rawls, J.(1972), *A Theory of Justice*, Oxford University Press, p. 13.
4. Adkins, A. W. H. (1960), *Merit and Responsibility: A Study in Greek Values*, Oxford University Press, and (1972), *Moral Value and Political Behaviour in Ancient Greece*, Chatto & Windus, London. For a recent version of this general argument see for example Salkever, S. G. (1974), 'Virtue, obligation and politics', *American Political Science Review*, **LXVIII**, 78–92.
5. Reid, W. M. and Henderson, J. S. (1976), 'Political obligation: an empirical approach', *Polity*, **IX**, 2, 238 and 252.
6. Schumpeter, J. A. (1952), *Capitalism, Socialism and Democracy*, Allen and Unwin, London, 5th ed., pp. 244–5. On the introduction of universal suffrage in the western liberal democracies see Therborn, G. (1977), 'The rule of capital and the rise of democracy', *New Left Review*, **103**, 3–41.
7. See McPherson (1967), pp. 84–5.
8. I have borrowed the term from Connolly, W. E. (1973), 'Theoretical self-consciousness', *Polity*, **VI**, 5–35.
9. An excellent article has now appeared on this topic; however, it does not cover the aspects of contract theory which I discuss below: Gauthier, D. (1977), 'The social contract as ideology', *Philosophy and Public Affairs*, **6**, 2, 130–64.
10. See, for example, Walzer, M. (1971), *Obligations*, Simon and Schuster, New York; Zweibach, B. (1975), *Civility and Disobedience*, Cambridge University Press; Johnson, K. (1975), 'Political obligation and the voluntary association model of the state', *Ethics*, **86**, 17–29; Dagger, R. K. (1977), 'What is political obligation?', *American Political Science Review*, **LXXI**, 1, 86–94.
11. For these terms see for example Walzer (1971), p. 207; Pranger, R. J. (1968), *The Eclipse of Citizenship*, Holt, Reinhart and Winston, New York, p. 29; Arendt, H. (1973), 'Civil disobedience', in *Crises of the Republic*, Penguin, Middlesex, pp. 69–70.

Chapter 1

1. Hobbes, T. (1968), *Leviathan*, Ed. C. B. Macpherson, Penguin, Middlesex, p. 268.
2. See Connolly, W. E. (1974), *The Terms of Political Discourse*, Heath, Lexington, Mass., and MacIntyre, A. (1967), *A Short History of Ethics*, Routledge, London.
3. More generally on the development of 'individualism' see Lukes, S. (1973), *Individualism*, Blackwell, Oxford.

196

4. I have criticized this denial in more detail in Pateman, C. (1973), 'Political obligation and conceptual analysis', *Political Studies*, XXI, 199–218.
5. Pitkin (1972), p. 80; 84.
6. Sesonske, A. (1964), *Value and Obligation*, Oxford University Press, p. 80.
7. Tussman, J. (1960), *Obligation and the Body Politic*, Oxford University Press, especially p. 37.
8. I have adapted the term from Pitkin's (1972) 'hypothetical consent'.
9. Brandt, R. B. (1964), 'The concepts of obligation and duty', *Mind*, **73**, 386.
10. Rawls (1972), p. 113.
11. Singer, P. (1973), *Democracy and Disobedience*, Oxford University Press, p. 50.
12. Verba, S., and Nie, N. H. (1972), *Participation in America*, Harper and Row, New York, p. 106.
13. I should like to thank Gordon Schochet for allowing me to read his unpublished paper, 'Contract, Consent and Political Obligation', which alerted me to the importance of this distinction. See also Schochet, G. J. (1975), *Patriarchalism in Political Thought*, Blackwell, Oxford, p. 9; 262.

Chapter 2

1. Braybrooke, D. (1975), 'Through epistemology to the depths of political illusion', paper presented to the Annual Meeting of the American Political Science Association.
2. Pitkin (1972), p. 74.
3. Hume, D. (1953), 'Of the original contract', in *Political Essays*, Ed. C. W. Hendel, Library of Liberal Arts, p. 56 (first published 1748).
4. See, for example, Pitkin (1972); my discussion of promising is indebted to Pitkin's work. On the idea of promising as a performative utterance see Austin, J. L. (1962), *How to do Things with Words*, Oxford University Press; and on promising as a speech act see Searle, J. R. (1969), *Speech Acts*, Cambridge University Press.
5. The term is taken from Gauthier, D. (1977), pp. 153–7.
6. Taylor, C. (1976), 'Hermeneutics and politics', in P. Connerton (Ed.), *Critical Sociology*, Penguin, Middlesex, p. 177.
7. The nearest we can come to an 'abstract' individual is probably the feral child. This only shows the oddity of abstract individualism, an oddity illustrated in Truffaut's film *L'Enfant Sauvage* and Herzog's film *The Enigma of Kaspar Hauser*.
8. Pitkin (1972), p. 77.
9. Rawls, J. (1972), pp. 345–6. Compare Flathman, R. E. (1972), *Political Obligation*, Atheneum, New York, p. 141.
10. The conceptual argument can be found, for example, in McPherson, T. (1967), and Pitkin (1972).
11. I have been helped in thinking about this distinction by Sesonske, A. (1964) and Beran, H. (1972), 'Ought, obligation and duty', *Australasian Journal of Philosophy*, **50**, 207–21.
12. Pitkin (1972), p. 81.
13. Flathman (1972), p. 214.
14. I have borrowed the phrases from Thomson, J. J. (1973), 'A defense of abortion' in J. Feinberg (Ed.), *The Problem of Abortion*, Wadsworth, Belmont, California, pp. 35–7. If references are frequently made to individuals' 'consent' where it is superfluous, the consent of women is often deemed irrelevant (or appropriately assessed by someone else) in cases such as abortion and rape where it vitally affects her person and interests.
15. This is graphically illustrated in Titmuss, R. M. (1970), *The Gift Relationship*, Allen and Unwin, London.
16. Flathman (1972), p. 197.
17. Hume (1953), p. 45.
18. Bradley, F. H. (1927), 'My station and its duties', in *Ethical Studies*, Oxford University

Press, 2nd ed., p. 162. On duty see also, for example, Brandt (1964) and Beran (1972).
19. Rawls (1972), p. 345.
20. Pitkin (1972), p. 74, footnote.
21. For empirical arguments and evidence about the feasibility of participatory democracy see Pateman, C. (1970), *Participation and Democratic Theory*, Cambridge University Press.

Chapter 3

1. Oakeshott, M. (1975), *Hobbes on Civil Association*, Blackwell, Oxford, p. 63.
2. Macpherson, C. B. (1962), *The Political Theory of Possessive Individualism*, Oxford University Press, p. 30.
3. References in brackets in the text are to chapter and page number of Hobbes (1968), *Leviathan*, Ed. C. B. Macpherson.
4. Another way of putting this argument is that a 'private language' is not possible; this has been a subject of discussion among philosophers under the impetus of Wittgenstein's theories. See for example Winch, P. (1958), *The Idea of a Social Science*, Routledge, London, especially pp. 33–9.
5. Cf. the comments on the capacity to make promises in Gauthier, D. (1969), *The Logic of Leviathan: The Moral and Political Theory of Thomas Hobbes*, Oxford University Press, p. 43.
6. See Macpherson, C. B. (1968), 'Introduction' to *Leviathan*, p. 40, and (1962), pp. 34–5.
7. McNeilly, F. S. (1968), *The Anatomy of Leviathan*, Macmillan, London, p. 188.
8. For a more detailed discussion (but which does not take account of the distinction between 'ought' and 'obligation') see Beackon, S., and Reeve, A. (1976), 'The benefits of reasonable conduct: the *Leviathan* theory of obligation', *Political Theory*, 4, 4, 423–38.
9. 'There could, if Hobbes is to be taken strictly, be no performative utterances in the state of nature. If, *per impossible*, there could be performatives, they would be "void" ': Parry, G. (1967), 'Performative utterances and obligation in Hobbes', *Philosophical Quarterly*, 17, 251–2.
10. See, for example, Barry, B. M. (1972), 'Warrender and his critics', in M. Cranston and R. S. Peters (Eds), *Hobbes and Rousseau: A Collection of Critical Essays*, Anchor, New York, p. 51.
11. Compare Gauthier (1977), pp. 150–57, and Taylor, M. (1976), Chapter 6.
12. Riley, P. (1973a); 'Will and legitimacy in the philosophy of Hobbes: is he a consent theorist?', *Political Studies*, XXI, 4, 504.
13. See also the discussion of the 'society of sorts' that might arise between (social) individuals each acting solely on the basis of self-interest in Braybrooke, D. (1974), 'The Social Contract Returns, This Time as an Elusive Public Good', paper presented to the Annual Meeting of the American Political Science Association.
14. Watkins, J. W. N. (1973), *Hobbes's System of Ideas*, Hutchinson, London, 2nd ed., Chapter 5; McNeilly (1968), Chapter 8; Warrender, H. (1957), *The Political Philosophy of Hobbes: His Theory of Obligation*, Oxford University Press.
15. Gauthier (1969), pp. 70–1.
16. Warrender (1957), p. 237.
17. Warrender (1957), pp. 280–1. For this interpretation see also Plamenatz, J. (1963), *Man and Society*, Longmans, London, Vol. 1, pp. 125–8.
18. Warrender (1957), p. 70.
19. Macpherson (1962), p. 271.
20. Macpherson (1962), p. 83; see also p. 272.
21. Macpherson (1962), p. 273.
22. Macpherson (1962), p. 276.
23. See Winch, P. (1972), 'Man and society in Hobbes and Rousseau', in M. Cranston and

198

R. S. Peters (Eds), p. 250. I shall leave aside the question of how Hobbes' 'natural' individuals could ever agree who is to be authorized as Leviathan—unless he already is their conqueror.

24. Watkins (1973), p. 110.
25. See Brennan, T., and Pateman, C. (forthcoming) ' "Mere Auxiliaries to the Commonwealth": Women and Liberalism', *Political Studies*. On Hobbes' conception of the family as an artificial unit see Chapman, R. A. (1975), '*Leviathan* writ small: Thomas Hobbes on the family', *American Political Science Review*, **LXIX**, 1, 76–90.
26. Watkins (1973), p. 114.
27. Flathman (1972), p. 239.
28. Flathman (1972), pp. 239–40.
29. Cohen, C. (1971), *Civil Disobedience*, Columbia University Press, p. 87. There is a large, repetitive and often tedious literature on civil disobedience. Cohen's book covers most of the topics usually discussed under this heading.
30. I have borrowed the description from James, G. G. (1973), 'The orthodox theory of civil disobedience', *Social Theory and Practice*, **2**, 475–98. Some writers would even confine the term 'civil disobedience' to actions aimed at 'testing' the constitutional or legal status of particular laws.
31. Barry, B. M. (1973), *The Liberal Theory of Justice*, Oxford University Press, p. 153. Rawls' account of civil disobedience can be found in Sections 55, 57, and 59 of *A Theory of Justice*.
32. Schochet, G. J. (1972), 'The morality of resisting the penalty', in V. Held, K. Nielsen and C. Parsons (Eds), *Philosophy and Political Action*, Oxford University Press.
33. Hall, R. T. (1971), 'Legal toleration of civil disobedience', *Ethics*, **81**, 128–42.

Chapter 4

1. Plamenatz, J. (1963), *Man and Society*, Longmans, London, Vol. 1, p. 241.
2. Wolin, S. (1961), *Politics and Vision*, Allen and Unwin, London, p. 294.
3. Locke, J. (1967), 'First treatise of government', in P. Laslett (Ed.), *Two Treatises of Government*, Cambridge University Press, 2nd edition, paragraph 43. (There is some controversy about the date at which Locke wrote the two treatises, but Laslett suggests that the 'Second Treatise' was written first, about 1679–81.)
4. See Ashcraft, R.. (1968), 'Locke's state of nature: historical fact or moral fiction?', *American Political Science Review*, **LXII**, 898–915.
5. References in brackets in the text are to paragraphs of the 'Second Treatise' in Locke (1967).
6. Ashcraft (1968), pp. 902–3.
7. Locke, J. (1965), 'A letter concerning toleration', in M. Cranston (Ed.), *Locke on Politics, Religion, and Education*, Collier, New York, p. 140.
8. See Ashcraft (1968), pp. 904–5.
9. It is discussed in Pateman, C. (1975), 'Sublimation and reification: Locke, Wolin and the liberal democratic conception of the political', *Politics and Society*, **5**, 441–67. My arguments in the present chapter draw on this paper.
10. See Pitkin (1972).
11. On the importance of the invention of money see Macpherson, C. B. (1962), pp. 203–20; 233–5.
12. I refer to 'capital' because more is involved in the consent to money than its use as a medium of exchange; on this point see Poole, R.(1977), 'Locke and the Bourgeois State', Paper presented to the Annual Meeting of the Australasian Philosophy Association, especially Section iv.
13. Schochet, G. J. (1975), *Patriarchalism in Political Thought*, p. 259.

14. Dunn, J. (1969), *The Political Thought of John Locke*, Cambridge University Press, p. 106.
15. Schumpeter (1952), pp. 242–3.
16. See Laslett's 'Introduction' to the *Two Treatises of Government*, pp. 112–4; also, more recently, Abbott, P. (1976), *The Shotgun Behind the Door*, University of Georgia Press, pp. 149–51.
17. Macpherson (1962), p. 227. Wood, E. M. (1972), *Mind and Politics: An Approach to the Meaning of Liberal and Socialist Individualism*, University of California Press, p. 117, notes that in 1696 a bill passed through the English Parliament to establish, for the first time, a property qualification for MPs.
18. The phrase comes from Dunn, J. (1971), 'Consent in the political theory of John Locke', in G. J. Schochet (Ed.), *Life, Liberty and Property: Essays on Locke's Political Ideas*, Wadsworth, Belmont, p. 145.
19. Wolin, S. (1961), p. 311.
20. Hume, D. (1963), p. 51.
21. For recent examples see Simmons, A. J. (1976), 'Tacit consent and political obligation', *Philosophy and Public Affairs*, 5, pp. 274–91; Abbott (1976), pp. 115–20. Cf. Dunn (1971), p. 139, and Richards, D. A. J. (1971), *A Theory of Reasons for Action*, Oxford University Press, pp. 153–5.
22. This is discussed in more detail in Brennan and Pateman (forthcoming).
23. 'First Treatise', paragraph 47.
24. 'First Treatise', paragraph 48.
25. Macpherson (1962), pp. 232–8.
26. Schochet, G. J. (1975), *Patriarchalism in Political Thought*, Blackwell, Oxford, p. 12.
27. Cited by Schochet (1975), p. 202.
28. Dunn (1969), p. 182.
29. Locke, J.(1967a), *Two Tracts on Government*, Ed. P. Abrams, Cambridge University Press, p. 154.
30. Locke (1967a), p. 137.
31. Locke (1967a), 'Introduction', p. 99.
32. On Locke's transformation of conscience into interest or private property, see Wolin (1961), pp. 331–42.
33. Locke (1965), pp. 136–7.
34. Dunn (1971), p. 137.
35. Historically, religious toleration and religious refusal led to the establishment of the legal status of conscientious objector in the liberal democracies.
36. Rawls (1972), pp. 372–3. The orthodox account of civil disobedience ignores the historical realities of this form of political action. Martin Luther King sought to gain civil rights for blacks that were, in principle, already theirs, but, of the other 'classic' disobedients, Gandhi was an anti-imperialist who proposed radical changes in Indian society, and Thoreau was a radical individualist who took consent seriously and defended John Brown.

Chapter 5

1. Partridge, P. H. (1971), *Consent and Consensus*, Macmillan, London, p. 23.
2. Plamenatz, J. P. (1968), *Consent, Freedom and Political Obligation*, Oxford University Press, 2nd edition, p. 3.
3. Tussman, J. (1960), *Obligation and the Body Politic*, p. 37.
4. Partridge (1971), p. 23.
5. Cassinelli, C. W., (1961), *The Politics of Freedom: An Analysis of the Modern Democratic State*, University of Washington Press, p. 99; 112. Statements such as

'consent can simply be a need of strong government' can also be found: Crick, B. (1964), *In Defence of Politics*, Penguin, Middlesex, p. 179.

6. Flathman, R. (1972), *Political Obligation*, p. 230.
7. Flathman (1972), p. 232.
8. Flathman (1972), p. 216.
9. Plamenatz (1968), pp. 9–10; 16–17.
10. Plamenatz (1968), p. 10.
11. Plamenatz (1968), p. 24.
12. See also Greenawalt, K. (1970), 'A conceptual approach to disobedience', in J. R. Pennock and J. W. Chapman (Eds), *Political and Legal Obligation*, Nomos XII, Atherton, New York, pp. 344–5.
13. Jenkins, J. J. (1970), 'Political Consent', *Philosophical Quarterly*, **20**, 63.
14. Gewirth A., (1962), 'Political justice', in R. B. Brandt (Ed.), *Social Justice*, Prentice-Hall, New Jersey, p. 138.
15. Plamenatz (1968), p. 167.
16. Plamenatz, J. (1963), *Man and Society*, Vol. 1, p. 238.
17. Plamenatz (1963), p. 240.
18. Gewirth (1962), p. 138.
19. Two of the best known statements can be found in Berelson, B. R., *et al.* (1954), *Voting*, University of Chicago Press, Chapter 14; and Almond, G. A., and Verba, S. (1963), *The Civic Culture*, Princeton University Press, Chapter 15.
20. One is not legally required to cast a valid vote. 'Compulsory voting' does not apply to non-naturalized residents from outside the British Commonwealth nor to the Australian Aboriginal population. See also the comments on legal compulsion in Singer, P. (1973), *Democracy and Disobedience*, p. 56.
21. I have commented in more detail on this aspect of empirical political science in Pateman, C. (1974), 'To them that hath shall be given', *Politics*, **ix**, 139–45; and 'The civic culture: a philosophic critique', in G. Almond and L. Rose (Eds), *The Civic Culture Revisited* (forthcoming).
22. These two statements are taken respectively from McClosky H., (1970), 'Consensus and ideology in American politics', in R. E. Wolfinger (Ed.), *Readings in American Political Behavior*, Prentice-Hall, New Jersey, p. 396; Dennis, J. (1970), 'Support for the institution of elections by the mass public', *American Political Science Review*, **LXIV**, 828–9.
23. Lipsitz, L. (1970), 'On political belief: the grievances of the poor', in P. Green and S. Levinson (Eds), *Power and Community*, Vintage Books, New York, p. 165.
24. Cited in Parenti, M.(1974), *Democracy for the Few*, St Martin's Press, New York, p. 160. (From Kimball, P. (1972), *The Disconnected*, Columbia University Press, p. 17.) Parenti argues that electoral abstention is a rational response to the social inequalities of liberal democracies; see Chapter 10.
25. Verba, S., and Nie, N. H. (1972), *Participation in America: Political Democracy and Social Equality*, Harper and Row, New York, p. 338 (my emphasis).
26. See, for example, Bourque, S. C., and Grossholtz, J. (1974), 'Politics an unnatural practice: political science looks at female participation', *Politics and Society*, **4**, 2, 225–66; Goot, M., and Reid, E. (1975), 'Women and Voting Studies', *Sage Contemporary Political Sociology Series*, Vol. 1.
27. The question is asked by Jaquette in the 'Introduction' to Jaquette, J. S. (Ed.) (1974), *Women in Politics*, Wiley, New York, p. xix. In the same volume see also Iglitzin, L. B. 'The making of the apolitical woman', p. 34.
28. Lane, R. E. (1959), *Political Life*, Free Press, New York, p. 212.
29. Plamenatz (1963), p. 239.
30. The example comes from Cohen, M. (1972), 'Liberalism and disobedience', *Philosophy and Public Affairs*, **1**, 3, 312.
31. Partridge (1971), p. 40; terms such as 'manufacture' of consent occur throughout the

book, see for example pp. 41–3; 150–2.

32. See Bachrach, P., and Baratz, M. S. (1970), *Power and Poverty*, Oxford University Press; Crenson, M. A. (1971), *The Un-Politics of Air Pollution*, John Hopkins, Baltimore.

33. The phrase comes from Arendt, H. (1973), 'Lying in politics', in *Crises of the Republic*, Penguin, Middlesex.

34. The paradoxes are discussed in more detail in Pateman, C. (1975), 'Sublimation and reification', *Politics and Society*, 451–7.

35. Schumpeter, J. (1952), p. 282.

36. Marx, K. (1967), 'On the Jewish question', in L. M. Easton and K. M. Guddat (Eds), *Writings of the Young Marx on Philosophy and Society*, Anchor, New York, p. 226.

37. Prewitt, K. (1970), 'Political ambitions, volunteerism, and electoral accountability', *American Political Science Review*, **LXIV**, 1, 16.

38. Plamenatz (1968), p. 169.

39. Edelman, M. (1964), *The Symbolic Uses of Politics*, University of Illinois Press.

40. Rose, R., and Mossawir, H. (1969), 'Voting and elections; a functional analysis', in C. F. Cnudde and D. E. Neubauer (Eds), *Empirical Democratic Theory*, Markham, Chicago, p. 82. On voting as a duty see also for example di Palma, G. (1970), *Apathy and Participation*, Free Press, New York, p. 202, 'For many political participation is … the fulfillment of a duty rather than a precise calculation or a response to an immediate wrong or reward'; and Dennis (1970).

41. Plamenatz (1963), p. 241.

42. Partridge (1971), p. 65.

43. Partridge (1971), p. 149; 148.

44. Partridge (1971), p. 56. Partridge distinguishes consent from consensus, but as it turns out that consensus is 'weak' or 'low-level' consent and consent is 'supportive' consensus (p. 139; 150) I have ignored consensus.

45. Page references in the text are to Walzer, M. (1971), *Obligations: Essays on Disobedience, War and Citizenship*.

46. Plamenatz (1968), p. 24.

47. Cole, G. D. H. (1915), 'Conflicting social obligations', *Proceedings of the Aristotelian Society*, **XV**, 157.

48. Walzer, M. (1968), 'Politics in the welfare state', *Dissent*, **15**, 33.

49. Euben, J. P. (1972), 'Walzer's *Obligations*', *Philosophy and Public Affairs*, **1**, 454.

50. Johnson, K. (1975), 'Political obligation and the voluntary association model of the state', *Ethics*, **86**, p. 20; 28.

51. See Beran, H. (1977), 'In defense of the consent theory of political obligation and authority', *Ethics*, **87**, 3, especially p. 269.

52. Perhaps Walzer means something like this when he refers to the need to 'hollow out' and drain the state of 'whatever superfluous moral content and unnecessary political power it has usurped', and to reduce it 'to a transparent administrative shell': Walzer (1968), p. 37.

'Postscript' to Chapter 5

1. Salkever, S. G. (1974), 'Virtue, obligation and politics', p. 78.

2. The phrase is taken from Gouldner, A. W. (1967), *Enter Plato*, Routledge, London, p. 195. I owe thanks to Conal Condren for comments on an earlier draft of this material.

3. Adkins, A. W. H. (1960), *Merit and Responsibility*; and (1972), *Moral Value and Political Behaviour in Ancient Greece*.

4. It is also significant that Antigone made her sacrifice for a brother, a truly 'womanly' act; see Hegel, G. W. F. (1949), *The Phenomenology of Mind*, trans. J. B. Baillie, Allen and Unwin, London, pp. 475–7; and Pomeroy, S. B. (1975), *Goddesses, Whores, Wives*

202

and Slaves, Schoken, New York, pp. 99–103. For a fascinating and witty study of political disobedience in the ancient world (though it is doubtful if the examples should be called 'civil' disobedience) see Daube, D. (1972), *Civil Disobedience in Antiquity*, Edinburgh University Press.

5. Greenberg, N. A. (1965), 'Socrates' choice in the *Crito*', *Harvard Studies in Classical Philology*, **LXX**, 1, 76.
6. Rosen, F. (1973), 'Obligation and friendship in Plato's *Crito*', *Political Theory*, **1**, 3, 310.
7. Plato (1969), 'Apology' and 'Crito', in H. Tredennick (trans.), *The Last Days of Socrates*, Penguin, Middlesex, p. 68.
8. Plato (1969), p. 86.
9. Plato (1969), p. 92.
10. McIlwain, C. H. (1932), *The Growth of Political Thought in the West*, Macmillan, New York, p. 292.
11. Taylor, G. R. (1959), *Sex in History*, Thames and Hudson, London, p. 132.
12. Ullman, W. (1966), *The Individual and Society in the Middle Ages*, John Hopkins, Maryland, p. 59.
13. Aquinas, St Thomas (1965), *Selected Political Writings*, Ed. A. P. D'Entreves, Blackwell, Oxford, p. 145.
14. It has been claimed that 'the really permanent attainment of individualism was due to a religious and not a secular movement', but this seems an overstatement. Cited in Lukes (1973), *Individualism*, p. 94 (from Troeltsch, E., *The Social Teaching of the Christian Churches*, Vol. 1, p. 381).
15. See Hill, C. (1972), *The World Turned Upside Down*, Temple Smith, London.
16. Walzer, M. (1972), *The Revolution of the Saints*, Atheneum, New York, p. 57.
17. For an account, and criticism, of this claim, see Lipsitz, L. (1968): 'If, as Verba says, the state functions as a Religion, what are we to do then to save our souls?', *American Political Science Review*, **LXII**, 527–35.

Chapter 6

1. Pitkin (1972), 'Obligation and consent', p. 74.
2. McPherson (1967), *Political Obligation*, pp. 42–3. He argues that the idea of political obligation is superfluous, but I fail to see how this can be reconciled with his argument that it is conceptually necessary. The terms 'collectivist' and 'organic' are McPherson's and Macdonald's (1960).
3. McPherson (1967), p. 64.
4. See Taylor, C. (1975), *Hegel*, Cambridge University Press, pp. 449–55; Ilting, K.-H. (1971), 'The structure of Hegel's *Philosophy of Right*,' in Z. A. Pelczynski (Ed.), *Hegel's Political Philosophy*, Cambridge University Press, p. 103; 108.
5. Riley, P. (1973b), 'Hegel on consent and social contract theory: does he "cancel and preserve" the will?', *The Western Political Quarterly*, **XXVI**, 134.
6. References in brackets in the text are to the paragraphs and additions to paragraphs (AS …) of Hegel,, G. W. F. (1952), *Philosophy of Right*, trans. T. M. Knox, Oxford University Press.
7. See Walzer (1971), p. 219. More generally on Hegel's pluralism see Avineri, S. (1972), *Hegel's Theory of the Modern State*, Cambridge University Press, pp. 167–75.
8. MacIntyre, A. (1966), *A Short History of Ethics*, p. 205.
9. Although Hegel's argument about political obedience depends upon the separation of civil society and the state, he claims, of course, that his theory overcomes and transcends the separation; a claim which Marx disputed a long time ago.
10. The proposed basis of the franchise was one of Hegel's main criticisms of the Reform Act in England (in 1832). See also comments in his discussion of Wurtemberg, in Hegel (1964), *Hegel's Political Writings*, Ed. Z. A. Pelczynski, Oxford University Press, pp. 262–5; 295–330.

11. Avineri (1972), p. 172; on the relationship between the Estates and the bureaucracy see Riley (1973b), pp. 158–9.
12. Plant, R. (1973), *Hegel*, Allen and Unwin, London, p. 192.
13. See Riley (1973b), p. 160; also on the monarch Marcuse, H. (1955), *Reason and Revolution*, 2nd ed., pp. 217–8.
14. Riley (1973b), p. 156.
15. Avineri (1972), p. 154.
16. Lubasz, H. (1976), 'Marx's initial problematic: the problem of poverty', *Political Studies*, **XXIV**, 1, 29. I have taken the distinction between the 'incorporated' poor and the 'masterless men' from Lubasz, who notes that the latter were nearly two-thirds of the population in Prussia in 1846.
17. The quotation is from Hegel's Berlin lectures of 1818–19: cited by Riedel, M. (1971), 'Nature and freedom in Hegel's *Philosophy of Right*', in *Hegel's Political Philosophy*, p. 146.
18. Hegel's fear of the impact of women on political life seems to be based on the very ancient fear of the socially subversive effects of female sexuality; see Hegel (1949), *The Phenomenology*, pp. 496–7.
19. Plamenatz (1963), *Man and Society*, Vol. II, p. 225.
20. Pelczynski, Z. A. (1971), 'The Hegelian conception of the state', in *Hegel's Political Philosophy*, p. 27.
21. References in brackets in the text are to page numbers of Rawls, J. (1972), *A Theory of Justice*.
22. Chapman, J. W. (1975), 'Rawls' theory of justice', *American Political Science Review*, **LXIX**, 588.
23. Kant, I.(1971), *Kant's Political Writings*, Ed. H. Reiss, Cambridge University Press, p. 143.
24. Kant (1971), p. 79; p. 139–40; 78.
25. Bloom, A. (1975), 'Justice: John Rawls vs. the tradition of political philosophy', *American Political Science Review*, **LXIX**, 651.
26. Hare, R. M. (1975), 'Rawls' theory of justice', in N. Daniels (Ed.), *Reading Rawls*, Blackwell, Oxford, p. 82, points out that Rawls states that the view of the 'reader and author' are the ones that count. How does he picture his readers? Largely, it seems, as male professionals; see also Wolff, R. P. (1977), *Understanding Rawls*, Princeton University Press, pp. 138–9. Not only is Rawls' theory, as Hare argues, subjectivist, but it is, rather amusingly, based on male intuitions.
27. Barber, B.(1975), 'Justifying justice: problems of psychology, politics and measurement in Rawls', in *Reading Rawls*, p. 295.
28. This is because Rawls' 'social contract' is treated as part of game theory, not as a consequence of the social conditions of the state of nature. The individuals who are postulated in game theory are our old friends, abstract, possessive individuals, but an abstract 'game' leads to a concern with 'random freeloading', not systematically structured inequalities. See Fisk, M. (1975), 'History and reason in Rawls' moral theory', in *Reading Rawls*, pp. 61–2.
29. See Macpherson, C. B. (1973), 'Revisionist liberalism', in *Democratic Theory: Essays in Retrieval*, Oxford University Press, pp. 93–4. It might be objected that Rawls allows for other than a capitalist economy. However, his view of 'socialism' is very narrow, indeed liberal; state-owned industry plus the market is not much of an advance on liberal democracy, and, according to Rawls, possessive individuals will be at home in this 'socialism'.
30. Pitkin (1972), p. 62.
31. Singer, P. (1973), *Democracy and Disobedience*, p. 46.
32. Singer (1973), p. 124.
33. Hart, H. L. A. (1967), 'Are there any natural rights?', in A. Quinton (Ed.), *Political Philosophy*, Oxford University Press, p. 61.

34. Flathman (1972), *Political Obligation*, p. 288.
35. Walzer (1972), p. 207.
36. Antonovsky, A. (1974), 'Class and the chance for life', in L. Rainwater (Ed.), *Social Problems and Public Policy: Inequality and Justice*, Aldine, Chicago, p. 177; 178.
37. Kinnersly, P. (1973), *The Hazards of Work*, Pluto Press, London, p. 13. 'Protecting your protection' in the most extreme fashion also makes its contribution; see Zeitlin, M., Lutterman, K. G., and Russell, J. W. (1973), 'Death in Vietnam: class, poverty and the risks of war', *Politics and Society*, **3**, 313–28.
38. Chambliss, W. J., and Seidman, R. B. (1971), *Law, Order and Power*, Addison-Wesley, Mass., p. 475; 484.
39. The state of South Australia made history in 1976 when the Criminal Law (Sexual Offences) Amendment was passed, making it possible for a wife to prosecute her husband for rape.
40. On brutality, see for example Pizzey, E. (1974), *Scream Quietly or the Neighbours Will Hear*, Penguin, Middlesex. On rape, see for example Toner, B. (1977), *The Facts of Rape*, Arrow Books, London; Brownmiller, S. (1975), *Against Our Will*, Simon and Schuster, New York. Summers, A. (1975), *Damned Whores and God's Police*, Penguin, Victoria, cites the case of the judge in 1973, in Sydney, who told two trainee nurses, raped by three men who offered them a lift at night when they were unable to use public transport, 'these young women, who are prepared to get into a car late at night, ... It is like placing a saucer of milk before a hungry cat and expecting it not to drink it' (p. 212).
41. See the Judgement of the Court of Appeal in R v Holdsworth, *The Times*, June 22, 1977. Women are also advised to submit to rape to avoid further violence, and perhaps death—yet submission, in good Hobbesian fashion, is then widely interpreted as 'consent'.
42. Daniels, N. (1975), 'Equal liberty and unequal worth of liberty', in *Reading Rawls*, p. 254.
43. The connection was suggested to me by the discussion of charity, gift-giving, the problem of the 'indiscriminate alms-giver', and the separation of the classes in nineteenth-century London, in Stedman Jones, G. (1976), *Outcast London*, Penguin, Middlesex, Chapter 13.
44. Rawls' (p. 204) only 'argument' is that the lesser worth is 'compensated for' since the working class would be worse off if they did not accept 'the existing inequalities whenever the difference principle is satisfied'. Daniels (1975) shows that the 'parties' have no good reason for 'choosing' that liberty should be of unequal worth.
45. Singer (1973), p. 49.
46. Singer (1973), p. 54.
47. Singer (1973), p. 125.
48. Voting by these citizens can be seen as a case of rational error; for this concept see Pateman, T. (1975), *Language, Truth and Politics*, Stroud and Pateman, Devon, Chapter 11.
49. Singer (1973), p. 128; 130.
50. Wertheimer, A. P. (1972), 'Political coercion and political obligation', in J. R. Pennock and J. W. Chapman (Eds), Nomos XIV, *Coercion*, p. 229.
51. Wolff (1977), p. 201.
52. Sennett, R., and Cobb, J. (1973), *The Hidden Injuries of Class*, Random House, New York, provide a different view of class and self-worth.
53. Georgakas, D., and Surkin, M. (1975), *Detroit: I Do Mind Dying*, St Martin's Press, New York; Benyon, A. (1973), *Working for Ford*, Penguin, Middlesex.
54. Wedderburn, D., and Craig, C. (1974), 'Relative deprivation in work', in D. Wedderburn (Ed.), *Poverty, Inequality and Class Structure*, Cambridge University Press, p. 141.
55. Benyon (1973), p. 253.

56. Participatory democracy in the workplace requires more radical changes both in authority structure and in the organization of the work process; see my comments in Pateman (1970) and (1975a). The realities of the historical development of the everyday work process, and the magnitude of the changes required, are discussed in Braverman, H. (1974), *Labor and Monopoly Capitalism*, Monthly Review Press, New York.

Chapter 7

1. Abbott (1976), *The Shotgun Behind the Door*, p. 74.
2. Wolff, R. P. (1970), *In Defense of Anarchism*, Harper and Row, New York, p. 6.
3. Pitkin (1972), 'Obligation and consent', p. 79.
4. Connolly, W. E. (1974), *The Terms of Political Discourse*, D. C. Heath, Lexington, Mass., p. 108.
5. On this distinction see Connolly (1974), Chapter 3; Lukes, S. (1974), *Power: A Radical View*, Macmillan, London, p. 31.
6. Bachrach, P., and Baratz, M. S. (1970), *Power and Poverty: Theory and Practice*, Oxford University Press, p. 34.
7. Wolff (1970), p. 19.
8. Wolff (1970), p. 6; 40.
9. Wolff (1970), p. 71; 27. There has always been a strong radical individualist tradition in the USA. Its adherents have been divided between those who drew anarchist, egalitarian conclusions, and those who reduced political life to the capitalist economy writ large, to a series of exchanges between unequally situated individuals. The most recent example of the latter approach is Nozick, R. (1974), *Anarchy, State, and Utopia*, Blackwell, Oxford. The historical tradition is explored in Martin, J. J. (1970), *Men Against the State*, Ralph Myles, Colorado Springs.
10. References in brackets in the text are to the pages of Godwin, W. (1976), *Enquiry Concerning Political Justice*, Ed. I. Kramnick, Penguin, Middlesex. (The Penguin edition follows the revised 3rd edition of 1798; the 1st edition of the *Enquiry* was published in 1793.)
11. Godwin's novel *Caleb Williams* has the subtitle 'Things as They Are' and provides a fascinating fictional illustration of his philosophical arguments.
12. Wolff (1970), p. 18.
13. Wolff (1970), p. 72; 78.
14. Kropotkin P., (1970), 'Anarchism: its philosophy and ideal' in R. N. Baldwin (Ed.), *Kropotkin's Revolutionary Pamphlets*, Dover, New York, p. 137.
15. Flathman (1972), *Political Obligation*, p. 103.
16. Kroptkin (1970), p. 46 ('Anarchist communism: its basis and principles').
17. Kropotkin, P. (1969), *The State: Its Historic Role*, Freedom Press, London, p. 10.
18. Kropotkin, P. (1939), *Mutual Aid*, Penguin, Middlesex, p. 232.
19. Kropotkin, P. (1970a), 'Must we occupy ourselves with an examination of the ideal of a future system?', in M. A. Miller (Ed.), *Selected Writings on Anarchism and Revolution*, MIT Press, Cambridge, Mass., and London, p. 69. Cf. the discussion in Friedrich, C. J. (1972), *Tradition and Authority*, Macmillan, London, Chapter 9; the account of anarchist organizations in Leval, G. (1975), *Collectives in the Spanish Revolution*, Freedom Press, London; the excellent fictional account of an anarchist society in Le Guin, U. (1975), *The Dispossessed*, Panther, Frogmore, Herts.
20. Durkheim, E. (1965), *Montesquieu and Rousseau*, Ann Arbor Paperback, p. 80.
21. Page references are to Rousseau, J. J. (1964), 'Discourse on the origin and foundations of inequality', in R. D. Masters (Ed.), *The First and Second Discourses*, St Martin's Press, New York (first published in 1755).
22. Fetscher, I. (1962), 'Rousseau's concepts of freedom in the light of his philosophy of history', in C. J. Friedrich (Ed.), Nomos IV, *Liberty*, Atherton, New York, p. 53. See

206

also Colletti, L. (1972), *From Rousseau to Lenin*, New Left Books, London, pp. 149–55.

23. See Winch, P. (1972), 'Man and society in Hobbes and Rousseau', in M. Cranston and R. S. Peters (Eds), *Hobbes and Rousseau: A Collection of Critical Essays*, Anchor, New York, especially pp. 235–43.

24. Rousseau's conception is not quite that of Locke, since he takes little account of the economic development of the capitalist economy: 'Rousseau ... was convinced that one man's wealth arose *directly* from the impoverishment of another'—Fetscher (1962), pp. 40–1. Nevertheless, his critique of competition and the transformation of social relationships into those of self-interest anticipates many aspects of Marx's critique of bourgeois political economy; see Colletti (1972), pp. 155–71.

25. MacAdam, J. I. (1972), 'The discourse on inequality and the social contract', *Philosophy*, **47**, 315. MacAdam notes that Rousseau foreshadows Marx's discussion of money in *The Economic and Philosophic Manuscripts*.

26. Hall, J. C. (1973), *Rousseau: An Introduction to his Political Philosophy*, Macmillan, London, pp. 47–8.

27. Shklar, J. N. (1969), *Men and Citizens: A Study of Rousseau's Social Theory*, Cambridge University Press, p. 3.

28. MacAdam (1972), pp. 313–4.

29. Cited in Riley, P. (1970), 'A possible explanation of Rousseau's general will', *American Political Science Review*, **LXIV**, 89 (from the sixth 'Lettre de la Montagne', *Oeuvres Complètes*, Gallimard, Paris, Vol. III, pp. 806–7).

30. Page references are to Rousseau, J. J. (1968), *The Social Contract*, trans. M. Cranston, Penguin, Middlesex (first published in 1762).

31. Durkheim (1965), p. 130.

32. In so doing it reveals the 'astonishing properties' of political associations. A decision about the membership of the government is a 'particular act', or act of 'government', so the sovereign temporarily turns itself into a democracy (in Rousseau's sense), chooses its representatives, and then reconstitutes itself as a legislative assembly (p. 145).

33. Ellenburg, S. (1976), *Rousseau's Political Philosophy*, Cornell University Press, p. 126.

34. Riley (1970), p. 96.

35. Riley (1970), p. 93.

36. Riley (1970), p. 87.

37. Zwiebach, B. (1975), *Civility and Disobedience*, Cambridge University Press, p. 40.

38. McBride, W. L. (1969), 'Voluntary association: the basis of an ideal model, and the "Democratic" Failure', in J. R. Pennock and J. W. Chapman (Eds), Nomos XI, *Voluntary Associations*, Atherton, New York, p. 210.

39. Hall (1973), p. 145.

40. Charvet, J. (1974), *The Social Problem in the Philosophy of Rousseau*, Cambridge University Press, p. 118.

41. Riley (1970), p. 92. Riley attributes this to the inherently contradictory nature of the notion of a 'general' will, a will always being individual or particular. However, nothing in my argument hinges on the acceptability of the term 'general will'.

42. Ellenburg (1976), p. 247.

43. Rousseau, J.-J. (1911), *Emile*, trans. B. Foxley, Dent, London, p. 322; 332.

44. Rousseau (1911), pp. 442–3.

45. Ellenburg (1976), p. 307.

46. I owe this point, and the following comment on the family as a 'sectional association', to the excellent and detailed account of Rousseau's views on the role of women in Moller Okin, S. *Women in Western Political Thought* (forthcoming).

47. Rousseau (1964), p. 147.

48. Basically, the threat arises from their 'boundless passion', or sexuality. Rousseau blames women for the growth and destructive nature of the social sentiment of 'love'; in the *Discourse* (p. 135) he notes that it is used 'by women in order to establish their ascendancy and make dominant the sex that ought to obey'. This aspect of Rousseau's

theory is fully discussed by Moller Okin.

49. See the detailed discussion of this point in Goldschmidt, M. L. (1969), 'Rousseau on intermediate associations', in Nomos XI.
50. Rousseau (1911), pp. 324–5.
51. 'Evidently, it is moral liberty that Rousseau has in mind when he utters his notorious paradox about a man's being forced to be free': Plamenatz, J. (1972), 'Ce qui ne signifie autre chose sinon qu'on le forcera d'être libre', in M. Cranston and R. S. Peters (Eds), *Hobbes and Rousseau*, p. 324.
52. Barry, B. M. (1967), 'The public interest', in A. Quinton (Ed.), *Political Philosophy*, p. 122.

Chapter 8

1. Bentham, J. (1967), *A Fragment on Government*, Ed. W. Harrison, Blackwell, Oxford, p. 51.
2. Schumpeter, J. A. (1952), *Capitalism, Socialism and Democracy*, p. 297.
3. Bentham (1967), p. 55.
4. The phrase is used about philosophical anarchism by Barber, B. (1972), *Superman and Common Men*, Penguin, Middlesex, p. 93.
5. Taylor, M. (1976), *Anarchy and Cooperation*, shows that, given a dynamic interpretation of the game, it is rational to cooperate. However, he also criticizes abstractly individualist assumptions: 'If the activities of the state may result in changes in individual preferences, then clearly it cannot be deduced from the structure of preferences in the absence of the state that the state is desirable. ... the effect of the state is to exacerbate the very conditions which are claimed to provide its justification ...' (pp. 129–30).
6. Gauthier, D. (1977), 'The social contract as ideology', p. 160.
7. Gauthier (1977), p. 163.
8. See, for example, the discussion of tendencies towards such a technocratic conception of politics and its implications for the 'end of the individual' in Habermas, J. (1976), *Legitimation Crisis*, Heinemann, London, especially Part III, Chapters 4–6.
9. This may be a legacy of Marx's unwillingness to admit that he had learnt from Rousseau; on this point see the discussion in Colletti, L. (1972), *From Rousseau to Lenin*, New Left Books, London, p. 179 and pp. 185–93.
10. Habermas (1976), p. 22. See also Habermas, J. (1971), 'Technology and science as "ideology" ', in *Towards a Rational Society*, Heinemann, London, pp. 97–100.
11. Habermas (1976), p. 69.
12. Habermas (1976), p. 74.
13. Habermas (1976), pp. 36–7; see also p. 74.
14. Cf. Walzer (1971), p. 91.
15. All this raises the extremely difficult question of the compatibility of the market and participatory democracy. There is an interesting discussion in Miller, D. (1977), 'Socialism and the market', *Political Theory*, 5, 4, 473–90. See also the comment on Yugoslavia by Zukin, S. (1975), *Beyond Marx and Tito*, Cambridge University Press, p. 250: 'they have instituted equality to the extent that citizens enjoy the same formal political rights, and liberty to the degree that people are free to be economically unequal. This compromise between liberty and equality is called liberalism'.
16. I have borrowed this term from Bernstein, R. J. (1976), *The Restructuring of Social and Political Theory*, Blackwell, Oxford.
17 There is now a good deal of interest in industrial democracy and an increasing amount of evidence available: see, for example, Hunnius, G., Garson, G. D., and Case, J. (Eds), (1973), *Workers' Control*, Vintage Books, New York; *Participation and Self-Management* (1972–3), 6 Vols., Institute for Social Research, Zagreb; Garson, G. D.

208

(1974), 'On democratic administration and socialist self-management', *Sage Professional Papers in Administrative and Policy Studies*; Vanek, J. (Ed.) (1975), *Self-Management*, Penguin, Middlesex.

18. Connolly, W. E. (1974), *The Terms of Political Discourse*, p. 203.
19. Zwiebach, B. (1975), *Civility and Disobedience*, pp. 75–6.
20. Wolfe, A. (1974), 'New directions in the Marxist theory of politics', *Politics and Society*, **4**, 2, 149.
21. I have taken the phrase from Taylor, C. (1975), *Hegel*, p. 461.
22. Compare: 'When, in the course of development, class distinctions have disappeared, ... the public power will lose its political character', Marx, K., and Engels, F. (1968), 'The Communist Manifesto', in *Selected Works*, Lawrence and Wishart, London, p. 53. See also the comments in Miliband, R. (1977), *Marxism and Politics*, Oxford University Press, pp. 6–15.
23. McBride, W. L. (1969), 'Voluntary association', pp. 222–3.
24. Taylor, C. (1975), p. 457, footnote. On freedom see Connolly (1974), Chapter 4, and Lukes (1973), *Individualism*, Part Three.
25. The question is asked of Habermas by his reviewer, J. Miller (1975), *Telos*, **25**, 213.
26. Rousseau (1968), *The Social Contract*, p. 87.
27. Shklar (1969), p. 128. Compare the role of Odo in Le Guin's *The Dispossessed*.
28. See Taylor, M. (1976), p. 141.
29. Nor is elucidation assisted when the actions of the state are ignored or given privileged treatment; see Arblaster, A. (1975), 'What is violence?', *The Socialist Register*, and (1977), 'Terrorism: myths, meaning and morals', *Political Studies*, **XXV**, 3, 413–24.
30. Fox Piven, F. (1976), 'The social structuring of political protest', *Politics and Society*, **6**, 299. There are also some hard questions to be answered about the present role of political parties and their place in a self-managing democracy; see the comments in Macpherson, C. B. (1977), *The Life and Times of Liberal Democracy*, Oxford University Press, pp. 64–9; 113–4.
31. Compare Pranger (1968), *The Eclipse of Citizenship*, pp. 44–5. Legitimacy has been defined as 'the capacity of the system to engender and maintain the belief that the existing political institutions are the most appropriate ones for the society': Lipset, S. M. (1960), *Political Man*, Doubleday, New York, p. 77.
32. Pateman, T. (1975), *Language, Truth and Politics*, p. 80.
33. Habermas (1971), pp. 92–4; (1976), pp. 8–12. For criticisms of Habermas see for example Miller (1975), pp. 216–8; Bernstein (1976), pp 221–5; Keane, J. (1977), On turning theory against itself', *Theory and Society*, **4**, 4, 561–72.

References

1979

Abbott, P. (1976), *The Shotgun Behind the Door: Liberalism and the Problem of Political Obligation*, University of Georgia Press.

Adkins, A. W. H. (1960), *Merit and Responsibility: A Study in Greek Values*, Oxford University Press.

Adkins, A. W. H. (1972), *Moral Values and Political Behaviour in Ancient Greece*, Chatto and Windus, London.

Almond, G. A., and Verba, S. (1963), *The Civic Culture: Political Attitudes and Democracy in Five Nations*, Princeton University Press.

Antonovsky, A. (1974), 'Class and the chance for life', in L. Rainwater (Ed.), *Social Problems and Public Policy: Inequality and Justice*, Aldine, Chicago.

Arblaster, A. (1975), 'What is violence?', in R. Miliband and J. Saville (Eds), *The Socialist Register*, Merlin, London.

Arblaster, A. (1977), 'Terrorism: myths, meaning and morals', *Political Studies*, **XXV**, 3, 413–24.

Arendt, H. (1973), 'Civil disobedience' and 'Lying in politics', in *Crises of the Republic*, Penguin, Middlesex.

Ashcraft, R. (1968), 'Locke's state of nature: historical fact or moral fiction?', *American Political Science Review*, **LXII**, 898–915.

Austin, J. L. (1962), *How to do Things with Words*, Oxford University Press.

Avineri, S. (1972), *Hegel's Theory of the Modern State*, Cambridge University Press.

Bachrach, P., and Baratz, M. S. (1970), *Power and Poverty: Theory and Practice*, Oxford University Press.

Barber, B. (1972), *Superman and Common Men*, Penguin, Middlesex.

Barber, B. (1975), 'Justifying justice: problems of psychology, politics and measurement in Rawls', in N. Daniels (Ed.), *Reading Rawls*, Blackwell, Oxford.

Barry, B. M. (1967), 'The public interest', in A. Quinton (Ed.), *Political Philosophy*, Oxford University Press.

Barry, B. M. (1972), 'Warrender and his critics', in M. Cranston and R. Peters (Eds), *Hobbes and Rousseau: A Collection of Critical Essays*, Anchor, New York.

Barry, B. M. (1973), *The Liberal Theory of Justice*, Oxford University Press.

Beackon, S., and Reeve, A. (1976), 'The benefits of reasonable conduct: the *Leviathan* theory of obligation', *Political Theory*, **4**, 4, 423–38.

Bentham, J. (1967), *A Fragment on Government*, Ed. W. Harrison, Blackwell, Oxford.

Benyon, A. (1973), *Working for Ford*, Penguin, Middlesex.

Beran, H. (1972), 'Ought, obligation and duty', *Australasian Journal of Philosophy*, **50**, 3, 207–21.

Beran, H. (1977), 'In defense of the consent theory of political obligation and authority', *Ethics*, **87**, 3, 260–71.

Berelson, B. R., Lazarsfeld, P. F., and McPhee, W. N. (1954), *Voting: A Study of Opinion Formation in a Presidential Campaign*, University of Chicago Press.

Bernstein, R. J. (1976), *The Restructuring of Social and Political Theory*, Blackwell, Oxford.

Bloom, A. (1975), 'Justice: John Rawls vs the tradition of political philosophy', *American Political Science Review*, **LXIX**, 648–62.

Bourque, S. C., and Grossholtz, J. (1974), 'Politics an unnatural practice: political science looks at female participation', *Politics and Society*, **4**, 2, 225–66.

Bradley, F. H. (1927), 'My station and its duties', *Ethical Studies*, 2nd ed., Oxford University Press.

Brandt, R. B. (1964), 'The concepts of obligation and duty', *Mind*, **73**, 374–93.

Braverman, H. (1974), *Labor and Monopoly Capitalism: The Degradation of Work in the Twentieth Century*, Monthly Review Press, New York.

Braybrooke, D. (1974), 'The Social Contract Returns, This Time as an Elusive Public Good', paper presented to Annual Meeting of the American Political Science Association.

Braybrooke, D. (1975), 'Through Epistemology to the Depths of Political Illusion', paper presented to Annual Meeting of the American Political Science Association.

Brennan, T., and Pateman, C. (forthcoming), ' "Mere Auxiliaries to the Commonwealth": Women and the Origins of Liberalism', *Political Studies*.

Brownmiller, S. (1975), *Against our Will: Men, Women and Rape*, Simon and Schuster, New York.

Cassinelli, C. W. (1961), *The Politics of Freedom: An Analysis of the Modern Democratic State*, University of Washington Press.

Chambliss, W. J., and Seidman, R. B. (1971), *Law, Order and Power*, Addison-Wesley, Mass.

Chapman, J. W. (1975), 'Rawls's theory of justice', *American Political Science Review*, **LXIX**, 588–93.

Chapman, R. A. (1975), '*Leviathan* writ small: Thomas Hobbes on the family', *American Political Science Review*, **LXIX**, 76–90.

Charvet, J. (1974), *The Social Problem in the Philosophy of Rousseau*, Cambridge University Press.

Cobb, J., and Sennett, R. (1973), *The Hidden Injuries of Class*, Random House, New York.

Cohen, C. (1971), *Civil Disobedience: Conscience, Tactics and the Law*, Columbia University Press.

Cohen, M. (1972), 'Liberalism and disobedience', *Philosophy and Public Affairs*, **1**, 3, 283–314.

Cole, G. D. H. (1915), 'Conflicting social obligations', *Proceedings of the Aristotelian Society*, **XV**, 140–59.

Colletti, L. (1972), *From Rousseau to Lenin: Studies in Ideology and Society*, New Left Books, London.

Connolly, W. E. (1973), 'Theoretical self-consciousness', *Polity*, **VI**, 5–35.

Connolly, W. E. (1974), *The Terms of Political Discourse*, D. C. Heath, Lexington, Mass.

Crenson, M. A. (1971), *The Un-Politics of Air Pollution*, John Hopkins, Baltimore.

Crick, B. (1964), *In Defence of Politics*, Penguin, Middlesex.

Dagger, R. K. (1977), 'What is political obligation?', *American Political Science Review*, **LXXI**, 86–94.

Daniels, N. (1975), 'Equal liberty and unequal worth of liberty', in *Reading Rawls*, Blackwell, Oxford.

Daube, D. (1972), *Civil Disobedience in Antiquity*, Edinburgh University Press.

Dennis, J. (1970), 'Support for the institution of elections by the mass public', *American Political Science Review*, **LXIV**, 819–35.

di Palma, G. (1970), *Apathy and Participation*, Free Press, New York.

Dunn, J. (1969), *The Political Thought of John Locke: An Historical Account of the Argument of the 'Two Treatises of Government'*, Cambridge University Press.

Dunn, J. (1971), 'Consent in the political theory of John Locke', in G. J. Schochet (Ed.), *Life, Liberty and Property: Essays on Locke's Political Ideas*, Wadsworth, Belmont, California.

Durkheim, E. (1965), *Montesquieu and Rousseau*, Ann Arbor Paperback, Michigan.

Edelman, M. (1964), *The Symbolic Uses of Politics*, University of Illinois Press.

Ellenburg, S. (1976), *Rousseau's Political Philosophy: An Interpretation From Within*, Cornell University Press.

Euben, J. P. (1972), 'Walzer's *Obligations*', *Philosophy and Public Affairs*, 1, 4, 438–59.

Fetscher, I. (1962), 'Rousseau's concepts of freedom in the light of his philosophy of history', in C. J. Friedrich (Ed.), Nomos IV, *Liberty*, Atherton, New York.

Fisk, M. (1975), 'History and reason in Rawls' moral theory', in N. Daniels (Ed.), *Reading Rawls*, Blackwell, Oxford.

Flathman, R. E. (1972), *Political Obligation*, Atheneum, New York.

Friedrich, C. J. (1972), *Tradition and Authority*, Macmillan, London.

Garson, G. D. (1974), 'On democratic administration and socialist self-management: a comparative survey emphasising the Yugoslav experience', *Sage Professional Papers in Administrative and Policy Studies*, Sage Publications, Beverley Hills and London.

Gauthier, D. (1969), *The Logic of Leviathan: The Moral and Political Theory of Thomas Hobbes*, Oxford University Press.

Gauthier, D. (1977), 'The social contract as ideology', *Philosophy and Public Affairs*, **6**, 2, 130–64.

Georgakas, D., and Surkin, M. (1975), *Detroit: I do Mind Dying*, St Martin's Press, New York.

Gewirth, A. (1962), 'Political justice', in R. B. Brandt (Ed.), *Social Justice*, Prentice-Hall, New Jersey.

Godwin, W. (1966), *Caleb Williams or Things as They are*, New English Library, London.

Godwin, W. (1976), *Enquiry Concerning Political Justice And its Influence on Modern Morals and Happiness*, Ed. I. Kramnick, Penguin, Middlesex.

Goldschmidt, M. L. (1969), 'Rousseau on intermediate associations', in J. R. Pennock and J. W. Chapman (Eds), Nomos XI, *Voluntary Associations*, Atherton, New York.

Goot, M., and Reid, E. (1975), 'Women and voting studies: mindless matrons or sexist scientism?', *Sage Contemporary Political Sociology Series*, Vol. 1, Sage Publications, Beverley Hills and London.

Gouldner, A. W. (1967), *Enter Plato: Classical Greece and the Origins of Social Theory*, Routledge and Kegan Paul, London.

Greenawalt, K. (1970), 'A conceptual approach to disobedience', in J. R. Pennock and J. W. Chapman (Eds), Nomos XII, *Political and Legal Obligation*, Atherton, New York.

Greenberg, N. A. (1965), 'Socrates' choice in the *Crito*', *Harvard Studies in Classical Philology*, **LXX**, 1, 45–82.

Habermas, J. (1971), 'Technology and science as "ideology"', in *Toward a Rational Society: Student Protest, Science, and Politics*', trans. J. J. Shapiro, Heinemann, London.

Habermas, J. (1976), *Legitimation Crisis*, trans. T. McCarthy, Heinemann, London.

Hall, J. C. (1973), *Rousseau: An Introduction to his Political Philosophy*, Macmillan, London.

Hall, R. T. (1971), 'Legal toleration of civil disobedience', *Ethics*, **81**, 128–42.

Hare, R. M. (1975), 'Rawls' theory of justice', in N. Daniels (Ed.), *Reading Rawls*, Blackwell, Oxford.

Hart, H. L. A. (1967), 'Are there any natural rights?', in A. Quinton (Ed.), *Political Philosophy*, Oxford University Press.

Hegel, G. W. F. (1949), *The Phenomenology of Mind*, trans. J. B. Baillie, Allen and Unwin, London.

Hegel, G. W. F. (1952), *Philosophy of Right*, trans. T. M. Knox, Oxford University Press.

Hegel, G. W. F. (1964), *Hegel's Political Writings*, Ed. Z. A. Pelczynski, Oxford University Press.

Hill, C. (1972), *The World Turned Upside Down: Radical Ideas During the English Revolution*, Temple Smith, London.

Hobbes, T. (1968), *Leviathan*, Ed. C. B. Macpherson, Penguin, Middlesex.

Hume, D. (1953), 'Of the original contract', in C. W. Hendel (Ed.), *Political Essays*, Library of Liberal Arts, Bobs-Merrill, New York.

Hunnius, G., Garson, G. D. and Case, J. (Eds) (1973), *Workers' Control: A Reader on Labor and Social Change*, Vintage Books, New York.

Iglitzin, L. B. (1974), 'The making of the apolitical woman', in J. S. Jaquette (Ed.), *Women in Politics*, Wiley, New York.

Ilting, K. H. (1971), 'The structure of Hegel's *Philosophy of Right*', in Z. A. Pelczynski (Ed.), *Hegel's Political Philosophy*, Cambridge University Press.

Institute for Social Research, Zagreb, *Participation and Self-Management* (1972–73) (6 vols.).

James, G. G. (1973), 'The orthodox theory of civil disobedience', *Social Theory and Practice*, **2**, 475–98.

Jaquette, J. S. (1974) (Ed.), *Women in Politics*, Wiley, New York.

Jenkins, J. J. (1970), 'Political consent', *Philosophical Quarterly*, **20**, 60–6.

Johnson, K. (1975), 'Political obligation and the voluntary association model of the state', *Ethics*, **86**, 17–29.

Kant, I. (1971), *Kant's Political Writings*, Ed. H. Reiss, Cambridge University Press.

Keane, J. (1977), 'On turning theory against itself', *Theory and Society*, **4**, 4, 561–72.

Kinnersly, P. (1973), *The Hazards of Work*, Pluto Press, London.

Kropotkin, P. (1939), *Mutual Aid*, Penguin, Middlesex.

Kropotkin, P. (1969), *The State: Its Historic Role*, Freedom Press, London.

Kropotkin, P. (1970), *Kropotkin's Revolutionary Pamphlets*, Ed. R. N. Baldwin, Dover, New York.

Kropotkin, P. (1970a), *Selected Writings on Anarchism and Revolution*, Ed. M. A. Miller, MIT Press, Cambridge, Mass.

Lane, R. E. (1959), *Political Life: Why and How People get Involved in Politics*, Free Press, New York.

Le Guin, U. (1975), *The Dispossessed*, Panther, Frogmore, Herts.

Leval, G. (1975), *Collectives in the Spanish Revolution*, Freedom Press, London.

Lipset, S. M. (1960), *Political Man*, Doubleday, New York.

Lipsitz, L. (1968), 'If as Verba says, the state functions as a religion, what are we to do then to save our souls?', *American Political Science Review*, **LXII**, 527–35.

Lipsitz, L. (1970), 'On political belief: the grievances of the poor', in P. Green and S. Levinson (Eds), *Power and Community*, Vintage Books, New York.

Locke, J. (1965), 'A letter concerning toleration' in M. Cranston (Ed.), *Locke on Politics, Religion, and Education*, Collier, New York.

Locke, J. (1967), *Two Treatises of Government*, Ed. P. Laslett, 2nd ed., Cambridge University Press.

Locke, J. (1967a), *Two Tracts on Government*, Ed. P. Abrams, Cambridge University Press.

Lubasz, H. (1976), 'Marx's initial problematic: the problem of poverty', *Political Studies*, **XXIV**, 1, 24–42.

Lukes, S. (1973), *Individualism*, Blackwell, Oxford.

Lukes, S. (1974), *Power: A Radical View*, Macmillan, London.

MacAdam, J. I. (1972), 'The discourse on inequality and the social contract', *Philosophy*, **47**, 308–21.

McBride, W. L. (1969), 'Voluntary association: the basis of an ideal model, and the "democratic" failure', in J. R. Pennock and J. W. Chapman (Eds), Nomos XI, *Voluntary Associations*, Atherton, New York.

McClosky, H. (1970), 'Consensus and ideology in American politics', in R. E. Wolfinger (Ed.), *Readings in American Political Behavior*, 2nd ed., Prentice-Hall, New Jersey.

Macdonald, M. (1960), 'The language of political theory', in A. Flew (Ed.), *Logic and Language*, First Series, Blackwell, Oxford.

McIlwain, C. H. (1932), *The Growth of Political Thought in the West: From the Greeks to the End of the Middle Ages*, Macmillan, New York.

MacIntyre, A. (1967), *A Short History of Ethics*, Routledge and Kegan Paul, London.

McNeilly, F. S. (1968), *The Anatomy of Leviathan*, Macmillan, London.

Macpherson, C. B. (1962), *The Political Theory of Possessive Individualism: Hobbes to Locke*, Oxford University Press.

Macpherson, C. B. (1973), 'Revisionist liberalism', in *Democratic Theory: Essays in Retrieval*, Oxford University Press.

Macpherson, C. B. (1977), *The Life and Times of Liberal Democracy*, Oxford University Press.

McPherson, T. (1967), *Political Obligation*, Routledge and Kegan Paul, London.

Marcuse, H. (1955), *Reason and Revolution: Hegel and the Rise of Social Theory*, 2nd Ed., Routledge and Kegan Paul, London.

Martin, J. J. (1970), *Men Against the State: The Expositors of Individualist Anarchism in America*, 1827–1908, Ralph Myles, Colorado Springs.

Marx, K. (1967), 'On the Jewish question', in L. M. Easton and K. M. Guddat (Ed.), *Writings of the Young Marx on Philosophy and Society*, Anchor, New York.

Marx, K., and Engels, F. (1968), 'The Communist Manifesto', in *Selected Works*, one vol., Lawrence and Wishart, London.

Miliband, R. (1977), *Marxism and Politics*, Oxford University Press.

Miller, D. (1977), 'Socialism and the market', *Political Theory*, 5, 4, 473–90.

Miller, J. (1975), 'Review of J. Habermas' *Legitimation Crisis*', *Telos*, 25, 210–20.

Okin, S. M. (forthcoming), *Women in Western Political Thought*, Princeton University Press.

Nozick, R. (1974), *Anarchy, State, and Utopia*, Blackwell, Oxford.

Parenti, M. (1974), *Democracy for the Few*, St Martin's Press, New York.

Parry, G. (1967), 'Performative utterances and obligation in Hobbes', *Philosophical Quarterly*, 17, 246–52.

Partridge, P. H. (1971), *Consent and Consensus*, Macmillan, London.

Pateman, C. (1970), *Participation and Democratic Theory*, Cambridge University Press.

Pateman, C. (1973), 'Political obligation and conceptual analysis', *Political Studies*, XXI, 2, 199–218.

Pateman, C. (1974), 'To them that hath shall be given: on Verba and Nie's *Participation in America*', *Politics*, IX, 139–45.

Pateman, C. (1975), 'Sublimation and reification: Locke, Wolin and the liberal democratic conception of the political', *Politics and Society*, 5, 441–67.

Pateman, C. (1975a), 'A contribution to the political theory of organizational democracy', *Administration and Society*, 7, 5–26.

Pateman, C. (forthcoming), 'The civic culture: a philosophic critique', in G. A. Almond and L. Rose (Eds), *The Civic Culture Revisited*, Princeton University Press.

Pateman, T. (1975), *Language, Truth and Logic*, Stroud and Patman, Devon.

Pelczynski, Z. A. (1971), 'The Hegelian conception of the state', in *Hegel's Political Philosophy*, Cambridge University Press.

Pitkin, H. (1972), 'Obligation and consent', in P. Laslett, W. G. Runciman and Q. Skinner (Eds), *Philosophy, Politics and Society*, Fourth Series, Blackwell, Oxford.

Piven, F. F. (1976), 'The social structuring of political protest', *Politics and Society*, 6, 297–326.

Pizzey, E. (1974), *Scream Quietly or the Neighbours will Hear*, Penguin, Middlesex.

Plamenatz, J. (1963), *Man and Society: A Critical Examination of Some Important Social and Political Theories from Machiavelli to Marx*, 2 vols., Longmans, London.

Plamenatz, J. (1968), *Consent, Freedom and Political Obligation*, Oxford University Press, 2nd ed.

Plamenatz, J. (1972), 'Ce qui ne signifie autre chose sinon qu'on le forcera d' être libre', in M. Cranston and R. S. Peters (Eds), *Hobbes and Rousseau*, Anchor, New York.

Plant, R. (1973), *Hegel*, Allen and Unwin, London.

Plato (1969), trans. H. Tredennick, *The Last Days of Socrates*, Penguin, Middlesex.

Pomeroy, S. B. (1975), *Goddesses, Whores, Wives and Slaves: Women in Classical Antiquity*, Schocken, New York.

Poole, R. (1977), 'Locke and the Bourgeois State', paper presented to the Annual Meeting of the Australasian Philosophy Association.

Pranger, R. J. (1968), *The Eclipse of Citizenship: Power and Participation in Contemporary Politics*, Holt, Rinehart and Winston, New York.

Prewitt, K. (1970), 'Political ambitions, volunteerism, and electoral accountability', *American Political Science Review*, LXIV, 5–17.

Rawls, J. (1972), *A Theory of Justice*, Oxford University Press.

Reid, W. M., and Henderson, J. S. (1976), 'Political obligation: an empirical approach', *Polity*, IX, 2, 237–52.

Richards, D. A. J. (1971), *A Theory of Reasons for Action*, Oxford University Press.

Riedel, M. (1971), 'Nature and freedom in Hegel's *Philosophy of Right*', in Z. A. Pelczynski (Ed.), *Hegel's Political Philosophy*, Cambridge University Press.

Riley, P. (1970), 'A possible explanation of Rousseau's general will', *American Political Science Review*, **LXIV**, 86–97.

Riley, P. (1973), 'How coherent is the social contract tradition?', *Journal of the History of Ideas*, **XXXIV**, 4, 543–62.

Riley, P. (1973a), 'Will and legitimacy in the philosophy of Hobbes: is he a consent theorist?', *Political Studies*, **XXI**, 4, 500–22.

Riley, P. (1973b), 'Hegel on consent and social contract theory: does he "cancel and preserve the will"?', *The Western Political Quarterly*, **XXVI**, 130–61.

Rose, R., and Mossawir, H. (1969), 'Voting and elections: a functional analysis', in C. F. Cnudde and D. E. Neubauer (Eds), *Empirical Democratic Theory*, Markham, Chicago.

Rosen, F. (1973), 'Obligation and friendship in Plato's *Crito*', *Political Theory*, 1, 3, 307–16.

Rousseau, J.-J. (1911), *Emile*, trans. B. Foxley, Dent, London.

Rousseau, J.-J. (1964), *The First and Second Discourses*, Ed. R. D. Masters, St Martin's Press, New York.

Rousseau, J.-J. (1968), *The Social Contract*, trans. M. Cranston, Penguin, Middlesex.

St Thomas Aquinas (1965), *Selected Political Writings*, ed. A. P. D'Entreves, Blackwell, Oxford.

Salkever, S. G. (1974), 'Virtue, obligation and politics', *American Political Science Review*, **LXVIII**, 78–92.

Schochet, G. J. (1972), 'The morality of resisting the penalty', in V. Held, K. Nielsen and C. Parsons (Eds), *Philosophy and Political Action*, Oxford University Press.

Schochet, G. J. (1975), *Patriarchalism in Political Thought*, Blackwell, Oxford.

Schumpeter, J. A. (1952), *Capitalism, Socialism and Democracy*, 5th ed., Allen and Unwin, London.

Searle, J. (1969), *Speech Acts*, Cambridge University Press.

Sesonske, A. (1964), *Value and Obligation*, Oxford University Press.

Shklar, J. N. (1969), *Men and Citizens: A Study of Rousseau's Social Theory*, Cambridge University Press.

Simmons, A. J. (1976), 'Tacit consent and political obligation', *Philosophy and Public Affairs*, 5, 3, 274–91.

Singer, P. (1973), *Democracy and Disobedience*, Oxford University Press.

Stedman Jones, G. (1976), *Outcast London: A Study in the Relationship between Classes in Victorian Society*, Penguin, Middlesex.

Summers, A. (1975), *Damned Whores and God's Police: The Colonisation of Women in Australia*, Penguin, Melbourne.

Taylor, C. (1975), *Hegel*, Cambridge University Press.

Taylor, C. (1976), 'Hermeneutics and politics', P. Connerton (Ed.), *Critical Sociology*, Penguin, Middlesex.

Taylor, G. R. (1959), *Sex in History*, Thames and Hudson, London.

Taylor, M. (1976), *Anarchy and Cooperation*, Wiley, London.

Therborn, G. (1977), 'The rule of capital and the rise of democracy', *New Left Review*, **103**, 3–41.

Thomson, J. J. (1973), 'A defense of abortion', in J. Feinberg (Ed.), *The Problem of Abortion*, Wadsworth, Belmont, California.

Titmuss, R. M. (1970), *The Gift Relationship*, Allen and Unwin, London.

Toner, B. (1977), *The Facts of Rape*, Arrow, London.

Tussman, J. (1960), *Obligation and the Body Politic*, Oxford University Press.

Ullman, W. (1966), *The Individual and Society in the Middle Ages*, John Hopkins, Baltimore.

Vanek, J. (1975), (Ed.), *Self-Management: Economic Liberation of Man*, Penguin, Middlesex.

Verba, S., and Nie, N. H. (1972), *Participation in America: Political Democracy and Social Equality*, Harper and Row, New York.

Walzer, M. (1968), 'Politics in the welfare state', *Dissent*, **15**, 26–40.

Walzer, M. (1971), *Obligations: Essays on Disobedience, War, and Citizenship*, Simon and Schuster, New York.

Walzer, M. (1972), *The Revolution of the Saints: A Study in the Origins of Radical Politics*, Atheneum, New York.

Warrender, H. (1957), *The Political Philosophy of Hobbes: His Theory of Obligation*, Oxford University Press.

Watkins, J. W. N. (1973), *Hobbes's System of Ideas: A Study in the Political Significance of Philosophical Theories*, 2nd ed., Hutchinson, London.

Wedderburn, D., and Craig, C. (1974), 'Relative deprivation in work' in D. Wedderburn (Ed.), *Poverty, Inequality and Class Structure*, Cambridge University Press.

Werthcimer, A. P. (1972), 'Political coercion and political obligation', in J. R. Pennock and J. W. Chapman (Eds), Nomos XIV, *Coercion*, Aldine, Atherton, Chicago.

Winch, P. (1958), *The Idea of a Social Science and Its Relation to Philosophy*, Routledge and Kegan Paul, London.

Winch, P. (1972), 'Man and society in Hobbes and Rousseau', in M. Cranston and R. S. Peters (Eds), *Hobbes and Rousseau: A Collection of Critical Essays*, Anchor, New York.

Wolfe, A. (1974), 'New directions in the Marxist theory of politics', *Politics and Society*, 4, 2, 131–59.

Wolff, R. P. (1970), *In Defense of Anarchism*, Harper and Row, New York.

Wolff, R. P. (1977), *Understanding Rawls: A Reconstruction and Critique of 'A Theory of Justice'*, Princeton University Press.

Wolin, S. (1961), *Politics and Vision: Continuity and Innovation in Western Political Thought*, Allen and Unwin, London.

Wood, E. M. (1972), *Mind and Politics: An Approach to the Meaning of Liberal and Socialist Individualism*, University of California Press.

Zeitlin, M., Lutterman, K. G., and Russell, J. W. (1973), 'Death in Vietnam: class, poverty, and the risks of war', *Politics and Society*, 3, 3, 313–28.

Zukin, S. (1975), *Beyond Marx and Tito: Theory and Practice in Yugoslav Socialism*, Cambridge University Press.

Zwiebach, B. (1975), *Civility and Disobedience*, Cambridge University Press.

216

1985

Beiner, R. (1983), *Political Judgement*, Methuen, London.
Brennan, T., and Pateman, C. (1979), ' "Mere Auxiliaries to the Commonwealth": Women and the Origins of Liberalism', *Political Studies*, **XXVII**, 2, 183−200.
Coleman, J. (1985), 'The Formalist Challenge to the Liberal Theory of Democracy', presented to the Weingart Conference on Explanation and Justification in Social Theory, California Institute of Technology. (Forthcoming in *Ethics* 1986.)
Dagger, R. (1980), 'Review', *Political Theory*, **8**, 3, 409−13.
Dunn, J. (1980), 'Political Obligations and Political Possibilities', in *Political Obligation in its Historical Context: Essays in Political Theory*, Cambridge University Press.
Fishkin, J. S. (1982), *The Limits of Obligation*, Yale University Press.
Mansbridge, J. (1980), 'Review', *American Political Science Review*, **74**, 488−90.
Markus, G. (1982), 'A Radical Theory on Classical Political Obligation', *Radical Philosophy*, **32**, 35−8.
Pateman, C. (1980a), ' "The Disorder of Women": Women, Love, and the Sense of Justice', *Ethics*, **91**, 20−34.
Pateman, C. (1980b), 'Women and Consent', *Political Theory*, **8**, 2, 149−68.
Pateman, C. (1983a), 'Feminist Critiques of the Public/Private Dichotomy', in S. I. Benn and G. F. Caus (Eds), *Public and Private in Social Life*, Croom Helm, London and Canberra.
Pateman, C. (1983b), 'Feminism and Democracy', in G. Duncan (Ed), *Democratic Theory and Practice*, Cambridge University Press.
Pateman, C. (1984), 'The Shame of the Marriage Contract', in J. Stiehm (Ed), *Women's Views of the Political World of Men*, Transnational Publishers, New York.
Pateman, C. (1985), 'Women and Democratic Citizenship', The Jefferson Memorial Lectures, University of California, Berkeley.
Riker, W. H. (1982), *Liberalism Against Populism: A Confrontation Between the Theory of Democracy and the Theory of Social Choice*, W. H. Freeman and Co., San Francisco.
Rogowski, R. (1981), 'The Obligations of Liberalism: Pateman on Participation and Promising', *Ethics*, **91**, 296−301.
Simmons, A. J. (1979), *Moral Principles and Political Obligations*, Princeton University Press.
Steinberg, J. (1978), *Locke, Rousseau, and the Idea of Consent: An Inquiry Into the Liberal Democratic Theory of Political Obligation*, Greenwood Press, Westport and London.
Unger, R. M. (1984), *Passion: An Essay on Personality*, Free Press, New York.

Further Reading

Abbott, P. (1976), 'With equality and virtue for all: John Rawls and the liberal tradition', *Polity*, **VIII**, 3, 339–57.

Arendt, H. (1968), 'What is authority?', in *Between Past and Future*, Viking, New York.

Ballestrem, K. G. (1972), 'The radicalism of Robert Paul Wolff', *The Review of Politics*, **34**, 16–19

Bates, S. (1973), 'Laws, habits of obedience and obligation', *Philosophical Quarterly*, **23**, 41–51.

Bay, C. (1971), 'Foundations of the liberal make-believe: some implications of contract theory *versus* freedom theory', *Inquiry*, **14**, 213–43.

Berger, F. R. (1970), ' "Law and order" and civil disobedience', *Inquiry*, **13**, 254–73.

Blaine, H. R., and Kettler, D. (1971), 'Law as a political weapon', *Politics and Society*, **1**, 4, 479–526.

Bookman, J. T. (1972), 'Plato on political obligation, *Western Political Quarterly*, **25**, 260–68.

Brown, K. C. (1965) (Ed.), *Hobbes Studies*, Blackwell, Oxford.

Cameron, J. R. (1971), 'Ought and institutional obligation', *Philosophy*, **XLVI**, 309–23.

Cameron, J. R. (1972), 'The nature of institutional obligation', *Philosophical Quarterly*, **22**, 318–32.

Care, N. S. (1969), 'Contractualism and moral criticism', *Review of Metaphysics*, **XXIII**, 85–101.

Carnes, J. R. (1970), 'Myths, bliks, and the social contract', *Journal of Value Inquiry*, **V**, 105–18.

Carr, S. (1975), 'Rawls, contractarianism, and our moral intuitions', *The Personalist*, Winter, 83–95.

Carter, A. (1971), *The Political Theory of Anarchism*, Routledge and Kegan Paul, London.

Craig, L. H. (1975), 'Contra contract: a brief against John Rawls' *A Theory of Justice*', *Canadian Journal of Political Science*, **VIII**, 1, 63–81.

David-Hillel, R. (1972), 'Tacit promising', *Ethics*, **83**, 71–9.

d'Entreves, A. P. (1968), 'On the nature of political obligation', *Philosophy*, **XLIII**, 309–23.

Earle, W. (1970), 'Some paradoxes of conscience as a political guide', *Ethics*, **80**, 306–12.

Engels, F. (1969), 'On authority', in K. Marx and F. Engels, *Selected Works*, Vol. II, Progress Publishers, Moscow.

Feinberg, J. (1973), 'Duty and obligation in the non-ideal world', *Journal of Philosophy*, **70**, 263–75.

Finley, M. I. (1973), *Democracy Ancient and Modern*, Chatto and Windus, London.

Finley, M. I. (1973a), *The Ancient Economy*, Chatto and Windus, London.

Frankel, C. (1972), 'Political disobedience and denial of political authority', *Social Theory and Practice*, **2**, 1, 85–98.

Frazier, C. (1972), 'Between obedience and revolution', *Philosophy and Public Affairs*, **1**, 3, 315–34.

Gauthier, D. (1975), 'Reason and maximization', *Canadian Journal of Philosophy*, **4**, 3, 411–33.

Gendin, S. (1972), 'Governmental toleration of civil disobedience' in V. Held, K. Nielsen, and C. Parsons (Eds), *Philosophy and Political Action*, Oxford University Press.

Gierke, O. (1958), *Political Theories of the Middle Age*, Beacon, Boston.

Goldsmith, M. M. (1966), *Hobbes's Science of Politics*, Columbia University Press.

Gough, J. W. (1957), *The Social Contract*, 2nd ed., Oxford University Press.

Green, T. H. (1941), *Lectures on the Principles of Political Obligation*, Longmans, London.

Hart, H. L. A. (1961), *The Concept of Law*, Oxford University Press.

Hart, H. L. A. (1973), 'Legal and moral obligation', in R. E. Flathman (Ed.), *Concepts in Social and Political Philosophy*, Macmillan, New York.

Hundert, E. J. (1972), 'The making of *Homo Faber*: John Locke between ideology and history', *Journal of History of Ideas*, XXXIII, 1, 3–22.

Hunter, J. F. M. (1966), 'The logic of social contracts', *Dialogue*, V, 31–46.

Johnson, K. (1974), 'Perspectives on political obligation: a critique and a proposal', *Western Political Quarterly*, XXVII, 3, 320–35.

Jones, A. H. M. (1960), *Athenian Democracy*, Blackwell, Oxford.

Kelly, G. A. (1976), 'Politics and philosophy in Hegel', *Polity*, IX, 1, 3–18.

Ladd, J. (1970), 'Legal and moral obligation', in J. R. Pennock and J. W. Chapman (Eds), Nomos XII, *Political and Legal Obligation*, Atherton, New York.

Le Baron, B. (1967), 'Real and mythic obligations', *Ethics*, **78**, 62–76.

Le Baron, B. (1973), 'Three components of political obligation', *Canadian Journal of Political Science*, VI, 3, 478–93.

Levin, M. (1970), 'Rousseau on independence', *Political Studies*, XVIII, 4, 496–513.

McBride, W. L. (1972), 'Non-coercive society: some doubts, Leninist and contemporary', in J. R. Pennock and J. W. Chapman (Eds), Nomos XIV, *Coercion*, Aldine, Atherton, Chicago.

MacCormick, N., and Raz, J. (1972), 'Voluntary obligations and Normative Powers', *The Proceedings of The Aristotelian Society*, Supp. Vol. XLVI, 59–102.

McWilliams, W. C. (1969), 'Civil disobedience and contemporary constitutionalism', *Comparative Politics*, **1**, 2, 211–27.

Mansfield, H. C. (1971), 'Hobbes and the science of indirect government', *American Political Science Review*, LXV, 97–110.

Martin, R. (1970), 'Socrates on disobedience to law', *Review of Metaphysics*, XXIV, 21–38.

Martin, R. (1974), 'Wolff's defense of philosophical anarchism', *Philosophical Quarterly*, **24**, 140–9.

Martin, R. (1975), 'Two models for justifying political authority', *Ethics*, **86**, 70–5.

Masters, R. D. (1968), *The Political Philosophy of Rousseau*, Princeton University Press.

Milgram, S. (1974), *Obedience to Authority: An Experimental View*, Tavistock, London.

Miliband, R. (1969), *The State in Capitalist Society*, Weidenfeld and Nicholson, London.

Moore, S. (1971), 'Hobbes on obligation, moral and political', Part 1, *Journal of History of Philosophy*, IX, 43–61.

Moore, S. (1972), 'Hobbes on obligation, moral and political', Part 2, *Journal of History of Philosophy*, X, 29–41.

Pitkin, H. (1972), *Wittgenstein and Justice: On the Significance of Ludwig Wittgenstein for Social and Political Thought*, University of California Press.

Pocklington, T. (1970), 'Protest, resistance, and political obligation', *Canadian Journal of Political Science*, III, 1, 1–17.

Rawls, J. (1971), 'Legal obligation and the duty of fair-play', in J. G. Murphy, *Civil Disobedience and Violence*, Wadsworth, California.

Rees, J. C. (1954), 'The limitations of political theory', *Political Studies*, II, 3, 242–57.

Reiman, J. H. (1972), *In Defense of Political Philosophy*, Harper and Row, New York.

Riley, P. (1973), 'On Kant as the most adequate of the social contract theorists', *Political Theory*, **1**, 4, 450–71.

Riley, P. (1974), 'On finding an equilibrium between consent and natural law in Locke's political philosophy', *Political Studies*, XXII, 4, 432–52.

Riley, P. (1976), 'Locke on "voluntary agreement" and political power', *Western Political Quarterly*, XXIX, 1, 136–45.

Ryan, A. (1965), 'Locke and the dictatorship of the bourgeoisie', *Political Studies*, XIII, 219–30.

219

Schaar, J. H. (1970), 'Legitimacy in the modern state', in P. Green and S. Levinson (Ed.), *Power and Community: Dissenting Essays in Political Science*, Vintage Books, New York.

Schaefer, D. L. (1974), 'A critique of Rawls' contract doctrine', *The Review of Metaphysics*, **XXVIII**, 89–115.

Schrag, F. (1975), 'The child's status in the democratic state', *Political Theory*, **3**, 4, 441–57.

Seliger, M. (1968), *The Liberal Politics of John Locke*, Allen and Unwin, London.

Skillen, T. (1972), 'The statist conception of politics', *Radical Philosophy*, **2**, 2–6.

Spooner, L. (1966), *No Treason: The Constitution of No Authority*, Pine Tree Press, Colorado.

Stillman, P. G. (1974), 'Hegel's critique of liberal theories of rights', *American Political Science Review*, **LXVIII**, 1086–92.

Taylor, R. (1973), *Freedom, Anarchy, and the Law: An Introduction to Political Philosophy*, Prentice-Hall, New Jersey.

Thoreau, H. D. (1969) *Civil Disobedience*, in H. A. Bedau (Ed), *Civil Disobedience: Theory and Practice*, Pegasus, New York.

Zashin, E. M. (1972) *Civil Disobedience and Democracy*, The Free Press, New York.

Index